– WHEN TO USE THIS BOOK –

ALWAYS:
- In preparing for your annual performance review.
  (Go over questions that might be asked of you, and other
  questions you might want to ask your boss.)

PERIODICALLY:
- When you sense a promotion or transfer,
- Get a new boss,
- Are restless about a move,
- A recruiter gets you interested.

OR WHEN:
- You're not sure your job is "doable,"
- You're having trouble with your boss,
- You're uneasy about your top management,
- You're checking your company against competition,
- You're looking at your compensation.

AND AT LEAST:
- Every 18 months if one of the above hasn't happened.

* * *

WHAT YOUR BOSS CAN'T TELL YOU

HOW TO EVALUATE
- YOUR COMPANY
- YOUR JOB
- YOUR GOALS
- YOUR PERFORMANCE

KENT L. STRAAT
with Nellie Sabin

amacom
American Management Association

This book is available at a special
discount when ordered in bulk quantities.
For information, contact Special Sales Department,
AMACOM, a division of American Management Association,
135 West 50th Street, New York, NY 10020.

Library of Congress Cataloging-in-Publication Data

Straat, Kent L.
    What your boss can't tell you.

    Includes index.
    1. Career development. 2. Self-evaluation.
I. Sabin, Nellie. II. Title.
HF5549.5.C35S76   1988   650.1'4   87-47851
ISBN 0-8144-7704-6

Printing number

10   9   8   7   6   5   4   3   2   1

To
my mother,
an English teacher,
who never would have believed it.

Acknowledgments

This book was started with enthusiasm and a minimal understanding of the effort ahead. It was continued with support from many friends, clients, and colleagues who provided insights, critiqued chapters, and encouraged me on. It was brought to fruition with the assistance of wonderful professionals.

Early on, Alan D. Kohn, Richard Lindenmuth, Joseph M. Fox, and Alexander Burnham provided thoughtful suggestions, and Colin Gabriel was a consistent inspiration.

Renni Browne of the Editorial Department introduced me to the professional side of publishing. (Being a bit of a renegade, I thought I could do it my way. I couldn't!) Renni introduced me to Nellie Sabin, whom I met with some trepidation, only to begin a year-plus relationship of building what I thought was good into something so much better.

Nellie forced me to embellish thoughts I used as throwaways; she took the spoken jargon that I loved and wrote and made it so much easier to read; she took the thoughts that I wrestled with and made them clear. In essence, if you can imagine a bobsled veering from rim to rim while careening down an icy track, Nellie took the wheel and carved the sled to a finish in the center of the track.

Doe Coover, my agent, lent another level of insight in shaping the book, creating the proposal, and much more.

Ron Mallis, my publisher, has been constantly stimulating and encouraging. He, too, improved the book.

My wife, Donna, only now speaks of getting a husband back, having lost me to the word processor night after night and on weekends. I so easily accepted her support and that of my children, Hilary and Ted. My father, Lou Bredice, seemed to know that the project would end well. My Yankee uncle, George Fish, was a bit more succinct. "Well," he would say, "you may as well get it out of your system!"

My one regret is that my mother passed away before the book came to completion. It would have been a special treat for her.

Contents

Introduction   **xi**

Part I: Appreciating Your Assets: Identifying the Job Factors You Control   1

1 How Well Are You Managing Your Manager?   3
2 Is Your Performance as Good as You Think It Is?   24
3 Do Your Working Relationships Work?   47
4 How Do Others Perceive You?   69
5 How Well Do You Know Yourself?   88

Part II: Taking Stock: Checking Out the Company   107

6 What Makes the Company Tick?   109
7 How Strong Are the Products and Markets?   126
8 How Good Are the People and How Well Does the Company Develop Them?   141
9 Who's in Charge Here?   159
10 How Good Is Your Company's Financial Health?   178

Part III: Reviewing the Balance Sheet: Putting It All in Perspective   197

11 Is the Job Doable?   199
12 What Do You Get for What You Give?   217
13 What Is Your Career Fitness Index?   236
14 How Do You Know If It's Time to Make a Move?   265

Index   **273**

Introduction

Nothing against your boss, but he or she can't possibly tell you everything you need to know to manage your career to maximum advantage. To get ahead in today's treacherous corporate environment, even simply to keep your job while others are losing theirs, you need to wise up to the entire range of elements that affect the course of your career. Grapple with them, monitor them, and know their implications. Most people take entirely too much for granted. Those who excel see the larger picture and respond as factors change within it. You can—indeed, you must—learn to monitor these variables yourself, for no one else, including your boss, will do it for you.

Your boss wants you to succeed, but on his or her terms—not yours. Even the most well-intentioned boss cannot be expected to abandon his or her priorities for yours. There are important things your boss knows but cannot or will not share with you, and there undoubtedly is essential information of which he or she is not even aware. Your boss knows more than you do but cannot necessarily protect your job, nor is he or she a career adviser.

I'm a headhunter. I came into recruiting after working with Bethlehem Steel, IBM, Ogilvy & Mather, and Clark Dodge & Company. The year 1973 was the time of the generalist in recruiting and I am still close to that today. I've done unusual searches, such as for chief economists, general counsels, and a manager of an international airport, and I've done the expected ones for presidents, group executives, and vice presidents for marketing, finance, manufacturing, sales, human resources, administration, research and development, as well as the senior people reporting to these positions. I've searched for consultants for major consulting firms and for lawyers for major law firms. I've searched in most industries; from ladies hosiery through publishing and telecommunications to steel foundries, although I do seem to have an affinity for technically oriented searches.

In 14 years of recruiting, I've interviewed thousands of executives. I've found that people seldom realize exactly where they stand. They certainly don't get the whole truth from their employers. I've discovered that:

• People don't know how good—or bad—they are. Repeatedly, a candidate's words and résumé simply do not match what I hear, see, and read about that person. Often people don't understand their track record or achievements, or recognize their own personal interests or limitations, particularly if they rely solely on their boss's evaluations. *This lack of self-awareness is correctable.*

• People get sandbagged by problems that could have been avoided had they known what to look for and had they been paying attention. Bosses can telegraph only so much, and most of us are too trusting. Some surprises cannot be anticipated, but many can. In fact, *a great deal can be done to head off career crises.*

• The changes that have occurred in business are putting vast new pressures on individual careers today. There is no assurance that once you start working for a company you can stay there; that five, ten, or twenty years down the road the company will still have room for you. Navigating a career today can be tricky, but by performing well and anticipating problems, *you can build your own job security.*

• People don't know how to evaluate job offers—how to compare a prospective job or unusual promotion against what they already have. When you are faced with a job offer, neither your present nor your prospective boss can be depended upon to furnish you with all the information you need to make the best decision. Consequently, you end up making pivotal career decisions in the dark. These choices don't come up often enough— at least, they shouldn't—for you to become skilled at handling them, and serious mistakes can result. *These mistakes can be avoided.*

• People make job changes for invalid reasons, often realizing too late that they have thrown away a huge investment in their previous company—in relationships, knowledge of company procedures, and dollars—for a job that fails to turn out as expected. The true situation is not what it appeared to be during the courtship, and no honeymoon follows. I have seen many executives become enraptured by a prospective boss's promises, only to find they didn't materialize. *These disappointing job changes need not occur.*

The Importance of Taking Charge

We like to think that we are in charge of our lives. We read self-help books and do-it-yourself manuals, use at-home medical tests and procedures, make careful decisions about where to live and how to spend our time and money. But amazingly, we lose track of our work life. A career becomes something that happens to us rather than something we control. This amounts to self-sabotage. It doesn't have to happen.

Championship athletes and celebrities have managers and agents to look out for their every move. Businesspeople need the same kind of guidance, but it's not available. You certainly can't look for it from your boss. You have only yourself to rely upon. Who else really knows you? Who else has your best interests at heart?

In every complex or costly endeavor, a periodic audit is standard—for example, you wouldn't invest in a company without an annual report. Yet most people fail to take time to evaluate the strengths, weaknesses, progress, or deterioration of their careers.

Think for a moment. When was the last time you really scrutinized your job? Your career progress? You probably put more thought into buying a car than managing your career. You spend half an hour working out each day, 45 minutes eating, and another hour scheming over how to save 10 percent on a $300 purchase. Why not spend an hour or two each year systematically reviewing the career that makes everything possible?

Now consider something else. What might you have found if you'd performed a career checkup last year? For each of the last five years?

Think of this book as a career physical, like an annual medical checkup. In this case, however, you are both patient and doctor; you write the prescription for your own career's good health. Using this book, you first diagnose the condition of your career, then take corrective measures. *What Your Boss Can't Tell You* is not a panacea; it's a tool. The repair work comes later.

The Bottom Line Now Governs Your Career

In today's turbulent corporate environment, no one can guarantee that your company won't go under or be sold, merged, taken over, or split up. All jobs are at risk—including your boss's and your own. A good relationship with your boss helps but ultimately cannot protect you. Even fine companies that try to manage their operations for everyone's benefit are forced to lay off employees. Profitability of the company must come first.

Out of this changing corporate environment comes increased interest in a concept called "employment at will." In principle, it's simple enough: When an individual is hired for an indefinite period, as most are, either the employee or the employer may terminate that relationship without cause or notice. This idea has already had significant consequences. Most companies have eliminated all references to career employment and stability from their hiring and counseling materials. Companies are gently trying to let you know that they can't take care of you the way you've expected in the past and, more important, that you must take responsibility for some of that care yourself.

The message is simple, and disturbing: You can't afford to take your career for granted. Your best defense is to make sure you're as valuable to your company as possible and visible to the "right" people in that company. This is where this book will help. There *are* ways to keep your career on the ascent through unpredictable times.

To Get the Right Answer, Ask the Right Question

As a recruiter, I hear a continuous flow of sensitive information from people who have been burned or caught in messy situations.

During an interview, I ask each professional what he or she has achieved and how; why he or she made certain moves. All have war stories—different wars, different stories. They ask me different questions, depending upon what happened to them. In turn, I ask them a battery of questions, to assess their strengths and draw out their true talents and inclinations. Over the years, a pattern of questions has emerged, and it is these questions that I offer in this book so that you can benefit from the hard-earned experience of others.

What Your Boss Can't Tell You provides a framework for a complete career review and acts as a checklist for danger signs. Each chapter raises questions for you to consider and offers general advice on how to take corrective measures should you discover a problem.

In general, the optimal response to each question is clearly implied. If your private answer is positive and encouraging, you can be confident; if you're unsettled or disturbed, you've pinpointed a possible sign that all is not well. Your responses to those questions which are most important for your situation—including those in areas you may previously have overlooked—form the foundation of your career evaluation.

What Your Boss Can't Tell You is most helpful when all the points are considered together. A complete review yields a more accurate picture, and you can see whether a weakness is offset elsewhere by an advantage. Even if a particular section seems not to apply, at least glance at the questions, since you cannot know which ones will trigger your most valuable insights.

New Information Can Be Disruptive

Don't expect reading this book to be painless, for it is designed to bring you face to face with new information and to pinpoint factors that are (or should be) disquieting as well as encouraging to you professionally. You'll be surprised by the results of your first career checkup. You'll begin your review with some preconceived ideas about how you or your company are doing, but your in-depth analysis will turn up much more for you to think about.

Your first review may unsettle you with factors you've never before considered, and your first reaction to some of the topics may be that you aren't equipped to make judgments about them. Maybe you aren't, but by being alerted to them, at least you'll seek more information on which to base your opinions. It's a first step toward taking responsibility for your own job security. Do the best you can while you have time to do something constructive in your present situation.

A career is partly planned, partly managed, and partly chance. You want to avoid trouble, capitalize on opportunities—and give luck its chance to work, as well. To do this, you need to be as realistic and informed as possible. Using *What Your Boss Can't Tell You,* you'll identify all the variables that affect your career—internal or external, under your control or out of your hands—and keep these factors in perspective as circumstances change.

The purpose of this book is to help you make the most of the job you have, protect what you've achieved, and enhance your greatest asset, the aggregate value of your career—which could total in the millions. *What Your Boss Can't Tell You* can also help you evaluate any job you're offered, so you can be assured that any move you make will be the best.

Using this book as a reference, you'll be able to make timely, informed decisions about your career, recognize career pressure points, and see when something is going wrong. You'll learn to anticipate rather than respond. You'll learn to spot turning points—so obvious in hindsight but so difficult to see at the time. You'll learn to move out of situations in which your contribution is less meaningful and into those in which your skills are in short supply. You'll learn how to recognize what you need to succeed, all of which lessens your chances of being fired or displaced by a company upheaval. *What Your Boss Can't Tell You* will lead you to a new job awareness that will last through the rest of your career. You'll never look at your job—or any job—the same way again.

I've found that the special ingredient in successful career planning is attention to detail. Even the clearest objectives are useless if you're cut off by something you hadn't anticipated, and the finest strategy is irrelevant if you have no stable starting place. (Would you stand on a soggy milk carton in a damp cellar to change a light bulb?) *What Your Boss Can't Tell You* will help you establish a secure platform from which to reach out.

A Note About Women in Business

Any general use of *he* and *him,* rather than the preferable but sometimes awkward *he or she* and *himself or herself,* carries no sexist intent. I hope the reader will forgive this concession to readability, for without question this career review applies equally to men and women.

Winning in business is open to anyone, male or female, who wants to play the game. Still, women have at least two problems in business that men generally do not: They may experience discrimination in the workplace, and many of them come to the corporate arena with backgrounds that are different from those of most men.

I find, however, that women have the edge over men when it comes to career development. They don't hide behind a three-piece facade. Women make a greater effort in managing their careers, are openly interested in doing so, and attend seminars on the subject in greater numbers. Most men want everyone to think they know what they're doing, they've already arrived, or their success is virtually assured. This kind of posturing is actually self-defeating.

Using *What Your Boss Can't Tell You*

It's almost time to begin. In performing your career checkup, be honest. Strip away your business image as you tackle the uncomfortable questions. You need not share your thoughts with anyone. Your career checkup is an exercise for you alone; it is your own inner voice you want to hear.

You may think you know where you are and where you want to go, but quite possibly you don't. You may believe your company is healthy, but perhaps it isn't. It's so easy to get the facade mixed up with reality. You want to know the truth, because, even if the news is bad, this way, you can do something about it.

In the final analysis, your individual performance over time is the only security you really have, the only investment that walks out the door with you. What matters is what you can take away from a job and apply to another one—what you have learned, how you operate, how you see things, how you let others see you.

In today's changing corporate environment, employees need to be knowledgeable. I believe we will be seeing an unprecedented amount of activity in the workplace as people go where their skills are needed—and are dismissed when their contributions are no longer valuable. We will see more flurries of hirings and firings, more jobs terminated, more job offers made, more recruiting by headhunters. Greater career risks will be taken by individuals at all levels, whether they are comfortable with these risks or not. And behind the roar of all this activity, I hear the scythe of the grim reaper—the doctrine of employment at will—forcing you to take control of your own livelihood.

This book is meant to improve your chances of finding career success in a turbulent time. The competition is fierce, and everyone is working to the limits of his or her abilities. To distinguish yourself, you need not necessarily *do* more, but you must *know* more: what is expected of you, what factors are helping you, what elements may sabotage you, what changes are occurring—and of course, what your boss can't tell you.

Part I
Appreciating Your Assets:
Identifying the Job Factors You Control

I find that most people are not aware of all the things they can do to ensure their professional success. The following five chapters encourage you to review all of the elements of your job situation so that you can manipulate them to advantage.

You control so much of your career that you probably forget many of the things you can do to speed things along, just as you forget to take into account many of the things upon which you are being judged. Part I includes practical pointers on how you can get the most out of your boss, how to evaluate your real contribution to your company, what relationships you should nurture, how you can control the impression you make on others, and how to make sure you have your personal values in perspective.

You do control all of what follows, although it may come as a surprise. The starting point of your career checkup is you.

1

How Well Are You Managing Your Manager?

Set the scene. In professional sports, a manager must win to keep his job. It's not much different in corporate life.

For better or worse, your boss plays a pivotal role in your career success. He uses your performance to achieve the goals he has been given; consequently, it's his responsibility to make you as productive as possible. However, as the junior member of this team, it is your responsibility to find a way to work effectively with your boss and to make that association as mutually rewarding as possible.

In an ideal situation, your boss is outstanding, the two of you have an excellent rapport, he's promoted frequently, and he always asks you to follow. This is one of the easiest routes to success, but not a common one. If you are in this fortunate situation, you're probably already aware that it almost never holds throughout a career—nor would you want it to.

More likely, your boss has some quirks and your relationship could use some work. Your boss may be demanding, quick to criticize, intimidating, or dictatorial. He may be aloof, self-centered, or totally insensitive to those around him. He may be abusive but a superior decision maker; he may be a thoroughly nice guy but not too bright. A boss can possess any combination of qualities. You need to recognize his particular mix, good and bad, strong and weak, so you can focus more clearly on how the two of you complement each other, what you can expect to gain from your relationship, and how to achieve the results you want.

As a beginning, consider your boss's personal foibles. Crazy things do happen with bosses, and as any employee can tell you, a boss's pet peeves are important simply because you have to learn to live with them. I recall one legendary publisher, renowned for being particular about office expenditures, who became ill at work and asked her assistant to run out for some over-the-counter medication. When the assistant returned, he was horrified to discover his boss lying prostrate on the floor, pale and in obvious discomfort. Still, as he bent down, she managed to lift her head and whisper, *"Did you get the receipt?"*

If you're typical, the only question you've asked yourself about your boss is, "Does he like me?" Go beyond this. By asking yourself sharp, specific questions about your boss, you can see how you might shape and change your relationship. Use this chapter to turn around any problems you may have with him. An unsatisfactory relationship with your boss doesn't have to remain that way.

If your boss is a well-rounded high-achiever, you may be able to keep your relationship on track simply by turning in a strong performance and making sure you maintain contact with him at whatever frequency he prefers. If you're lucky, you'll be able to bask in his reflected glory. On the other hand, if your boss is a disorganized genius, an organized plodder, a poor communicator, or holding his current position only on account of his connections, you will need to do more and to know more—and that's the point of this chapter.

Your boss's traits, both good and bad, will be reflected on you; be sensitive to what that impact may be. Sometimes a boss can cast a long shadow over your efforts.

To explore your complex relationship with your boss, first put yourself in your boss's position. Try to see priorities and objectives from his point of view, recognize what's important to him and what irritates him. Next take an objective look at how he operates and what he's like. Consider how your personalities mesh, then factor in any hunches you may have. Once you have assembled all this information, it's surprising what you can accomplish by keeping it in mind.

Examine Your Relationship with Your Boss

○ Are you and your boss comfortable talking with each other?

○ Do you respect each other, relative to the job you must accomplish together?

○ With which of your peers does your boss spend more time than he does with you?

○ Does your boss use you in any special way?

○ Are you trying to become your boss's friend?

On a person-to-person level, you need to get along with your boss. You need a personal chemistry between you that works. Without it, you add a dimension of apprehension that slows the communication process and raises a psychological barrier in your working relationship. The two of you do not, however, need to be friends or drinking buddies. Trying to be your boss's friend can create more problems than advantages.

Does your boss respect you? If so, you can't help but benefit. Ignore for the time being whether your boss is a fast-tracker or not; what's important here is how well your boss thinks of you and speaks of you. If possible, you want him to respect you more than he does your peers—not to the detriment of the team effort, but for your ultimate advancement.

Are you at ease with your boss, and he with you? Comfort in a relationship is subtle but helps act as a buffer when tensions arise. Ideally, you want to develop a comfort level that encourages your boss to use you as a sounding board before he makes decisions.

What is the personal chemistry between you and your boss? Personality differences can be difficult to judge, particularly with a superior. Sometimes they don't even exist but are imagined by the junior person. Whether they exist or not, you have the most to gain by eliminating any sense of difference. The sooner you bridge the gap between your personality types, the better.

I have seen some executives so deferential they make it all but impossible for their superiors to have an easy relationship with them. Both you and your boss will benefit if you are respectful rather than deferential. *Are you in awe of your boss?*

If you are, you'll never be part of the informal decision-making process. Try thinking of him as a customer. You project confidence with your customers; your boss wants to see some of the same. Play the role of the problem solver, and pay close attention to the clues that constitute a valuable source of feedback.

Bosses aren't stupid. They know when a hotshot has come in under them and will be passing beyond them. They just don't want to get hurt in the process. *Is your boss threatened by you?* Instead of competing with your boss, ask yourself how you can help him. Make him see you as an asset to be developed rather than a threat. If your relationship with your boss is strained, the ball is in your court. Know what he expects and when.

How does your boss like to see himself? Do you know his idiosyncracies as well as his special work habits? If you don't take his pet peeves into consideration, you may irritate him unnecessarily. As you become sensitive to your boss's preferences, the potential for your developing a comfortable working relationship increases. How do you like to have your subordinates deal with you? Maybe your boss feels the same way.

How do you get along with others of equal or higher status than your boss? If these relationships are mutually satisfying and your opinions are respected, consider what may be preventing you from having the same kind of relationship with your boss.

Now step into the future for a moment. *How might you interact with your boss if you left the company and met him at a party a year from now?* With the tension out of your relationship, you would probably discover a lot of commonality. Project what that might be, and see how much of it you can use now.

Consider Your Boss's Personal Interests

○ What telephone calls will your boss allow to interrupt a meeting?

○ What activities of his does his secretary joke about?

○ To which charitable, civic, or cultural activities does he contribute his time and energy?

○ What sport does he enjoy most?

○ What does he do in his spare time?

○ Is he fanatic about anything?

You can't ignore your boss's personal interests because he certainly doesn't. As a recruiter, I've seen a person hired because he played tennis—and this isn't as crazy as it sounds. If two candidates are equally qualified for a position, the swing factor can be as trivial as which one of them likes whatever the boss likes. Let me emphasize that playing tennis is not the way to get a job; however, being sensitive to your boss's interests is a way to facilitate your relationship. Your boss may want people around him whose attitudes are closely in sync with his own.

If your boss is one of those rare people whose job is all-consuming, forget this section. More than likely, however, he will have some favorite activities and outside personal interests. It makes sense to figure out what they are.

What makes your boss tick? It may be the ego satisfaction he derives from achieving objectives, making more money and getting a bigger title, owning a yacht, or buying an island summer house. You should be sensitive to whatever it is.

Are you aware of your boss's priorities? Try to take into consideration this extra dimension he brings to his work. For example, you can avoid scheduling meetings during times when he would rather be elsewhere.

You don't have to go out of your way to become involved in something that interests your boss. You don't even have to agree with his priorities, only recognize them and make sure you pose no threat to them.

A word of caution: Remember that your boss's personal activities are private. You may not be welcome. Whether or not you participate in the same activities, a tactful sensitivity to your boss's interests can only reflect well on you.

Assess Your Boss's Management Style
- Does your boss stimulate communication or stifle it?
- Is he traditional, or does he innovate and aggressively seek out new ideas?
- Is he a detail person, or does he go for broad concepts?
- Does he delegate responsibility and the necessary authority?

○ Does he set a course, let you know what it is, and stick to it?

○ Is he accessible?

Style is subtle. No one advertises, "I'm a listener," "I'm a reader," "I'm aggressive," "I'm a workaholic," or "I'm one hell of an inside politician," but every boss (like every employee) has his own style and sense of priorities—an operating approach he feels comfortable with, that works for him. Identifying your boss's style makes it possible for you to adapt your own style to merge most effectively with his.

How does your boss get things done? How does his mind work? Some managers are highly analytical, good at sensing the issues upon which a matter turns. Some solicit a broad range of opinions before making a decision; others deliberate in private. Some are known for telephoning at all hours of the night, or scheduling meetings on weekends, or creating a frenzy when there is no cause for one—it's just their style.

There's no end to the questions you might ask yourself about your boss's management style. *Does he favor frequent and open communication or the occasional, strictly factual memo? What impresses him?* Simply determining how your boss operates can help you improve your own performance. It also can help free you from beating your head against the wall of a managerial style that is never going to change. And if you determine that your boss is truly talented, you may decide to be more tolerant of his other shortcomings.

To get a handle on your boss's style, talk with people who have worked with him in the past as well as those who work with him now. *What common factors exist in those who have succeeded under him and those who have failed? Who gets along best with him, and why?* Your subordinates don't have to admire your style, but they do have to cope with it. You have the same responsibility when it comes to your boss's style.

Study How Your Boss Handles Conflict

○ Have you seen your boss handle conflict?

○ Does conflict make him uncomfortable?

○ Does he search for the salient factors on each side?
○ Is he good at openly handling complex issues, or does he prefer one-on-one talks?
○ Does he encourage diverse opinions even though conflict might arise?
○ Do you feel comfortable bringing up new ideas to him?

How your boss handles conflict is an aspect of management style that warrants special mention. Openly dealing with a diversity of opinion does not come easily to many executives. They like to resolve matters in private and present only conclusions to groups. I remember one boss saying to me, "Don't worry. No decision will be announced until I talk to you." The real message was, "Don't bother me with facts until I make up my mind, and then we'll talk." By "then," of course, all that remained was announcing his decision.

Does your boss solicit diverse opinions and bring them up for comment in group meetings? If so, you're lucky. You have a forum for your ideas. If he treasures agreement, however, you'll have to build your case quietly, collect endorsements for your position, and be ready for your boss's first rebuttal. If your boss prefers to handle conflict privately, you might catch him as he walks by your office. Or if he is more receptive to a ground swell, you might drop hints with others and let the issue come up that way.

Does your boss create conflict? Some bosses like to pit colleagues against each other. Others create chaos by constantly changing their decisions. I recently interviewed a man who left his position as vice-president of a large and vigorous company after only eight months. He'd found he could not work effectively with the president, who kept changing his mind. He admitted he'd gotten himself into this bind by focusing on the opportunities the job had presented and failing to look beyond the president's charm. He now wishes he had delved into this president's management style before accepting the position. The signs were there, if only he had looked.

So much of how you get things done will depend on your boss's style. Recognizing how he likes to work will enable you both to prosper.

Watch How Your Boss Develops Others

○ Does your boss hire people who are better than he is?
○ Are his people sought internally? Externally?
○ Does he share responsibility, delegate, and give the authority needed to do the job?
○ Does he send subordinates to training programs or make other efforts to upgrade his people?
○ Does he make a sincere effort to get his people promoted and moved on to the best opportunities for them?

If your boss hires strong people, this indicates self-confidence as well as a desire to leave a stronger group after he moves on than the one that existed when he arrived. Other good signs are delegating, allowing you to develop expertise in some particular area, and sharing both the credit and the blame. *How much is your boss going to help you? How good is he at developing his people?*

Early in my career I worked for a president who was brought in to head up an excellent team. One by one, talented executives above me left for good positions elsewhere. Their career moves always seemed well chosen, but it finally dawned on me that I was witnessing an exodus. If these employees were so good— and indeed, they were—why were they leaving? Why were they *allowed* to leave? Soon it became clear to me that the president would rather let good people go than feel deficient in their presence. Eventually, I, too, left the corporation, and I learned some time later that the president had proceeded to run the company into the ground.

Does your boss encourage you to attend training sessions? Today, continuous training is crucial. If your boss is not willing to eat into short-term profits to benefit you and the company long-term, you have reason for concern. Changes in technology and products make it almost impossible to maintain a career without such updates. One of the by-products of the concept of "employment at will" is that you will need to be learning constantly in order to keep your skills up to date. A surge effort will not accomplish this.

Companies have very different attitudes about developing people. We'll look at company training policies in Chapter 8. Here you want to focus on your boss's attitude. *Does he recognize the importance of your keeping your skills up to date?*

How likely are you to advance under your boss? Your first promotion from entry level is the most important, and your boss can make a tremendous difference. For example, I recently interviewed a sales manager who made a point of getting at least one of his eight people promoted every year. Try not to leave your hiring manager until he has boosted you up that first step.

Your manager's desire to see you develop is not something you can control. If your boss gives you ample opportunity to express yourself and gain recognition, take advantage of it; if he doesn't, ask yourself what this may do to your long-term prospects.

Review Your Boss's Track Record
- ○ How do you regard the companies your boss has been with?
- ○ Are you impressed by the positions he has held?
- ○ Do you know what he accomplished in those positions?
- ○ How does he rank among his peers?
- ○ Is he one of the youngest in his position?
- ○ Is he known for consistently meeting his objectives?
- ○ Are there any signals that his power is weakening?

If your boss has been with impressive companies, that is to his credit. If he prospered in those companies, that is more to his credit. But what you really want to know is what he accomplished and how, whether he just rode a wave or caused the wave to happen. Has he handled a turnaround or solved an "impossible" situation? If so, that says a lot about his capabilities.

If you have been with your boss for at least six months or so, you may already know his track record. The information has a way of surfacing. If you're looking at a prospective boss in another division of your company, this information is relatively easy to get from friends.

Evaluating a prospective boss in a different company takes more effort and sensitivity, but it can be done. Talk with people who worked for him if you can, and with others who interacted with him and saw him in a broader perspective. To find these people, spin your Rolodex. Search for people you can call who have contacts at his former company or companies. Friends are generally honest with friends, but if you approached these contacts directly, they would probably be reluctant to speak freely with an outsider.

The ideal boss is one who is on the move. *How well is your boss handling his career? Is he moving up? Does he have a steady record of increasing responsibilities? How far do you think he's likely to go, and how fast?* Your best sources of information are people for whom your boss worked or who have worked for him. That is where recruiters go. Talk to people who have left the company, and when you hit a negative, check it with one or two other people before assuming it to be valid.

Is your boss on a fast track? If he is, he will generate excitement that creates opportunities for you. Although following a fast-tracker is usually to your advantage, it is not without risk. The fast-tracker—who often has greater responsibilities than his peers, gets involved in pivotal projects, is asked to serve on impressive committees, and is promoted at least every two or three years—can also be a threat to management, and therefore to you. Fast-track bosses often have difficult personalities and can be hard to work under. If your boss is insensitive and/or driven by a need for power and achievement, he may have little regard for lasting relationships.

On the other hand, few things are more unsettling than watching your boss slip from the ranks of the powerful. *Is your boss losing stature?* If so, doors that were once open to him are now closed, his budgets (and yours) are being cut, and a new level of anxiety appears within your group. You and others become preoccupied watching for the signals that your boss is topping out and moving toward the inevitable separation by "mutual consent." He may be out of favor at the top or have exceeded his level of efficiency. In this situation, you must be more careful, but your boss can still help you avoid the pitfalls he knows about that you don't—if you get along with him, and if he wants to help you.

In a corporation, you are known by the team you are on, and the team is known by the reputation and track record of its leader. Your boss's track record is far more important than his title. The sooner you know what it is, the sooner you can plan your actions to your best advantage.

Assess Your Boss's Corporate Goals

Short-Term Goals

○ What is the plan your boss has to make, and how is it broken up?
○ What is the toughest part of it?
○ How is his performance measured?
○ Can you think of anything extra you could do to help him?
○ Does he have a running battle with any particular colleague for a short-term advantage?

Long-Term Goals

○ Does your boss have a pet project that he is championing?
○ Where does he want to be in five years?
○ Who else is in the race for that same position?

Your concern for your boss's goals is not altruistic but realistic. By knowing his objectives, you can ensure that your performance makes the greatest contribution to the realization of a mutually beneficial goal.

Imagine for a moment that you are your boss. A manager who reports directly to you comes in for a meeting. In the course of your conversation, he asks you where his performance fits in with yours and how important his responsibilities are in getting your job done. You're probably impressed.

In another meeting, this manager asks you about your greatest problem in meeting the group's objective. You can't tell him everything, but you're pleased that he has a genuine concern for the bigger challenges you face.

Now stop role playing. *How much do you know about your boss's annual plan?* You'll probably need to do some homework to find out what he must achieve. *Who do you know who is close to your boss?* Try to identify someone who knows more than you do and will share what he knows with you. The more you know about the challenges your boss faces, the more helpful you can be. You need your boss's enthusiastic support to succeed, and one way of getting that support is by showing interest in where he is going.

In trying to pinpoint your boss's goals, keep an open mind. Ask delicately and watch carefully. Surprising things may turn up. You may find that your boss has an enemy in senior management he has to work around or that he wants a particular promotion badly. You may even find that he is a do-nothing manager, afraid to rock the boat for fear he won't get his next promotion. This situation, not uncommon in companies where seniority is more important than performance, makes it very difficult for you either to be helpful to your boss or to draw imaginative assistance from him.

Whatever type of boss you have, remember to ask yourself how any situation is likely to reflect on him and what it's likely to mean to you. You aren't playing politics, but you are using common sense.

Weigh Your Boss's Political Clout

- ○ How does your boss get along with the movers and shakers?
- ○ Is he well wired in?
- ○ Do his requests for additional budget usually get approved?
- ○ Does he spend more time than his peers do with the policy makers in the company?
- ○ Do senior executives use him as a sounding board before important decisions are made?
- ○ Does he maintain a broad range of good relationships, or does he play politics?

The political clout of your boss is particularly important because he can often leverage whatever power you have. If he is part of the informally acknowledged power structure in your company, he can introduce you to the right people and give you the job assignments with the best visibility.

Sometimes a political situation involving your boss is blatantly obvious. A new CEO comes in and slowly or not so slowly brings his own people aboard. The original employees, part of the old team, feel disenfranchised. They have a tough time trying to reestablish their positions. Sometimes they just wait, hoping the new team will burn itself out.

Politics in other situations can be more subtle. It is the good ol' boy network in action—associates choosing those they know over those they do not. *What are the power routes in your company? Is your boss on the right track?* At General Electric, early experience on the traveling audit staff is said to form bonds that hold throughout a career and that are essential for moving forward on the financial side of the company. At IBM, the traditional route to the top has been through sales. There's no great mystery here: The key is relationships—experiences shared and confidences established. Over time, you have seen certain people in action, you know how they respond, and most of all, you stay in touch.

How powerful is your boss? How he operates will tell you much about the power of his relationships, even if politics is not considered a factor in your company. A powerful person gets his requests for additional staff or budget approved quickly. He is asked to attend meetings that do not bear directly on his work and to review new policies before they are announced. He is visited by many people, often by those not directly related to his operation (good exposure for you). He stays in the mainstream of the company's business unless he accepts the challenge of a turnaround opportunity that affords great visibility. You have a lot to gain by being close to such a boss.

Your progress depends in part on your boss's ability to play the game at hand. Even if you try not to get involved in politics—and some people can pull this off—you should at least recognize how each player, especially your boss, is regarded and connected. *How well does your boss play the game? Does he have the power to take care of you?*

Represent Your Boss Effectively

○ How well do you represent your boss?
○ Do you communicate effectively, ask questions, and participate in a way that reflects well on him?
○ How well does your boss think you represent him?
○ Does he ask you to stand in for him at meetings?
○ Does he ask you to accompany him to meetings?

In representing your boss, you fall into what might be described as either the junior or senior level. If you are junior on your boss's team, much of how you represent your boss depends on your presentation, resourcefulness, and insights when you are sure of your ground. You will be noticed for your street smarts— how you handle yourself and protect your territory (your boss's territory, that is).

More is expected of you at the senior level. You have been around a while; you know your boss's feelings and priorities and should be able to represent him effectively. *Who does your boss select to stand in for him?* If he asks you to stand in more often than others, he is confident that you will conduct yourself in a manner worthy of him when he is not around. *Does your boss bring you to meetings?* This is even more significant. His willingness to appear with you and introduce you to others in his circle means he regards you highly, and it also gives you great visibility.

Bosses want to be represented well by their people. Presenting yourself well will reflect favorably both on him and on you.

Acquire Your Boss's Strengths

○ What is your boss known for?
○ What is his strongest point?
○ What does he have that allows him to be your boss?
○ What special knowledge or expertise does he possess?
○ Does he have peripheral experience in your field that could be useful to you?
○ How can you build his strengths into yourself?

You will work harder at your relationship with your boss if you recognize what can be learned by working closely with him. Anyone reaching your boss's level has to have *some* strengths— perseverance if nothing else, but most likely there are others. Identifying your boss's strengths presents you with a terrific learning opportunity. If your boss has few strengths, then a great element of challenge is missing from your environment.

I've grouped some attributes below to help you determine what strengths your boss has and how much you can gain from him. As you strive to put your boss in clearer perspective, be careful that you are not blinded by your own ego, and keep an open mind for attributes other than those listed.

Knowledge of:

> markets
> products
> customers, clients
> competition
> technology
> experts
> in-house operations

It may be your boss's knowledge that you need. He may be familiar with organizations and people, the network that conveys information. He may know facts and figures or have a special insight into products. These are all things you, too, can learn.

Skills, such as:

> decision making
> negotiating, compromising
> team building
> motivating

Personal characteristics, such as:

> good judgment
> excellent memory
> creativity

For what do you respect your boss? What does he do much better than you do? To identify your boss's strengths, stop focusing on how he appraises you and turn the tables. Step away from the personal aspects of his style and the things you can't stand about him and try to see why senior management values him. *What enables him to succeed?* Your view of a boss is all too easily obscured by the emotions that arise from trying to mix two styles. Keep those emotions and barriers out of it, since they stand in the way of your developing the relationship you want.

I remember a boss whose greatest attribute was his sincere charm, but because I was in a hot part of my career, I didn't recognize how much he accomplished with his manner rather than with his business skills, which were marginal. I focused on his weakness, not his strength. A number of years later I recognized my own rough edges and began working on smoothing them, a task that would have been much easier if I had started while working for that boss.

Much of the work in acquiring your boss's strengths is a matter of simply stripping away the negatives so that you are open and natural with each other. After that, you can carry the conversation just a little further than the pressing problem of the day.

Are you riding behind a mover and a shaker? If so, you can see how deals are struck and moves made. Your boss may have an unusually acute understanding of your industry; his expertise can help you as you build your own. He may know a broad array of clients or key people; by working closely with him, you can acquire some of these relationships and build on them. The abilities to negotiate skillfully, inspire confidence, hire and fire, and make firm decisions can all be acquired through observation as well as practice.

Once you identify your boss's strengths, drink them in. They are good to know, even if they are not your style. Most of them are transferable, and they are yours for the taking; it's an expected and free dividend of corporate life. Your efforts here can make the difference between your staying where you are or attaining a new level of success.

Does Your Boss Evaluate You Constructively?

○ Does your boss give you an evaluation?
○ Does he evaluate your performance at least every 12 months?
○ Are you impressed with his insights and comments?
○ Is he fair and objective?
○ Does he cover your weaknesses as well as your strengths?
○ Does he make an effort to be helpful?

Some bosses like to do evaluations, some don't. Some are good at them, some aren't. Some companies require them, some don't. Since federal laws require substantiation when people are held back or let go, more evaluations are being given these days, but this protect-your-backside approach is of little value to you. You want an evaluation that is designed to offer constructive criticism, provide feedback, and summarize both what you set out to achieve and what you did achieve. Ideally, the process is focused on improving your performance, and it can be extremely valuable to you as well as to management—not only in determining your compensation but also in clarifying your strengths, weaknesses, and prospects.

We'll look at your company's formal evaluation procedures in Chapter 8. A good procedure lays the groundwork for a constructive evaluation, but the deciding factor is your boss's attitude.

A solid evaluation takes a half hour or more. You and your boss sit down together and review a number of factors; your boss makes his observations, and you offer your opinions and/or rebuttals. A good manager will make recommendations and put forth possible courses of action that will strengthen your weaknesses—assuming, of course, that the value of your contribution outweighs your weaknesses by a good margin.

Such an evaluation takes time, insight, and concern, and not surprisingly, many bosses avoid it. They find evaluations messy and demanding of insight; they can cause repercussions and bruise egos. I remember a three-year period during which the closest I came to an evaluation was a handshake, a bonus check, and the comment, "You've done a great job; you earned this." Needless to say, I thought I had. One year my boss put his hand over the telephone and interrupted his conversation to give me this "evaluation." He wasn't a bad guy. He just had no interest in trying to work constructively with a subordinate—and he was president.

To progress and grow, you need constructive criticism. Your boss is not doing you a favor by failing to address your shortcomings until problems force them into the open sometime in the future. You need to fix them.

What if you don't get a meaningful evaluation? This is a problem, because you don't know how your boss sees your strengths and weaknesses, how he feels about you, or what he is saying about you to his superiors. You're adrift. To get some sense of how you are doing, try talking to your human resources executive, bearing in mind that although he has a good overview, he is not familiar with all the details. Then use this book to evaluate yourself.

Whether an evaluation is required and done formally at your company or is not required and is done informally, you are being evaluated by someone. Remember, there is no rule for when an observation becomes an evaluation. Periodically ask your boss questions to learn where you stand. Knowing how you are being evaluated can give you an important edge.

Do You Have the Potential to Succeed or Follow Your Boss?

○ Do you like where you're headed in your company?
○ Do you enjoy working for your boss?
○ Does he regard you highly?
○ Might he ask you to follow him if he moves?
○ Would you want to follow him, or are you tired of being behind him?

There's a difference between "succeed" and "follow." You could conceivably *succeed* your boss if management sees you as his successor or replacement. You may *follow* your boss if he reaches back for you as he moves ahead. The two forces at work here are the manpower continuity program of your company's human resources department, which focuses on your path through the company, and your boss's personal desires, which can move you within the confines of the company or beyond it if he is wooed away. Both paths have possibilities; each depends on a vast array of factors.

Are you aware of your company's plans for you? Desirable as it is to have succession plans in companies, they are not always made because they require time, work, and expense. Succession planning is covered in more detail in Chapter 8, but if you know you are well regarded in the succession plans, you are obviously doing something right. If succession planning is not a factor in your company, the matter of following your boss takes on more importance.

Would you want to follow your boss? What will you gain if you do? By now, you should have a feeling for the speed of your boss's progress and know a little about how he operates. You know where he wants to go, and you've identified his strengths. Now ask yourself what you'll give up by staying with him. If he's the best show in town, take your time deciding if and when you want to spin off from him.

Will your boss ask you to follow him? A tough question. If you are a confidant of your boss and talk frequently, you may well know the answer, but if that is not the case, look for other signs. Does your boss regularly ask your advice or ask you to accompany him to meetings or on trips? Is your skill important to him and key to his success? Do you get along well together? There is no guarantee that your boss will ask you to follow him, but your planning can be sharper if you have evaluated the probabilities.

COULD THIS BE YOU?

Norm was a great general manager, enthusiastic and successful. He was responsible for a $120-million division, and he reported to a group president who had three other general managers reporting to him. No matter how hard Norm worked, he could not get what he needed from the group president when he needed it in order to effectively run his division.

Norm was puzzled. His subordinates had a high regard for him, and he invested time in getting along well with his fellow managers. He knew he had what it took to do his job, but despite his strengths, he never developed a constructive rapport with his boss, Felix—and this was interfering with his performance.

Norm was on the brink of leaving the company. He thought he was doing everything he could, but he wasn't progressing. Norm also found himself outside the easy camaraderie Felix had with the other general managers, and he resented this.

One night over a drink at a convention, Norm learned why he wasn't breaking through. One of his fellow division managers said good-naturedly: "I gotta tell you, Norm, I love hearing stories about your going in and making those eloquent pitches but never getting what you want. You know, the only way you can get through to that guy is to send him a point-by-point memo of what you want to talk about before you meet with him."

Norm was stunned. Was it that simple? His last boss, whom he'd admired greatly, had hated memos. Norm thought he was helping Felix by going out of his way to avoid burdening him with paper—but it turned out Felix was a reader, not a listener.

"Don't bother me unless you have a problem," Norm's previous boss used to say, and Norm had made a point of not irritating him with trivia. He'd assumed Felix would appreciate the same approach, but now he began to wonder. Maybe Felix interpreted his self-sufficiency as remoteness or even unfriendliness.

Norm suddenly realized he might have made much faster progress in his company if he'd read his boss correctly—if he'd put as much time into developing his relationship with Felix as he had into his other working relationships. As he hit the lights that evening, he realized that he had a lot to do—but that redefining his relationship with Felix might yield even better career dividends than taking another job elsewhere.

PULLING IT TOGETHER

You should know your boss pretty well by now and have an accurate picture of how he feels about you. Your boss is human, with his own frailties; by knowing how you can support him and by capitalizing on his strengths, you can take action to ensure that you will prosper together.

You have also seen how this book works and the extent to which the value of *What Your Boss Can't Tell You* depends upon your active participation. *What specific problems have you pinpointed—and what remedies come to mind?* Chances are your boss isn't going to tell you how he feels about you, and most likely he won't go out of his way to explain his own management style. But the signals are there, if you look for them.

Search for areas in your relationship with your boss that you can improve upon. With some attention, a relationship can most definitely be strengthened—and your career prospects along with it.

What questions did you avoid answering? Everyone is less capable in some areas than others. While you do not need to publicize your weaknesses, it's important to recognize them privately. I have seen executives behave erratically because they were afraid to face their own inadequacies—and fearful that others would see them, too. It's better to open the closet door than to live with the feeling that you are hiding from something.

You may have felt that in this chapter you were asked to address matters that are out of your hands and therefore don't concern you. If these factors affect your career, however, then they *do* concern you, and you should review them periodically as best you can.

2

Is Your Performance as Good as You Think It Is?

It isn't easy to know how good you really are, but it's essential that you find out. What you do, how you do it, and who knows you do it is information crucial to any businessperson. There is no escaping the fact that your security and ability to command dollars are tied to the value of your performance. Whatever your performance level, you must take steps to protect what you have achieved even as you take steps to move forward.

Many factors affect your overall track record, and your performance is likely to have both strengths and weaknesses. The bottom line, however, is that you either succeed or you don't. If you're not succeeding, you obviously need to find out why. And if you are succeeding, it's just as important to find out how you can continue to succeed.

Frequently I encounter executives who describe their achievements overenthusiastically. Often they have not stopped to get a handle on their actual contribution.

The first step in heading off problems is to determine how well you are actually doing. Most bosses give you some kind of feedback, even if it's only at salary review time. Many companies have programs that require employees to evaluate their subordinates on a regular basis. The premise is good—that boss and worker meet to discuss openly how things are really going—but too often the procedure turns into a meaningless exercise.

You probably have had your share of glowing reviews, but you might also discover you've had periods of marking time or of helping your boss more than the company. These are things your boss isn't going to tell you. In addition, many managers are uncomfortable giving objective reviews. It is so much easier to leave out the bad news, to tell someone he is doing well— but this is a sugarcoated disservice. You need evaluations, particularly comparative evaluations relative to your peers, and these you must make yourself.

Evaluating performance in business is not like watching football on a wide-screen color television, with slow motion and multiple camera angles to isolate each member of the team. Your moves may not be obvious to your boss or even to you. Evaluating business performance is more like watching from the stands, where you see only the big plays—and then only if you are watching the right part of the field. In looking at your performance, you have to provide your own instant replays.

Individual performance is important, but you aren't working in a vacuum. As you review this chapter of your career checkup, focus on what you have accomplished, how you measure up against others, and who benefits from your activities. Be on the lookout for problems. Consider, too, your own satisfaction and comfort level with what you accomplished. If you put in your requisite number of hours, what do you have to show for it?

Assess the Value of Your Performance

- ○ Why is your performance valuable and to whom?
- ○ What would happen if your job weren't done?
- ○ Are you solving a problem or maintaining the status quo?
- ○ Did you make a contribution to the bottom line that is recognizable to those who know your work?
- ○ Have there been any indications that your work is valued by management?

The value of your performance—not your title or your niche— constitutes your job security. Safe niches are disappearing as managers face budget cuts and discover new ways to reduce expenses.

Most of the candidates I interview are successful, verbal, presentable, and well educated. It's hard to tell whether they have succeeded because of their own efforts or because of chance factors. Often they don't know the answer themselves, even those who see themselves as stars. They may simply have big egos or believe the corporate flattery they have received.

The test of your performance lies in your contribution to the bottom line—a point well illustrated by a CEO who hired me to find a division president. He had already targeted the additional revenue this new president would contribute, the after-tax earnings, the consequent increase in earnings per share, and the increase in share price with a price-earnings ratio of 10. Bottom-line orientation in the extreme.

Have you made a measurable contribution to the operating performance of your company? If you can say that you produced a certain benefit, this suggests that you're valuable. The contribution could have been in any area—new sales or products or acquisitions, legal matters resolved, increased production, reduced overhead. Think about what you have added to what you started with, new relationships you've forged, improved methods you've introduced. The further up the ladder you have made an impact, the better it is for you. If a new management group were to take over tomorrow (not unlikely these days), would your contribution show up as important or not?

What is your budget or revenue responsibility? Is it growing? This indicates the dimension of your responsibility in financial terms. It's another way of gauging your importance to your company, of determining whether or not your responsibilities have been increasing. Have you been given more capital to invest, facilities to manage or build, people to hire?

Consider, too, what important business decisions you made last year. *What was your best decision, and what was your worst?* If you made a number of big decisions, then you're in a position where judgment plays a key role. If your efforts were successful, you can be confident that your decisions were good ones. If you made few decisions, you may have avoided a responsibility that was expected of you, or little may have been expected of you, or you may simply have been the caretaker of a smoothly running operation.

What problems did you face? Solving a problem puts a high value on your performance because you are achieving what others didn't and are boosting the company's earning power to a higher plateau. Problem solving is one of the best ways to get recognition and can lead to your being asked to solve a bigger problem in the future.

What if you are just an ordinary performer? If this is the case, you have to search for the real value of your contribution—not how much you like what you're doing, but why your contribution matters and to whom in the company. Then ask yourself whether that person is important. Can you see the value of your performance moving on through that person to benefit the company itself? A danger in large corporations is that your performance may be important exclusively to your boss or division head.

It's not easy to calculate your impact on the bottom line in a business in which most of the work is a team effort. Still, someone is making a determination of your value and your contribution. *What do you think they are saying? How are you going to change that message if you don't like it?*

How Close Are You to the Primary Business of Your Company?

○ Where do the majority of company profits come from?
○ Where will they come from in five years?
○ What operations have been strengthened recently?
○ Where are the heavy-hitters? Are you with them?

The primary business of your company gets primary attention from Wall Street analysts, bankers, your competitors, and not surprisingly, your top management. It helps to be where everyone focuses his attention. There you will have a chance to work with the heavy-hitters in your company, who are often the people with the most powerful relationships.

Are you in the mainstream or on the periphery, where your performance is not as important? Recently, I was talking with a guy in Chicago who works in the corporate headquarters of a multibillion-dollar consumer electronics corporation. He was elated, having just discovered that a tricky career decision of his had paid off. Earlier in the year he'd been offered a promotion into a problematic division of the company in California, and while he didn't like to turn down a promotion, neither did he want to get stuck in a backwater of the corporation—a side effort that he regarded as a prime candidate for divestiture. With some trepidation, he'd declined the promotion and stayed in corporate headquarters. He'd just learned that morning that the division had been sold.

It's possible that you have been working hard on a project that management doesn't care much about or for a boss who's going nowhere. You're putting in a lot of effort in good faith—but in the wrong place! How hard you try has little to do with the actual value of your contribution. Long-term, you must be certain that your efforts are propelling you into the mainstream of your company.

Determine Your Annual Plan
○ Do you have an annual plan or set of objectives?
○ Do you assist in determining your plan?
○ Do you and your boss agree that the plan is fair?
○ Are there procedures to adjust the plan if major events disrupt its underlying assumptions?

You can't be measured if you don't have an annual plan, and if it is difficult to measure what you do, it will be difficult for the company to reward you. As you cope with whatever the situation is in your company, it is important to keep these two thoughts in mind:

1. If a plan is a company priority, try to get involved in the determining process.

2. If planning is not important to the company, make your own plan and track your performance.

How are responsibilities determined in your company? In companies where plans are important, the planning process is likely to be lengthy. Management will try to get as much input as possible before setting the goals—although as I write this, I remember when IBM determined where it wanted to go back in the 1960s and then just divided up that sales goal among the branch offices. That didn't stop sales reps from telling marketing managers tales of woe, trying to reduce the quotas.

What if you do not have an annual plan? What if your company is a seat-of-the-pants type? This throws the responsibility for making a plan to you. A plan is a way of pacing yourself and having something to talk about when troubles develop—and troubles do develop. It also gives you something to talk about at the end of the year if your compensation is not in line with your expectations. Without a plan, no one knows what you are expected to achieve, yourself included.

Once you have your plan, review it with your boss to make sure you're going in the right direction. If your plan is handed down to you by management, make sure you and your boss agree on what it is. Take into consideration any hidden agenda, any off-the-record objectives that your boss doesn't want to put in writing. Talk to your manager about your specific problems. Tell him what you see happening that he might not anticipate.

Do you have reason to believe you are falling behind? If you're not achieving your plan, management will question how you let yourself get into that situation. This, in turn, calls into question your business judgment, your ability to communicate with your boss, and your ability to set realistic objectives—which is every bit as important as achieving them.

Management edict will usually determine 90 percent of your plan, but try to get involved with tailoring that final 10 percent. Plans are designed to make you stretch, but see if you can't personalize that stretch. You are going to be measured on your plan, so you want to make sure it is as favorable for you as possible.

Achieve Your Objectives

○ To what do you attribute your success?

○ Were you simply lucky?

○ Do you usually achieve your objectives, even in bad times?

○ What percentage of your peers achieve their objectives?

When I interviewed a strong candidate for the presidency of an $800-million company, I asked him what he thought he was best known for, and he replied, "Making plans without wrecking the business, even in tough years." That was the first time I had heard that answer, and yes, he got the job. His history of making plans despite tough times impressed my client.

The ability to achieve under adverse circumstances is an important consideration to many senior managers when they appraise subordinates. They like to see people coming up who have handled a problem—either of their own creation or thanks to someone else—and worked out a satisfactory solution. It is your staying power management wants to see, because most problems don't turn around quickly in textbook fashion. If you did make a wrong decision but picked up the pieces and worked yourself out of the consequences, that's something you can be proud of.

You can learn from your mistakes *if* you're allowed to do so. I'm reminded of a former business associate of mine who made a very expensive mistake when personal computers were first introduced. Anxious for his department to be on the leading edge of technology, Bruce purchased several computers for office use before PC standards had been clearly established. The software he'd been assured of never materialized, the computer company failed, and Bruce was stuck with a lot of embarrassingly useless hardware. Management was not amused but decided to let Bruce work it out. Redoubling his efforts, Bruce applied himself again, this time becoming something of an expert on computer applications. He not only purchased new and better hardware but also went on to innovate a system for his department that was far better than management anticipated and ultimately was adapted for use by the whole company.

Have you met or exceeded your objectives? If you answer anything other than "yes"—including "yes, but . . ." and "no, but . . ."—ask yourself what happened. Achieving your plan puts you in a confident frame of mind and builds a good relationship with your boss and others. You get out from under management's gun and free yourself from having to make excuses. Even your complaints gain credibility.

Just how lucky were you? Maybe you answered the phone and there was your year-making order. At IBM we used to call orders that fell into our laps "bluebirds," although we didn't always admit to our managers that we hadn't worked for those orders. If you were fortunate and a number of factors beyond your control combined to make you a success, that's fine. Enjoy it. But admit it—to yourself, at least.

If you really worked to achieve your plan, brought the factors together, controlled their interaction, and nurtured the whole process—and you know the techniques you used and why they were successful—then you are in control and deserve to be confident.

Harold Geneen, the legendary ex-chairman of ITT, has often said that failure to make plans cannot be allowed—you must find a way. If you were president of an ITT operation having difficulties, he would ask you to present your problem in a large monthly operating meeting and then ask your fellow presidents for help. These meetings were brutal but effective. Strong medicine, but good to keep in mind during those down cycles and tough economic times that are the true test of your resourcefulness.

Weigh Your Performance Relative to That of Your Peers

○ Are your colleagues an impressive group?
○ Are you pleased to be a part of that group?
○ Do you have a stronger track record than they do?
○ How do your responsibilities compare with theirs?
○ How are you going to improve your position among your peers?
○ If a cut had to be made, why wouldn't it be you?

Your peers are a reflection of yourself. You chose them when you chose the company you work for, and you are seen as one of them by outsiders. Their reputation becomes your reputation.

For a moment, focus on how much you respect your peers and what you can learn from them. You can enjoy your colleagues without being impressed by them, but what you want is to be in a group you find challenging. If you are proud to introduce your colleagues to your friends and have accepted them with enthusiasm, you have a valuable relationship worth nurturing. If, on the other hand, you are neither stimulated by your colleagues nor eager to introduce them to your friends, you are underemployed—or possibly, poised to grab a position of leadership so you can upgrade the group. Take a chance. Do something, because sitting with uninspiring colleagues is a debilitating experience.

Winning organizations use the same dynamics you see in the sports pages. You are a member of a professional team, and you have a manager who, if necessary, will replace you—or find himself replaced in short order. He has a responsibility to make the team win and meet certain objectives, and he may have to move some people—possibly you—in order to do so. *What would the sportswriter be saying about you if he followed your team?* Even in business, somebody's watching.

Does your performance stand out? A winning attitude fosters competition between companies, between teams, and within a team. Whether it is acknowledged or not, competition within a team works. The trick is that you must work for the team and simultaneously distinguish yourself—even as the other members of the team are trying to do the same. It's easy to look good at someone else's expense and far more difficult to distinguish yourself solely on the basis of your performance.

To show yourself at your best amid a peer group you respect will take all your skills—all your intellect, determination, imagination, leadership, and persuasive and risk-taking abilities. You will have to be exceptional to win as your team wins, because your colleagues should be as smart as you are, work every bit as hard and as long, and want to be promoted every bit as much as you do.

What is your standing in your group? Your performance may satisfy you but rank low among your exceptionally well-qualified associates; or you may be at the top of that same group, an enviable position you can be proud of. You may even find that you are lucky to have the job you do.

Your basic concern in comparing your performance to that of your peers is to determine your relative position in the group. Keep an eye on what others are doing, no matter how busy you are. You do not want to be one of the weaker members of your team unless you are new or in training. In an outstanding group, it is not enough to be good. If you are only good, you're losing ground. If you're behind, do something while you still can.

Have you outdistanced your peers? If so, you have identified a problem. *How might you become part of a stronger group?*

Don't be surprised by an occasional dirty trick from a colleague. It happens. Take it as a compliment. He is worried that you are doing too well. Some people will do anything for a move up the ladder.

Have you checked your progress against that of your peers in similar positions elsewhere? These comparisons depend upon a broader range of variables, but they can still make you aware realistically of where you stand. With this knowledge, it is easier to take corrective action—or to be satisfied with where you are.

Assess Your Performance as a Manager and Leader

○ Do you enjoy coordinating the efforts of others?
○ Are you good at it, and recognized as such?
○ Are you a leader and motivator in addition to being a manager?
○ Do you command attention easily in a group?
○ Is your leadership admired for its results, the manner in which you achieve them, or both?

Managers push from behind; leaders clear the way ahead. The difference lies in your ability to motivate and inspire people, a talent above and beyond wrestling with the numbers to come up with the financial results. *How do you achieve your results through your people? How and why are you good at coordinating the efforts of others?*

Today, companies are putting more emphasis on making the best of their investment in their employees. They now recognize that changing people is costly and time-consuming; that it is better for them to build strength from within than to attempt to buy it when they need it. Your ability to get the most out of your people is more important than ever before.

You develop both skills and a reputation as you work, and while you will never know your reputation exactly, you can categorize your skills pretty definitively. Evaluate the "why" and "how" of your performance as a manager, for this enables you to appreciate your strengths and weaknesses as well as your chances for progressing inside or outside the company.

Managers, unlike owners, can't bank good fortune and live on it forever after. They are expected to continue to produce good results, coordinating all the times, dates, objectives, and people needed to meet deadlines. A good manager makes things happen.

A leader has the skills of a manager but adds to them the ability to motivate and inspire people, to cause excitement and stimulate imaginations. He draws a commitment from his people that allows his team to do the unexpected. Leaders have vision, enough to make them stand out from the crowd but not so much that they lose touch with those around them. Although leadership demands more skills and time from a manager, it is increasingly important in big organizations and is the driving force in start-ups and high-growth companies.

When you think of a leader, who comes to mind? You may think of a historical figure or someone in your company. *What qualities do you particularly admire in this person? Do you have— or can you acquire—the same skills?* A few years ago I had the privilege of meeting a two-star general in the air force whom I've never forgotten. He was tough, but his people loved and admired him. He could also join the band and grab a banjo, tell engaging stories, and trade repartee with the best. He made his people feel proud. Bold, sensitive, imaginative, smart—a powerful leader.

Are you following the pattern of most fast-trackers in your company? If not, why aren't you? Once you decide that you want to manage others rather than do a job yourself, it becomes obvious that you need a track record of growing responsibility for managing both people and money. You should already have demonstrated financial skill and the ability both to hire and fire and to fine-tune an organization. Progress toward general management involves managing greater numbers of people or, in a smaller company, broader involvement in different disciplines.

It is crucial that you have a realistic appreciation of your skills as a leader. Examine your skills. Can you control a meeting or take command of a tricky situation? Leaders get all kinds of things done. *Do you cross the line between manager and leader?* If you do, and are recognized for doing so, you should be a hot property.

Consider Your Performance as a Developer of People

○ Are people eager to work for you?
○ Are your people more successful after leaving you than those who have worked for your peers?
○ Do others in the company try to lure your people away?
○ Do you enjoy developing people and seeing them reach their optimum potential?

This special aspect of your performance as a manager may be distinct from both your leadership qualities and your profit-making potential. Your success or failure here may be more apparent to management than you think.

A record of developing people works for you in many ways. The people you have developed know it, no doubt think well of you, and stand ready to help you, formally or informally (and the latter is often more important than the former). Developing people is a form of networking, one with a substantial foundation. You are building a cadre of people who know they owe you something, and that is more important today than ever. Wherever these people go, or you go, that IOU between you remains, giving you a call on someone you might need someday. Recognition by management will, of course, come to you for being a team builder, as will a backhanded compliment: You will probably lose people as they are drawn away to fill other positions.

How accessible are you? How much attention do you give to developing your people? Caring, sharing, and delegating are the keys to developing people—but how few make the effort. It is so much easier to keep constantly on the move—well intentioned, of course, but busy with schedules and crises.

Do you share the communications coming to you that are not confidential? You can build a feeling of importance in your people by making them a part of sensitive developments.

Do you share the recognition? Let your people accompany you to meetings, give reports they helped prepare. Share the goodies, the trips south in the winter, the conventions, and the meetings offered by vendors. Being generous with your people actually increases your own clout. It also gives you the appearance of having recognition and authority to spare.

Do you delegate whenever you can as far as your authority permits? It's good for you and good for your people, as well. It provides another opportunity for them to do a job for you and be evaluated on the outcome.

Being known as a developer of people is a key ingredient to your progress, since a follow-on stream of good managers is essential to any organization. In any search I conduct, there is usually a list of six or seven factors upon which each candidate is rated, and one of these factors is invariably the ability to attract good people and to develop a team.

The final pleasure of having a reputation as a developer of people is that others in the organization want to join your team. It makes your job easier in the end.

What About Championing Something New?

○ Are you introducing a new discipline in your company?
○ Does it contribute to greater profitability?
○ Who in management recognizes this?
○ What is the life cycle of this new "thing"?
○ What are you going to learn?
○ Where are you going to be when interest in it peaks?

Championing something new is beautiful if you know when to get in and when to get out.

If you have been asked to champion something new, take it as a compliment. It shows that management feels you are credible in the organization. It also provides a chance to work with experts in learning new concepts and an opportunity to form relationships that can be long-lasting and valuable. Championing something new gives you a chance to demonstrate your capabilities to many to whom you wouldn't normally have access. You can see more of the company and be seen in the process—and it can be fun to be the guru. It can also mean you're expendable, since you are being pulled from your current duties. If so, you must consider it an opportunity for a fresh start.

Where is whatever you are championing in its development cycle? If you can, position yourself earlier in the cycle, when the technology or concept is hot and the experts with whom you are working will be closer to the strongest in the field. The benefits from this new concept are also likely to be greatest early on, and you will have more time to select the ideal situation to move into before the new concept peaks and becomes routine or outdated. At one point or another, operations research, personal computers, management by objective, data processing, and environmental control were all new; today's toys include electronic mail, local area networks, leverage buyout deal makers, and artificial intelligence. Each "thing" has its own life span, and each company has its own cycle for incorporating it into operations.

It's fun to ride the wave of recognition in introducing something new, but sooner or later all waves break. *Where will you be when your wave breaks?*

Assess Your Involvement in Outside Activities

○ Do you spend time during the day on outside activities?
○ Do you use company resources to support your activities?
○ Do these activities enhance your performance in the company and offset the expenses of supporting you?

○ Are your associates antagonized by your outside
   involvement?
○ Does management encourage you to pursue these
   activities?

You'll know it if this section applies to you. If you have a heavy
schedule of outside activities, recognize that this can be professionally risky.

Athletic, political, religious, civic, company, or industry activities take time—time to plan and time to participate. The
payoff can be tremendous, both in personal satisfaction and in
professional visibility, but there is a hitch. You are taking time
and energy away from your job.

*How much of your thinking time do you dedicate to outside
activities?* Thinking time can be expensive, and from my experience, the amount can be substantial. When I chaired the board
of managers of a museum, I was surprised to find out how much
thinking time this took, quite apart from the time I spent directly
involved in museum activities.

*How much time do you take from your workday for outside
activities?* While you might not think so, your associates and
your boss know how much time you take away from your work
for other pursuits.

The good news about outside activities is that they can
provide an avenue for both visibility and networking to those
who choose to actively participate. The bad news is that they
tend to grab you and demand more and more of your time. A
committee position leads to a board position, which leads to a
committee chairmanship, which leads to the presidency. Each
position is of greater responsibility and each is more personally
rewarding, but each takes more time as your importance grows.
As the organization depends more on you, you give more—and
this is where the bite comes with your job.

*Are your outside activities enhancing or damaging your profes-
sional prospects?* If you are a senior officer or president of your
company, you are expected to have outside involvements and
provide leadership in the community, and while you do so, your
company provides financial and manpower support for your efforts. Lee Iacocca did not hurt his position, for example, by

getting involved with the restoration of the Statue of Liberty. However, when you are not president, support is not available to you; your own time and effort are required. If your outside activities are very demanding, there is a possibility that you will damage your performance and that of your team. You may be perceived as out of touch in your workplace. You may miss things with which you would normally have been involved.

If the personal satisfaction of your outside activities is vital to you, you might also question why this satisfaction doesn't come from your job. *What's missing?*

Examine Your Track Record

○ Does your track record presell you?
○ Have you been in impressive places?
○ Have you done an outstanding job in each role you've had?
○ How would your former bosses describe your performance?
○ Have you been in unusual jobs, exceptional companies?
○ How does your track record read to those who don't know you?

A track record is a record of your performance, of when and where you did what, and the results you achieved. It is how people see you in their minds as well as on paper. It sits in the computer in your company's personnel department and may be held outside the company by your competitors, the media, or recruiters. It is not a résumé, which is a statement of fact that *you* write. A track record is what *others* say and write about you. You may or may not like it, and it may or may not be true, but it is what is perceived about you. It is based on the facts, but it can also be a reputation you have, regardless of the facts.

Do you look good on paper, or do you have to resell yourself every time? What concrete accomplishments can you claim? Recruiters want to know your track record. When I conduct a search, I look for "have done" people, not "can do" people. The "have done" candidates have been there before, know the problems, and have seen the risks. If they have done a job successfully once, they can probably do it again in a bigger role with more on the line. The "can do" candidate who says, "No problem, I can do that," but never has, scares the daylights out of me, since I'm being paid to find someone with a high predictability of immediate success. Maybe the "can do" candidate really can do the job, but without any precedent, "have done" is more comforting to anybody.

Do you know the message your track record sends? If it is not the message you want sent, anticipate the biases and draw attention to where you feel the emphasis should be.

What conclusions can people draw about you from your track record alone? Generally, it is difficult for me to persuade a corporation to take seriously a candidate with a flawed track record. When I start a search, I always ask for a description from the company of the ideal candidate—where this person should have been and what he should have done. For example, a major consulting firm recently needed a vice-president to focus on local communications. The company's ideal candidate had a degree in electrical engineering, an M.B.A., five years in a research environment like Bell Labs, and five years with an equipment vendor as product manager. That was the track record on paper that would excite the company. Looking behind it, the degree in electrical engineering indicated that the candidate was technical, the M.B.A., that this person was astute in marketing, the research experience, that he knew *how* things worked, and the years as product manager, that he knew *why* items were designed, priced, and marketed as they were. Further, the last position showed that the ideal candidate could manage, coordinate different departments, compromise as necessary, come out with a product that would beat the competition, and know how that product would probably evolve over three years.

In examining your own track record, try to visualize how you look at the backgrounds of others. If you are as quick and unforgiving with yourself as you are with them, you will probably have a clear idea of how others see your track record.

Gain Recognition for Your Performance

○ Do the "right" people know what you are doing?
○ Who among the policy makers takes the time to talk with you about your work or things in general?
○ Are you well recognized within your group?
○ Does your recognition extend beyond your immediate group?
○ How well are you known outside the company?
○ Are you satisfied with the amount of recognition you have received?

Recognition gives you visibility, and you need visibility to succeed in your company or move to another. You can't be sought out—either inside the company or from outside—if you aren't recognizable, and if you can't be sought out, your chances of being in the right place at the right time decrease. If you want to progress, you cannot afford to be casual about your recognition.

How much attention do you attract? If you have not received a promotion or job offer in three to four years, you can safely assume that your performance hasn't made much of an impression. Various factors could be to blame, but obviously, you must do something.

Are you a fast-tracker? Most companies maintain a list of high-potential employees they want to favor, and being on that list is a great way to be visible. In large companies, the list can be formal, and in small companies, it might simply be in the head of the president, but the important thing is to be on it. It will mean that alternatives will be presented to you.

How widely are you recognized? You want to be identifiable to people in your industry who don't know you personally. If you are going to assume greater responsibilities, people beyond your immediate sphere must know who you are. This requires some extroverted effort, but so do those new responsibilities you want.

Somewhere on the corporate playing field there may be an opportunity that is perfect for you. There is no way of telling where that opportunity is, but your goal is to maximize your chances of bumping into it. Don't forget, you are dependent upon others drawing you up the corporate ladder as you concentrate on your job.

How much effort do you put into being visible? Visibility builds upon itself after a while. You do something that causes you to be recognized, and in turn, you are asked to do something else that brings you greater visibility. Your efforts to step out can put you in a position where others start coming to you for information. The result is that you become something of an authority, because in acting as a clearinghouse for data, you learn more yourself and at the same time set the stage to go further.

I recall a situation in which a search for a general manager narrowed to two candidates who were equally well qualified. Both Charles and Ted had outstanding track records and personal attributes, and each could undoubtedly do a good job in the position that was available. However, my client recalled having heard Charles mentioned favorably in another context some time before—and that gave him the extra shade of comfort that led him to offer Charles the job.

There are ways to earn recognition and build a reputation in every discipline. It's the extra effort that makes the difference. *Have you volunteered for committees at either the company or industry level, given talks and presentations at meetings, or written articles?* Visibility is chancy to achieve in the short term, but long-term strategies can pay off handsomely. Have you taken on an unpleasant but pivotal assignment or led a task force?

Another way to achieve recognition is by working with a person who is on a very fast track and who himself has high visibility within the company. You gain by association. Your reputation is also affected by the corporate reputation and product quality of the company for which you work.

Consider the Transferability of Your Performance

○ Did you really do what people think you did?
○ Have unusual factors contributed to your success?

○ Did you control or cause those factors?
○ Were they unique to your company or industry?
○ Is it fair to assume that you are unique if you originated them?
○ Could you be successful in the same way again?
○ Do you want to be?

"I did it here, I can do it there." *Or can you?*

Transferability is the sum and substance of this whole chapter. Whether you move upward within your own company or outward to another, you need to know how good you are.

Assessing the transferability of your performance is a two-part process. First, you need to determine how good your performance really has been and why. Then you must determine whether or not you can duplicate this success in other circumstances.

How good are you? The feedback from those around you can be important in helping you decide, but you have a lot more insight than they do into what actually happened, and that is where the answer will come from. Seeing yourself as management sees you is important, but far more important is your own true evaluation of what you've done and how you've done it.

As a recruiter, I am actively involved in moving people into different positions. If you were on my search list, I would try to find out how good you are by talking with you and with others who know your work. I would evaluate whether or not you could transfer your skills and create a similar success in a situation that involves different associates, different support staffs, and different political structures. Only if I thought you could duplicate your success in another environment would I present you to my client.

For example, a European company asked me to find a president for its U.S. subsidiary. It wanted industry experience, a track record of achievement, and a Mr. Ambassador personality to suit the company's image of itself. Final interviews were under way, progressing so smoothly that I began calling other candidates to thank them for their interest, until one took me aggressively to task.

"I'm tailor-made for that job!" he said in the course of a stream of comments. He knew what he could do in that situation

and didn't hesitate to challenge me. "Did you review my credentials with your client?" I told him I had not, and the rest
of our conversation was sparky, to say the least.

As you might guess, I did mention him to my client, the
client did want to see him, he did get the position, and he has
done a great job. He is still no Mr. Ambassador, but he has
brought the parent company sharply increased profits with which
to enhance its image and his own.

Are you on target about your abilities? If you want to move
ahead, you cannot afford to be naive about either your talents
or your limitations. If you have a great feel for the market in
one industry and lead your group to success, think carefully
before you move into managing an unrelated business. By no
means am I suggesting that it is ill-advised to switch industries,
especially since that is in vogue right now. Many companies hire
experts from a different industry to gain new perspectives. Such
moves require strength and understanding from both the person
moving in and the established environment, however. Bodies
have been known to reject implants.

Being able to transfer what you do best from one work
situation into another is at the heart of managing your career
progress. If your efforts truly caused a distinctive accomplishment, your self-confidence should be high, even if the result was
not obvious to others.

COULD THIS BE YOU?

Things were not going well, and Vivian needed to think. She
headed for her favorite thinking place, the sun porch, and looked
out at the snow glistening in the afternoon sun. After eight years
of selling for a major consumer products company, Vivian had
switched to a different organization to make her mark. She'd
been with her new company for less than a year, but she had
the feeling she wasn't making much of an impression.

Vivian's main competitor on the sales force was Jack, a
consummate salesman who handled all the big-volume discount
chains. Jack's numbers were almost impossible to match, let
alone better. Vivian recognized she couldn't go head-to-head with

Jack—at least, not yet—and she didn't want to play politics and exploit some of the unsavory things she'd learned about his practices. Vivian badly wanted to distinguish herself, but how?

She knew the company was right and the product was right, but her performance wasn't making waves. Vivian continued to focus on where she could get big sales, and came up with no answers.

Then it came. She remembered some of the small but prestigious accounts she'd handled for her former company. The more Vivian pursued this idea, the more she liked it. She would go after upscale accounts, starting with those she knew already, and make a niche for herself. If she was successful—*when* she was successful—she would both improve the positioning of her new company's product and boost the company's reputation. She knew this would appeal to the president, who liked being told by his friends that they had seen his products in prestigious places.

Her new plan would benefit Vivian, too, of course. She hoped it would demonstrate that she was both creative and determined in sales. Although she would not catch up to Jack, she was willing to gamble that her numbers would be more than balanced by greater recognition for the company—and for her efforts.

PULLING IT TOGETHER

Quite possibly, you have come away from this chapter with both insights and doubts. You probably found things that you are not doing as well as you might, some that take great effort but aren't as important as you believed, and others that are important but aren't appreciated by the right people.

Have you found any surprises—unexpected soft spots or strengths? Look at your performance objectively, as someone might who is paying the bills to keep you on board. Then add your own insights. *Are you satisfied with your own performance? Could—should—it be improved?*

Problems may be building because you think you're better than you are or because others don't appreciate what you're doing. *How can you make the best of where you are now?* Ask yourself what you have accomplished lately and how you have improved. Note which factors are changing and the direction in which they are going, for these changes may have a profound impact on your work and your career.

"Heavy going," you might say. "I don't need these unsettling thoughts about how good I am. Everything is going well at the office."

My response is that you *do* need these thoughts. They should be in the back of your mind, gnawing gently. Remember, this review is preventive, a system for minimizing missteps so that you can concentrate on your opportunities. With insight and effort, a serious problem this year may be reduced to a minor complaint by next year. Once you have reviewed the factors in this chapter, you can judge their comparative importance—for now.

3

Do Your Working Relationships Work?

Success in business is more than a matter of how talented or bright you are. It's a matter of personal chemistry. Comfortable and well-cultivated working relationships are essential. It is not enough for you simply to be good; if you are to progress, people have to want to work with you. Your ability to get along with others can be the deciding factor in meeting your objectives or getting the job you want.

A vice-president once asked me at lunch, "What's the most important criterion in any search?" We were looking for that pivotal characteristic, the extra dimension above and beyond the prerequisites. I answered, "How someone gets along with others— his personal chemistry." He agreed. We both knew of situations in which people with sterling credentials and great experience just didn't work out. They failed to develop mutual trust with others, to find subtleties in common.

Recently, I attended a dinner party and was introduced to an attractive woman whose near-opening remark to me was, "I'm among the unemployed!" I thought I had been set up, but no, she did not know what I do for a living. She was simply thoroughly distressed, having recently taken a position as president of a promising company only to find herself out of work 11 months later. Brought on board as a change agent, she'd been unable to implement her programs because she had failed to gain the cooperation of her colleagues. She had been asked to resign and called it a terrible surprise. Indeed it was, but it need not have happened.

Personal chemistry in business is like oil in a Maserati, an essential ingredient for peak performance. Management teams work closely together in pursuing corporate objectives, sometimes under tense and unpredictable circumstances. When a group works well together, the members draw the best from each other, not out of friendliness but through an association that is free of friction and suspicion. They communicate freely and can depend on each other. You do not want your presence to disturb this smoothly running mechanism. If you create uncertainty in the minds of others, your opportunities will diminish precipitously.

As you examine your different relationships, think of both the short-term and long-term benefits they can bring. Try to see whether you are doing the best for yourself in your present job. Consider, too, whether or not you are doing enough to pave the way for any move you might make—up, down, or sideways, inside or outside your company. A little extra effort now prepares you for the unexpected and could make a tremendous difference later.

You depend upon myriad relationships in corporate life, each with the potential to be a trumpet in your favor or a whisper to your detriment. Many have been built up over the years, sometimes by close contact, sometimes only by telephone: You have worked together to establish mutual trust, and that trust gets things done. Other relationships are relatively new or shallow, but still important—and still dependent upon this sense of mutual confidence. Some people whom you have never met will have heard good things about you; when you call, they will respond to you because you have acquaintances in common.

Whatever your profession, your working relationships are critical to your success—and informal lines of communication are often more important than formal ones. Think of how you get the information you need and whom you depend on. How often do you look at all the relationships—inside or outside your company—that you take for granted? You probably don't think about them until you need them, and by then many of them could have gone dry. It's easy to keep in touch every year or so, but to reestablish contact after five or six years is difficult.

"I have no problem with this," you might say. "I get along with everyone." Your success may give you the confidence to feel that way, but why not make sure? I find out whether a candidate is well connected not by asking him but by checking with those who know him.

As you go through this chapter, ask yourself what makes your relationships work. If you feel enthusiastic about a particular colleague, take an extra minute to consider whether he or she feels the same way about you. If you were to construct a matrix of the respect you have for various people and the respect they have for you, a skewed pattern might develop that could hold an interesting message for you.

Whom do you need, and who needs you? If you feel unique as some kind of high-achiever, make sure you look carefully at all the relationships that play a part in your success.

Your relationship with your boss was discussed in the first chapter. Here, let's begin with you as the boss.

Examine Your Relationships with Your Subordinates

- Do your subordinates respect you and seek your advice?
- Do they bring problems to you before they become crises?
- Do they look out for you?
- Does your group have strong team spirit?
- Is your relationship with your subordinates the most effective it can be?
- Do your people prosper under you?

Your relationship with your subordinates will play a big role in your success, whatever you set out to accomplish. The respect you have for your people, and they for you, will determine how much you get out of them and when you get it. Friendship is not your goal, but rather the mutual respect of professionals in business together. *How do your people show their respect for you?*

In the previous chapter, you evaluated your performance as a leader and as a developer of people. Here, focus on the personal chemistry that allows you to work effectively through your people.

Do you create team spirit in your subordinates? You are the source of this extra measure of commitment and enthusiasm. *Do you inspire and motivate others beyond their own expectations?* If your people respond to you, they can and will do tremendous things for you when you give them the word. If you have ever felt proud as your boss talked about you and your group to others, then you know how your subordinates feel if you create this same sense of team spirit in them.

Are you easy or difficult to work for? You want the truth here, not your opinion but that of your subordinates. *Do you generate excitement as you work?* There is an element of zeal and fervor in the way leaders go about things.

What signals do you send? What signals are you getting from your people? If they have unshakable confidence and trust in you, and if you motivate them and make them feel more powerful by being with you, then your relationship is excellent. You have built confidence and self-esteem in them or nurtured what was already there.

Do you encourage two-way communication? You want your people to discuss minor problems with you before they become major, opportunities while they can still be seized, and personal problems before they damage performance.

Do your subordinates act as your eyes and ears? Surprises in business are dangerous, but you can often head off trouble if you see it coming. Every one of your subordinates is an antenna, a sensor in his particular part of the business. Your people can advise you of little developments that may have bigger implications. They know what is important, what will help or hinder them, and what will help or hurt you. You want that information—but you'll get it only if your door is open.

Do your subordinates speak well of you? You want their respect, so knowing what they have to say about you is important. It's also to your advantage if they put out good press about you. What may seem to be a private relationship between you and your people quickly becomes public as you all go your different ways with promotions and reassignments. What your subordinates think of you has a way of becoming known. A recruiter seeks it out, your superiors listen for it, or it just moves as scuttlebutt—but it moves. *Are your subordinates saying what you expect? Do the good ones regard you as a mentor?*

Looking at how you get along with your subordinates is like looking in the mirror. What you see is not always what you'd like, but you can change it.

Consider Your Relationship with Political Factions

○ What politics exist in your company?
○ Can you cope with this natural phenomenon?
○ Are you in the "right" political group, if you must be in one?
○ Can you work with both sides?

Politics is the detestable side of corporate life, and many corporations will not acknowledge that it exists, but of course, it does. As I mentioned earlier, politics simply comes down to relationships. At its most benign, it is the contacts and deals that keep business going. At its most vicious, politics can mean sabotage or open warfare between colleagues.

How strong is corporate politics in your company? What evidence do you see? Corporate politics is neither unnatural nor unusual; it's an unfortunate by-product of human frailty. It can begin with relatively simple situations—for example, when new employees are hired, either above or below you. New teams are created, new alliances formed, and rivalry begins. In older companies, politics thrives with the accepted order, and it can be difficult to make great strides forward without disturbing the status quo.

As you try to get a handle on the politics in your company, look behind the titles and organizational charts to see who is doing what to whom and why. If you are politically sharp, you know that politics is something you do not talk about casually.

We all recognize that there are "right" and "wrong" groups in most companies, and it makes a big difference which side you are on. *Which group are you in, and how strong is it?* Speaking pragmatically, the "right" group is the one in power, generally in the dominant area of the firm where those involved know they are contributing significantly to the company's profits. The members of this group understand each other, are comfortable with each other and their work. It's a natural selectivity. What is your group's cohesive factor? What might trigger a change in the group, and what would be its effect on you? Take a moment to identify the key people in your company and to consider how you interact with them.

How well connected are you? Even in a politically active environment, it pays to get yourself recognized as nonpolitical if you can, for this places you above much of the skirmishing. This will require not only that you be an outstanding performer but also that you communicate well with people on all sides, including some of the distinguished performers in the "wrong" camp. Do you maintain relationships outside of your group? If you are perceived as being able to function only within a certain clique, you appear to be dependent upon it and have set yourself up for trouble when circumstances change.

If you detest politics and won't play the game, this can work either for or against you, depending upon your environment. If you work in a hotbed of corporate politics, recognize that if you don't participate, you will probably fail. If your colleagues are not about to change their ways, you must either develop your political astuteness or get out.

The higher you climb, the more politicking you are likely to encounter. Being at the beginning of your career certainly does not insulate you from politics, but at senior levels, the stakes are higher, and there is no longer any question of your professional skills or managerial talent. You have proved that on your way up. Now the deciding factors include who gets along with whom and who gets along best on the outside, as well—networking at its highest level. Senior executives are survivors. They have seen it all before and therefore choose their battles—

and their colleagues—more carefully. The stronger your contacts and relationships across the board, the better off you'll be.

Politics is like rust and barnacles: It exists, you remove it, you take preventive measures, but it usually comes back. The best defense is a broad range of acquaintances and a good reputation in your field.

Assess Your Relationship with Your Peers

○ Do your peers voluntarily spend time with you?
○ Do you work enthusiastically with them?
○ Do you hold an informal position of leadership among them?
○ How well do you work with your peers?

In Chapter 2, you measured your performance against that of your peers to see if you are among the best in your group. Now take a look at how well you all get along.

Do your peers share confidences with you? If they are open with you and you maintain reasonably frequent contact, you will have a good idea of how they feel about you. *Do they think well of you?* If they seek your advice frequently or ask you to coordinate meetings, you have their respect and are well regarded. Instead of letting you coast, however, this esteem brings with it an obligation to spend extra time with your peers so that the views of each one are represented.

Do you take the time to visit with your peers? Your physical presence stimulates more communication than a phone call. You can share details, discuss recent developments, read each other's body language. If there's something that your colleagues might want to bring up, you're available. This was recognized even by a recently appointed president of a telephone company. Although he was given a state-of-the-art telephone with the best bells and whistles his company could offer, he still drops in on people throughout the office. He practices MBWA (management by walking around).

Remember that you are not an entrepreneur or an independent practitioner; you are a corporate employee and a team player. You depend on your peers to perform their functions well, as they depend on you. Your future in part depends on them—a far cry from being out on your own—so how you get along with them is critical.

Think About Your Relationship with Your Boss's Peers

○ Do you have any contacts with your boss's peers?
○ Are you at a level where they have a say in your promotions?
○ Might you want to work for or succeed one of them rather than your boss?
○ Are any of them handling more important areas than your boss is?
○ Does any one of them interest you particularly?
○ Do you feel closer to one of your boss's peers than to your boss?

Practically speaking, your relationship with your boss's peers within your company is your insurance policy against storms. Hurricanes do hit companies, and you need protection. Your performance provides protection, as well, but your relationships are important on a different and more subtle level.

When you think of insurance, you think of the dark side, of things that can go wrong. *What if your boss quits or gets fired? What if you need help getting around him?* A good relationship with a peer of his could be a pipeline to informal help and also ensures that you have a broader base of support in the company. *What if you have a problem with your boss, such as a personality clash or conflicting priorities?* The creative guy who senses a problem, seeks out a peer of his boss, and gets the promotion he wants manages to save his investment in his company and eliminate the risk of getting started in a new one.

Are you gunning for a particular promotion? If you are at a level in the company where the pyramid is narrowing and openings are few, you need the support of your boss's peers because each of them has his own candidates for advancement. Competition intensifies at this level, and personal chemistry becomes even more important. Your boss and his peers get together to compare notes on their subordinates and determine who will be promoted. A friend of mine at IBM told me that he has been in meetings where he found he had to reevaluate his feelings— good or bad—about his subordinates because his peers' appraisals were so different from his own.

Do your boss's peers know you and your work? If not, do something extra. Volunteer, join committees, stick your neck out and take a chance. Good things can happen if they know you— which means more than *your* knowing *them.*

Do you think you want to work for one of your boss's peers? If he seems to be getting more funding and attention from top management, he's in the mainstream, so that is where you may want to be. *Does he know you well enough to seek you out? Do you know him well enough to approach him?* You need to decide whether a transfer to his operation is more to your advantage than working for a promotion where you are. Try to determine which alternative could give you more two years down the road. If you're still interested, try to cultivate a relationship with him before you request a change. You can learn a lot about him without sacrificing your present position by having some inter- action with him on a committee or outside the office. Make sure his substance and his operation are as attractive as he may be personally.

You no doubt recognize that moving to a peer of your boss can be a sensitive situation and can bruise egos, but you have to judge the trade-off of whose egos they are and what the potential gain could be for you. Bear in mind that running from one boss in one company to another boss in another company has its own set of unpredictables.

Take Stock of Your Relationship with Senior Management

○ Does senior management know who you are?
○ Are you used as a sounding board for sensitive decisions before they are made?

○ Have you received that phone call down through the organization that presidents are known to make?

○ Can you gain exposure to senior management without alienating your boss or peers?

○ Have you been put on a senior-level task force?

What your "senior management" is depends on the size of your company, but in any organization, your objective is to get yourself known to the most senior people who can help you. If your immediate reaction is, "Hell, those guys don't even know I'm here," you have identified a less than perfect situation. You don't want to remain unknown to executives a level or two above your boss.

Are there any signs that you are on the inside track? Everyone would like to be on the inside track, but not many are. It's that level of policy or communication just beyond that with which you would normally be involved. Being on the inside track means that someone has reached out for you and brought you in.

How do the senior executives treat you? Do you get special attention? It's a good sign if senior management asks your opinions on important matters in your field or assigns you to task forces. For top executives to reach over the intervening levels in an organization to deal with you directly is indeed a compliment, but it can also be a two-edged sword: Your boss may resent being circumvented and put you under added scrutiny. Be happy that your senior management likes your approach, but take care to appease your boss—and for that matter, anyone else who was jumped over.

Let's face it, cultivating relationships with your senior executives is not without risk. It requires great sensitivity. If you're successful, your peers may see you as a goldbrick, or you may be cast as a special favorite. Being regarded as the fair-haired one—whether or not you are—can bring its own set of problems.

How soon do you learn of company developments? Are you privy to sensitive decisions before they are made? Including you in the decision-making process is the highest compliment your senior management can give you. It means you are trusted for your discretion and judgment, that senior management not only knows about you but values your input.

Being visible to senior management not only enhances your long-term prospects but can also have immediate benefits. Occasionally, management has to make quick decisions; if your senior executives are not familiar with you, you could get lost in the shuffle. When ITT discontinued one of its operations, an employee in the accounts receivable department encountered exactly this problem. For security reasons, ITT made and executed this decision rapidly, and hundreds of people were involved. In the process, the accounts receivable executive was let go. Because he was not visible, no one knew what he did. It wasn't until the bad debts and slow pays built up that senior management discovered how well he had handled his duties—but he should have been doing a lot more a lot earlier to cultivate his visibility with management.

In Chapter 9, you'll take a closer look at your company's top managers. Here, focus only on your relationship with them. There are no formulas for developing a relationship with senior management other than to volunteer, produce, speak, write, and take a risk. Eventually, you'll be noticed.

Examine Your Relationship with a Mentor

- Do you have a mentor—someone who speaks up for you and gives you good advice?
- Is your mentor respected by his peers?
- Does your progress depend more upon your mentor than on your own performance?
- How long can your mentor be helpful to you?
- If you do not have a mentor, is there anyone you consider a possibility?

Mentors are great. Everyone should have one. I never had a mentor; looking back, I don't think I ever wanted one. I thought it was macho to do things on my own. How foolish and wasteful—but then, I didn't really know what a mentor was or how the corporate game was played.

Finding a mentor is not easy. Most mentor relationships are formed early in a career, during the learning and growing period. Working for a person of excellent reputation allows a relationship to build while you learn. Newly graduated lawyers often clerk for distinguished judges. In corporations, personal chemistry plays a part in finding a mentor, as do local or family ties and experiences shared outside the company. If your boss develops confidence in your work and likes working with you, you've got a potential mentor.

A mentor looks out for you, smooths your path through the company, and occasionally even counsels you from outside your company. He is especially valuable if he has both a special interest in you and the inclination to share his knowledge and give you objective advice. Favoritism is not the point here. You've got to be good to develop a mentor, since he puts his reputation on the line every time he speaks up for you.

How much of your success is due to your mentor? If you're following closely behind a fast-tracker or being helped by a senior mentor who is looking out for you, enjoy this advantage, but know that you are vulnerable. Admit it to yourself, at least, and then consider how much of your success is due to your efforts and how much to others' pulling you along. Your mentor is a door opener, which is fine—so long as you are viable without his support.

There is much to be gained from having a mentor. Studies say you earn more money at a younger age, derive more satisfaction from your work, and are more likely to follow an efficient career path. But a mentor can also create problems for you. If his profile is too high, people may resent your relationship with him to the point that your peer support is undercut. Mentors' problems can also spill over onto you. Your mentor can lose a political battle or get hired away and leave you behind to weather more than your share of animosity.

It's also possible to believe you have a mentor when in fact you don't. One young woman of my acquaintance noticed that her boss's boss was taking an unusual interest in her work. When it developed that he was more interested in her attributes than her career, she was furious. Worse, her prospects within the company were compromised by what became a very delicate relationship with a senior executive.

A mentor is valuable, but keep a few eggs outside his basket.

Consider Your Relationship with Your Company's Human Resources Department

○ Do you respect your company's human resources department?

○ Is it truly involved in management or just a necessary evil?

○ Does your human resources director know what you are doing?

○ Are you comfortable opening up to him?

○ Do you help your human resources department help you?

○ Do you get the help you need, both as an individual and for your group?

You want those in your HR department to advise you, like you, and—in Broadway parlance—love you. HR guys can do things for you that you can't manage alone.

A good human resources department handles more than the particulars of hiring, firing, benefits, and compliance with state and federal laws. It is also involved with labor relations, training and improving skills at all levels of the company, and succession and organizational planning.

Personnel management, as it is sometimes called, is the task of trying to merge the goals of a company with the personal objectives of its employees so the company operates at peak proficiency. Your human resources department is the vehicle that will let you run to your greatest capacity and satisfaction within your company. Having a friend in HR is like having a friend in finance—it helps!

Let's start with the premise that your human resources department is strong, a key part of management, and involved in developing people for everyone's benefit. *Are you aware of how your HR group can help you?* If you have cultivated a relationship with your human resources director, he can give you little hints, bits of information that only someone who cares about you will pass along—not rumors, and not confidential information, but trends he sees first that you should know about. He can help you plan where you are going in the company, where your people are going, where you can get—and how you can keep—the talent you need to support you.

Your human resources person cuts across departments and titles. He is a confidant of management, involved in the early stages of company changes, and he knows what is happening where. He can be a great help, but only if he knows what you are doing and you allow him to help you. Tell him your ambitions. Discuss the strengths of the people under you, those you want to see promoted, those you might want to bring on board from elsewhere. Your human resources director can't help you unless he knows well in advance what you'll be needing. You must give him time, information, and attention—*before* you need him, not after.

Assess Your Relationship with Your Customers or Clients

○ Who are your customers?
○ How often do you interact with them?
○ Do they call you, or do you call them?
○ What is the "something extra" you give them or do for them?
○ Do you have long-standing relationships with your customers?
○ How many of them would follow you if you moved to another division or company?

Don't skip this section just because you aren't involved in direct sales. You probably have some kind of customers, inside or outside your company. A corporate lawyer's "customers" are the divisions he counsels. An inventory manager's "customers" are the manufacturing lines he supports.

If you're a salesman, you may find that your customers are more important to you than your company is. If your company has problems, you can move to another, and if your customers believe in you and trust you, they will follow. Of course, you can't do this too often, but many salespeople regard their close relationship with their buyers as an insurance policy. The same concept also applies in reverse: If your customers value your service, they may want to bring you along with them as they advance.

For ten years, I've been watching the progress of an executive who recently joined a new and larger firm. In her first three months, she brought in $1 million worth of business. She admitted that the amount thoroughly surprised and pleased her and said it was simply from clients she had worked with in the past few years who wanted to stay with her. Clients and customers often orient themselves to individuals rather than companies.

How important are relationships with customers in your company? Are they the key to your progress? I am reminded of a young IBM systems engineer who could not understand why an assistant vice-president of a small regional bank should be paid more than she when she was responsible for installing his entire computer system. The vice-president would take coffee breaks, come in late for various reasons, and leave early to get to his house at the shore—but he was well known with his customers. He would be at the bank long after the computer system was no longer new. His relationships earned him a higher wage than the hotshot's expertise.

In many service companies such as law, advertising, brokerage, and consulting firms, the biggest business getters are often made president. Sometimes the firms are forced to promote a high-producer in order to keep him, even though he may be less talented at directing the future of the firm and developing the people within it. The value of his productive relationships with customers is paramount.

Are your customers happy? Do they request your attention? If they respond well to you, you know you're giving good service. If they come back to you with repeat business, you can be sure that you're doing something right for them—and that you are highly valuable to your company. That "something right" is personal attention—frequent contact, getting in touch just before your client needs you because you have anticipated his needs, whether he is inside or outside your company. It's responding to his questions in a manner that not only informs him but also makes him feel good.

Having customers appreciate you protects and enhances not only your job but your career. It builds your reputation and establishes a basis for your success today and in the future.

Review Your Relationship with Experts in Your Field

○ Who are the best in your field?
○ Who are the most prominent?
○ Are you familiar with their work?
○ Are they familiar with yours?
○ Do you have any basis for working with these experts?
○ How can you meet them?

You need to be known by the experts, the best and the brightest. That is an elite cadre. The best are not always the most prominent, nor are the most prominent always the best, but those at the forefront of any field are the opinion shapers and trendsetters. They are easy to spot: They speak at conferences; their opinions are sought by the media, colleagues, and customers; they become the focal points as new information develops; their relationships are far-reaching. They have an impact on what is happening and who is involved. Recruiters go to these experts for their opinions and recommendations. Often there is not a single expert operating in a field but half a dozen, each with his own approach.

Do you presently have access to these experts? If you join a company that employs one or two, you have a chance to work with them and observe their style. You may hope to develop a mentor relationship with one of them, but with or without this, a relationship of respect is to your advantage. If and when either of you moves elsewhere, that relationship will remain.

How can you meet these experts? If the experts in your field are not in your company, you have to identify who they are and then find a way to get near them. For example, I have an invitation on my desk right now to a conference in an industry of interest to me that will cost a thousand dollars and three days' time. I don't want to forfeit either, nor am I certain that

I will meet the experts in the field who will be there. The first time out, I can't be sure and neither can you, but the gamble may pay off. Other approaches for meeting the experts are not surprising: Volunteer, write, speak, perform—do something extra. Make your energy and intellect available to those you respect and need to know.

Your interest in the experts is self-interest, and not only because you can learn from them. You want them to know you, appreciate your work, and mention your name. It's a way of building your own stature and that of your company.

Study Your Relationship with Former Associates

○ Do you keep up with former associates?
○ If there is an alumni group or directory, are you in it?
○ Do you make a point of staying in touch after you or a colleague leaves your company?
○ Can you name five people to whom you could turn for help?
○ Can you think of any valuable relationships that you have neglected lately?

"Keep in touch." How often one hears that phrase! The real message is, "I respect you. Maybe we can do something together in the future." You cannot know in advance which relationship will be valuable at what time, or to whom it will matter most, but the potential is there.

How much effort do you put into networking? Since there is no way to anticipate how to be in the right place at the right time, the best course is to make sure you are known and to keep in touch. Maintain a broad circle of acquaintances and keep the lines of communication open. The benefits far outweigh the effort it takes to do this. If your name comes to mind, you could be considered if something develops. If you're well connected, you'll keep current on the news within your company and industry and will be in a position to get information when you need it.

Spin your Rolodex occasionally. Stop when you see a name that makes you smile. Pick up the phone and give that person a call. Share the good feeling for just a minute. Ask how things are and then get back to work. You might be surprised at the responses you get, and you will have nurtured a relationship.

If you wait too long between calls, a relationship can go dry. *Do you give a call or drop a line every year or so? Do you send a word of congratulations to those who make a nice move?* Think how hard it is to call someone after you've fallen out of touch—particularly if you need something—compared to how easy it is to call once a year while the bond is still there. Your call is no great surprise, and no explanation of who you are (or were) is necessary.

The best businesspeople I know have their own card files of contacts that might be important to them or people they might want to hire. They are often very helpful to me as I conduct searches. Networking, so valuable in getting things done effectively and quickly, depends on sources, contacts, information, and insights.

With whom do you stay in touch? Former associates can be helpful, and the sooner in your career you recognize this, the broader your circle of acquaintances will be. Include in this circle those with whom you went to school or attended conferences, your former customers, and of course, those with whom you have worked. Some companies and many schools and universities make a point of keeping track of where people go; they recognize the value of long-term relationships and experiences shared. Colleges are understandably professional in their alumni follow-up for fund-raising purposes. If your former company or school puts out a directory, make sure you are in it—and that your address is current.

It pays to keep in touch with people before you need them, which one company president I know calls "networking while you're on top." I received a letter from him recently with a résumé and product brochure attached. When I called, he told me he was making a special mailing to recruiters. He felt he had been sandbagged in his earlier job after 17 years with the company and did not want that to happen again. This time he was deliberately building his visibility before he needed it.

Do you keep in touch before you need to?

Think About Your Relationship with Your Family

○ Which is more important to you, family or job?
○ How much invasion of your personal time and psychic space will you allow?
○ What is the effect of your job on your family?
○ Would your family be better off with more of you now or more of some "potential success" later on?
○ What is the likelihood of that success's being achieved?
○ What would be the cost to your family?

What you do and how you do it have a profound impact on those who are in any way dependent upon you. The reverse can also hold true—stresses within your family can disrupt your performance at work—but my focus here is on protecting the family.

Is your career plan as good for your family as it is for you? Try to move someone from one part of the country to another and family considerations come up very quickly. It becomes quite obvious that while work is important, family also ranks as high or higher.

While the logistical difficulties of moving are clear enough, it's more difficult to pinpoint the effect your present job has on you and the extent to which you allow that impact to carry through and affect your family. *Can you leave the stresses of your job at the office?* Your feelings at home are often a barometer for developments at work.

I'm working with a client right now who says with pride that on a Sunday morning he can ask a man to fly to Paris and encounter no question or objection. He really does ask people to do things like this, and his company is successful. That would cause problems in my family.

How hard can you work and how much stress can you bring home to your family before your job has a negative impact? At some point, sharing your presence, imagination, vitality, and love will be more valuable to your family—and to you—than the extra dollars, bigger perks, and larger house with less time to spend in it. *Is the success you're trying to achieve in the future a worthwhile trade-off for the present?* Consider the risk-reward ratio. What trade-offs are you willing to make? There is no easy answer to this continuing question, but consider it occasionally as you look at the direction your family is growing in and as you ask yourself if that is what you want for them.

How well are you getting along with your spouse and children? Is one or the other expecting more than you can give or deserving more than you're giving? Your work hours, travel, stress, and fatigue all take a toll on your family. If your job is disturbing your time with your family, try to figure out why. What are your alternatives?

Your family is easily taken for granted, especially when you're young and eager to perform for your company at any cost. If you don't hold back from anything the company asks you to do, at least be aware of the toll your all-out effort takes on your family. Children and spouses can get bruised. A little attention from you, recognizing that it is all you have to offer for the time being, can do a lot to alleviate these hurts.

COULD THIS BE YOU?

Stanley finished dinner and left his family to hole up in the den. He was disturbed, angry—and perplexed. He couldn't understand why his subordinates had set him up as they had. Oh, every one of them had been apologetic, each saying he thought another would have told him, but no one had. He'd heard about the trouble first from his boss, who'd called and asked why one of Stanley's projects had gone completely off track. Management had learned of the situation before Stanley, and that hurt him both personally and professionally.

Stanley was a mover. He was active in industry affairs and knew the top people in other companies as well as the experts in his field. He was well regarded within his company and carefully cultivated his relationships upward. He was social and part of the "right" group. These thoughts all came to him as he sat in the den, wondering how that one project could have gotten so far out of hand. By the time the situation had come to his attention, all kinds of problems had built up.

True, Stanley had been spending most of his time on a development project that had great potential. He saw it as a winner and didn't hesitate to delegate responsibility for his other projects to his subordinates—a sign, he felt, of a good manager. He expected to hear about any problems at his monthly staff meetings, if he hadn't already been advised of them directly. But no one had said a word about the fiasco that had been brewing upstate.

Or had they? Stanley began to wonder.

He thought back to the last staff meeting and tried to see himself as his people had. Sure he'd been smooth and had held control, but he also saw himself dominating the meeting. He hadn't questioned his managers as closely as he used to. He'd been so busy talking about his new project that he'd failed to pay attention to the others. Thinking back, he could even see that Bill, manager of the problem project, had been more quiet than usual, but Stanley hadn't noticed it then. He'd overpowered his own feedback system and set himself up for a fall.

As Stanley reflected, he saw that he'd been focusing too much on the power structure above and hadn't been spending enough time with his people—and they were the ones who were going to solve this mess with him. He decided to visit Bill the next morning and find out why things went wrong. He would also check in with his divisional human resources officer to see what he could pick up from that quarter. And he'd get back to the original philosophy of his monthly staff meetings: a thorough review of all operations. Last, he would curb his own preoccupation with the development project, at least for a while.

"Damage control," he thought. "Repair the damage, check all systems, and then get going again. Above all, don't sit dead in the water just because you've been hurt." Stanley wasn't happy as he thought this out, but he knew what he had to do to get back on track.

PULLING IT TOGETHER

This chapter should have reminded you of all the important relationships you have and of the good things that can come from them with a bit of nurturing. The more contacts you have, the more bits and pieces you can pick up and build upon as you remain attuned to the undercurrents in your company and your industry—and that is where things begin.

Your relationship with your boss, peers, and subordinates is only the basic level. Self-protection comes through staying in touch with former associates, and the pros know the value of maintaining more far-reaching contacts. It's an ever widening circle, all relating to personal chemistry.

If you can perform well and also have good personal chemistry with most people, you have a powerful combination of strengths, indeed—probably unbeatable. But most of us can't excel in every situation or get along with every person; it's good to take stock of what you can and can't do. *Are your relationships uneven?* You may have a great relationship with your subordinates but not with your clients or senior management, or a great relationship with one department but not with another. Ask yourself why.

Your immediate and long-term career success depends upon the strength of your various contacts, some of which I may not have mentioned. *What other relationships come to mind?*

Some people work in relative isolation and prefer it that way; others are highly social. *Where do you fall on the spectrum?* I find that relationships are often discarded too quickly by the fast-tracker who feels his performance is more important than getting along with the people around him. He strives for the numbers, shoots for the goals, and saves his close relationships for one or two trusted advisers. It's a tricky path, not for everyone but not impossible. At the other extreme is the stable traditionalist who may not be a superstar but who knows how to enlist people to get things done. A middle ground is best, but tigers and golden retrievers don't come half and half.

Take a moment to flip back through the headings in this chapter and note the strength of your different relationships. Have you found any surprises? What would happen if your key relationships changed suddenly? What can you do so they won't? Consider which relationships are the strongest and which are most important to your progress. Which need improving—and what are you going to do to improve them? Relationships take time to cultivate, true, but even slow nurturing can yield immediate dividends along the way.

4

How Do Others Perceive You?

People respond to what they see and hear. Instant impressions are formed in response to your tone of voice, how rapidly you speak, your mannerisms, stance, and appearance. These are all factors you can control. On a surface level, how others see you is how you *allow* them to see you.

Over time, other factors contribute to the overall impression people have of you—but that impression can be far from the reality. Your style and manner can either obscure good qualities or hide faults. If you want to present yourself in the best possible light, you need to recognize the signals you put out and, if necessary, work on them.

We live in an audiovisual age. You sense it while watching teenagers. Televisions are constantly on; image makers are always at work. The success of political candidates can be made or broken depending upon how well they master TV. You can't afford a political image maker yourself, but you can see how important impressions are. How many businesspeople do you know who are long on substance but short on sizzle—short on that unique aspect of a steak that everyone remembers? Sizzle is only sizzle, but it makes the initial, and sometimes lasting, impression.

We all have many ways of presenting ourselves, some fabricated because we enjoy them, some natural and open, some carefully crafted and defensive. We change under different circumstances. We construct armor to conceal things we don't want revealed—and despite our best efforts, there are chinks in that armor. Small wonder that others find it difficult to really know us and to see all our good qualities.

People unconsciously match their impressions of you to certain prejudices, opinions, and stereotypes—a salesman can't be trusted, a president should be handsome—and also add in hearsay and the biases of personal experience. You can't control all of these variables, but you can recognize how they work and turn many of them to your advantage. You may just as easily take advantage of a ready-made favorable impression as fall into a stereotype that works against you.

Like it or not, most people perceive you to be something other than what you really are. If you're nervous, you may talk too much; if under pressure, you may be sharp or abrupt—but neither kind of behavior may necessarily be indicative of your true manner. People don't know your life story or what kind of day you're having, but you do have a chance to tailor the impression you make. How do you come across? What thoughts are others walking away with?

Your voice, your clothes, and your body language make up the biggest part of how people perceive you—that initial impression, the first cut that either opens the door to further opportunity or closes it. Once beyond that first cut, the important impressions upon which you build business relationships go deeper. People form an idea of your judgment and foresight, your adeptness at handling risk, your ability to communicate effectively.

I recall a senior executive in the semiconductor industry—let's call him Martin—who had been an impressive candidate in a search I'd done. When Martin was cut loose from his job, I called my client on that search to keep him up-to-date. "Just about everyone let go over there has come to talk with us," he responded, "and the story on Martin surprisingly is not good." My client would not even speak with Martin because his former associates had cast him in an unfavorable light. If Martin had paid a little more attention to how these people regarded him, he could have avoided some, if not all, of this bad press.

What you are perceived to be, not what you are, is the focus of this chapter, although it is difficult to discuss one without the other. As you read, try to be sensitive to what you do that triggers impressions in other people and determine if those impressions are favorable or unfavorable. Then consider how you think of yourself. Do you recognize your best qualities? Are you hiding them? Are you putting forth the best you can? Where—and how—do you want to make changes? Whether you're in a meeting, at the watercooler, or on the squash court, you can determine the impression you make. Keep this in mind as you consider how others see you.

Take Stock of Your First Impression

○ What is the first thing people notice about you? Does this impression contribute to or detract from your effectiveness?
○ Is it the impression you want to make?
○ If not, can you change it?
○ Are you easily tagged as from a certain region or social class?
○ Are people drawn to you or put off by you?
○ Do you find that you have to explain yourself to people?

You don't get a second chance to make a first impression, nor can you choose the time or place you make it. It happens so quickly. Someone sees you, and he applies all he sees against what that image has meant in other people he knows. Then he hears you and makes another connection as a result. Sight and sound make the big impact. Later he will factor in what he knows or has heard about you, but the first impression has been made.

First impressions aren't fair, but they are unavoidable. *Does your image accurately reflect who you are and what you want?* Meeting people each day as I do, I know the inclination to make snap judgments, though I try to avoid them. It's great if you can get beyond a quick introduction so people can come to appreciate you, but often what others think of you is the result of a fragmentary impression.

Do you wear clothes that are customary and traditional for your work, and are you comfortable in them? Nice attire, not extravagant, sets you up to be whatever you want to be. You don't want your day-to-day appearance to be distracting—either truly impressive or questionable.

Assuming you are not a politician or game-show host—those who often dominate a room from the moment they enter—how you carry yourself says much about you. A casual presentation suggests you are relaxed about other things, and conversely, a trim impression suggests you are efficient and orderly. The way you look can immediately build confidence and lead to a strong rapport. *What personal attributes does your bearing convey?*

You make an impression walking into any group. What that impression is depends upon the people you are meeting, the purpose of the occasion, and the image you choose to project. *Are you going to be accepted immediately as part of the group, or will you stand out?* Your manner or some article of dress— say, your cowboy boots—could set you apart from the others.

"I can't know everyone's prejudices," you might say. No, you can't, but until you control your environment to your complete satisfaction, it pays to be sensitive to the impression you make on others. Know the first impression you make, and if it sends the wrong signals, do your darnedest to set the record straight.

Consider Your Body Language

O Are you sensitive to the moves, positions, and facial expressions of body language?

O Do you read these messages from others?

O Does your body language contradict your spoken language?

O Do you have any habits that others might find unsettling?

O Do you recognize when you are infringing upon someone's sense of space or holding his glance too long?

O Do you make body language work to your advantage?

Body language has a way of screaming a message without ever making a sound. It reveals information more quickly and clearly than spoken language. Think of your expression when you congratulate a colleague for getting a promotion that you had wanted. The disappointment is terribly difficult to hide.

According to Julius Fast, in his book *Body Language,* facial expressions for indicating interest, joy, surprise, fear, anger, distress, disgust, contempt, and shame are common across all cultures. We communicate certain emotions without ever learning how to do it.

On another level, our sophisticated society teaches us mannerisms that we fold into our natural lexicon. We may become more cosmopolitan, more polished, but at the same time more difficult to "read." Even if you pride yourself on being open and natural with your subordinates, you may have some mannerisms that tell a different story.

Body language is powerful. It can convey the clear, unvarnished truth, or it can be contrived—used to impress or distress. *Are you aware of all the messages you are unconsciously broadcasting? Do you read these subtle signals from others?*

Your body has a way of projecting power or weakness, and it also has a way of contradicting the words you use. *Has anyone ever commented upon your manner? Were you surprised at what he said?* I remember being part of a group in which one member was told that others were afraid he was going to hit them. He was shocked and replied, "The only guy who has ever moved away from me was the doorman at the Barbizon Hotel—and I didn't even swing at him!" The outburst of laughter got through to him, and he realized that he had the moves of a fighter, even though he was now a businessman. He had not been aware of what his body was telegraphing.

Body language is an important tool. You can say a lot with your body, and you can change the message to suit your needs. Be sensitive to both reading and sending these kinds of signals as you strive to present yourself in the most favorable manner and make others comfortable in your presence.

What About Your Eyes?

○ Do you share yourself through your eyes (what some call the window to the soul)?

○ Are you comfortable making eye contact with people as you talk with them?

○ Do you use your eyes to respond while you are listening?

○ Do you have any mannerisms that could put people off, such as squinting or looking away?

Think how you feel when someone shakes your hand and looks over your shoulder. It's all over in a second or two, but without eye contact you feel the coolness and know you don't rate. Another person might shake your hand and look at the floor or at a point just above your head. You can pick up a tremendous amount of information about others from the way they use eye contact—and they can do the same with you. *Under what circumstances do you avoid making eye contact?*

In conversation, the person who looks at you and holds your eyes with his conveys trust. Through his eyes, he opens himself to your examination. As you listen to him, your eyes confirm your understanding or lack of it, your agreement or discomfort. With so much information being exchanged on such a subtle level, the way you use eye contact reveals a great deal about you.

If you are aware of what a powerful tool eye contact can be, you can use it to advantage. Much of what we say with our eyes is unconscious, but eye contact is nonetheless a learned art. Your eyes are powerful communicators, and you can train them.

When does eye contact make you uncomfortable? Because it is so personal, eye contact can put you at ease or on edge. If someone you don't care for keeps trying to hold your look, you squirm or even get angry. If a colleague holds your glance too long, you wonder what your reaction is supposed to be. If he blinks too much, you get the impression he is trying to shut you out. Do you ever unwittingly make others uncomfortable with your eye contact?

Eye contact can forge a strong attachment between speaker and listener. *Do you deliberately work with eye contact when speaking in a group?* It has been proved that someone speaking in a small group can create a bond with you by maintaining eye contact for three to five seconds. A shorter glance makes little impression; you don't feel the speaker is talking to *you*. Anything longer generates discomfort; you feel he is giving you unusual attention.

Do you use eye contact to persuade or intimidate others? Salesmen use what they call the "power stare." This is heavy eye contact from a practiced communicator; use it carefully or you may overstep your boundary and intrude on your customer's private space. If this happens, you will be perceived as overbearing and aggressive. Used with discretion, however, the power stare is as effective as its name implies.

Listen to Your Voice

○ Do you have a regional accent?
○ Does it work to your advantage or to your detriment?
○ Does your way of speaking reveal your background?
○ Is there a smile in the sound of your voice?
○ Do you tend to build conversations with your responses or cut them off?
○ Does your voice reinforce the meaning of your words or detract from it?

Your voice can move mountains if you choose the right tone, tempo, inflection, and emphasis. It can convey joy or sorrow, love or hate, admiration or disdain. People respond to the voice more than to the words. A good listener will be searching for secondary messages—the note of panic or the tone that says, "You know I'm right."

How is your telephone manner? Many relationships are formed and sustained over the telephone—and not necessarily with leisurely conversations that show you to your best advantage. Voice mail, recording machines, and brief messages result in quick impressions, right or wrong. You have just moments to make the favorable impression that will do you the most good.

I spend a lot of time on the telephone, seldom speaking with someone for the first time in person. During an initial phone call, I am trying to decide if I want to get on an airplane and follow up with a personal meeting or not. To a great extent, how you impress me as a stranger suggests how you handle strangers in business.

Make a tape recording and listen to your voice. *How do you sound?* Do you speak rapidly or deliberately? Do you tend to hesitate or stumble? Evaluate your best asset and consider what should be changed. Does your pronunciation say anything special about you? Is it what you want said? The ideal speaking voice is measured, not rushed; resonant, not pinched.

People draw conclusions about you from the way you speak. You can probably think of any number of accents, including what we in the East call Locust Valley Lockjaw—used by the kind of person who speaks without opening his teeth and gives you an enthusiastic handshake by extending his hand a full six inches beyond his belt buckle! You can imagine how that goes over in Colorado.

Do you pay attention to your inflections? Deliberately modulating your voice can change the effect of what you say. This can become very complex when you are giving a speech, talking with foreigners, or selling a product. A particular emphasis can completely alter a sentence's meaning. "Thank you. Good-bye," with a little push in your voice, leaves a warm feeling. Saying the same thing with a falloff in tone and no enthusiasm conveys: "I'm done with you, and you're lucky I talked to you at all."

As long as you're paying attention to how you use your voice, check what you're saying. *Do you finish other people's questions for them? What stock phrases do you use or overuse?* I once heard someone say, "How are you?" twice to a woman he knew well who had just been blinded. It was shockingly tactless, but easy to do with our automatic social niceties.

How you use your voice can dramatically affect the import of your words. Get the most out of what you take the time to say.

Assess Your Judgment

○ How do others respond to the way you think?
○ Is your opinion sought by people you regard highly?
○ How is your track record of decisions?
○ Do others act upon your recommendations?
○ Is there any factor that could be preventing people from appreciating your good judgment?

It's a compliment to have people you regard highly ask for your opinion. If your judgment is frequently sought, you've no doubt earned the respect of others—something essential to your success. (In his book *Executive Qualities,* Joseph M. Fox made a study of the personal attributes most often found in successful executives. Not surprisingly, good judgment is one of them.)

What if your opinion isn't sought, and you don't find yourself making decisions of the scope you would like? The implication is that it is going to be difficult for you to take a leadership role because something is lacking. Hopefully, the missing ingredient is not a serious deficiency but rather an aspect of the way others see you that can be corrected—a presentation skill you lack, specific information you can learn, or a prejudice you hold or are thought to hold that you can eliminate. Perhaps you use too much humor and are considered a lightweight. You may tend to follow rather than initiate, suggesting weakness. Perhaps others find you too idealistic and removed from reality. Bad personal chemistry with your colleagues could also be the culprit, although pure self-interest would probably override that in people who truly need your opinion. Look for the signals that let you know how others see you.

Are you comfortable acting on your own decisions? If making choices puts you in a panic, if you consistently have trouble making up your mind, or if you make a decision and then spend days second-guessing yourself, you are not comfortable with your own judgment—and chances are no one else will be, either.

If your opinion isn't sought, why isn't it? Good judgment, a key quality in leaders, is something you want to possess and make sure others know you have. If you feel you have good judgment but others don't respect your opinion, ask yourself why. You may appear disinterested or overly emotional or rigid in your thinking. It helps to be associated with others whose opinions are valued. See what you can do to change how others perceive you. You want to be asked for your contribution.

Take Stock of Your Ability to Communicate
- ○ Are you asked to make presentations and give talks?
- ○ Are you regarded as long-winded or succinct?
- ○ What comments do you receive about your memos and letters?
- ○ Do people respond favorably to the tone of both your writing and your speaking?
- ○ Are people quick to share information with you?

At a political rally in a small Vermont town, Ned was standing at the back of the crowd. "What's he talkin' about, Ned?" asked Zeke. "He don't say," Ned responded.

It's what you get across that counts, not what you say, and the higher you go, the greater your need to be a good communicator. You can't be boring and advance. Communicating involves more than presenting your views; you must also be adept at receiving and synthesizing information, applying your knowledge and convictions to what you hear, and then effectively directing the activities of others. Communication is a two-way street, and more businesses are recognizing the need for communication between senior management and those in the field. Participation is in vogue; unquestioned direction from on high is not.

What opportunities do you have to show your communication skills? Speeches, presentations, reviews, and memorandums are all part of a manager's role in selling on the outside and motivating on the inside. "Communicating" can be as innocuous as entertaining a customer and his wife at dinner or as demanding as confronting your boss or the president of your company. It involves the ability to think quickly and creatively, then express your thoughts convincingly. Your particular style doesn't matter as much as your ability to communicate effectively and be recognized for it.

How practiced are you at public speaking? Being at ease before a group comes naturally to few people, but it can be learned. Can you "talk net" and "write net," being brief but precise? Clarity of expression indicates clarity of thought. People will be less inclined to value what you say if you ramble or use jargon. David Ogilvy once announced the opening of a company barber shop at Ogilvy & Mather with a one-line memo reading, "Hippity hop to the barber shop." No details; you could find them out easily.

Do you answer letters and questions promptly, or at least acknowledge them and indicate that you'll respond later? You can't always respond to others as rapidly as you or they would like, but you need to keep the lines of communication open until you have time to answer.

Do you know when to talk and when to listen? Can you convey empathy and boldness at the same time? Listening is the often-forgotten part of communicating. It should be taught. Listening is more than simply hearing. A good listener is alert for different shades of meaning and builds a rapport with the speaker. You aren't really communicating if you don't absorb someone's thoughts and let him know you understand his position before you go on with your own. You've no doubt experienced the person who appears to listen to you attentively but then starts off on his own tangent without any attempt to integrate what you've just said. It's infuriating; something good communicators never do. Are you known for taking the thoughts of others into account?

The payoff for being a good listener is all the information you will hear because people enjoy talking to you and sharing with you what they know. You needn't say much yourself if you don't want to—and the most active talker will still regard you as a great conversationalist!

Are You Persuasive?

○ Do others recognize the logic of your arguments?
○ Do you handle objections knowledgeably?

○ Are you convincing?
○ Do you enjoy taking the time to change someone's opinion?
○ Are you known for rarely giving up or getting discouraged?

Persuasion is a special and very important aspect of communicating. An opinion isn't worth much if you can't persuade people to accept it. There is a saying, "We are all salesmen regardless of what we do." To be effective in any field, you must be able to "sell" your ideas.

You may find *persuasiveness* a more palatable term than *sales ability*, but the skill is the same, and it's certainly respected if used with sensitivity. It is second nature to the salesman to build a bond of empathy, a bridge over which he can achieve his goals. He knows well that the first step toward persuasion is gaining a common understanding.

Can you protect your turf? Argue your case? The ability to defend your position suggests a certain toughness and resilience that is valuable. I probe for this during interviews. I appreciate the candidate who tells me that my client is mistaken on a certain point and gives me specific reasons for his opinion. He's strong. He's not falling at my feet for the job but is open to discussion.

What if selling and cajoling don't come easily to you? You can change that by taking a course or joining an organization that will help you build your skills. Dale Carnegie offers a number of courses tailored to different needs. At meetings of the Toastmasters Club, everyone gives a spontaneous two-minute talk, and three or four people give prepared six-minute talks. Participants gain not only frequent practice but also—even more important—feedback. I've been tagged for playing with my glasses, keeping my hand in my pocket, and putting so much into a talk that nothing could be remembered. It's great practice and a good way to get constructive criticism.

If you aren't outspoken, ask yourself why. *Are you reticent by nature? Do you lack confidence in your ability or your product?* If you aren't a good communicator, no one is going to ask you to argue a point in a meeting. You may be losing visibility because of a problem that could be corrected.

Consider Your Foresight

○ Are you recognized by your peers for having insight into trends that are gaining strength?
○ How often have you anticipated the correct turn of events?
○ Are you known for acting on your "hunches"?
○ Do others ask you what you see ahead?
○ Where is your specialty?

Foresight is the ability to see a need in the future. It is elemental in leaders and the driving force behind entrepreneurs, but it is not common.

Henry Ford and Walter Chrysler staked their futures on automobiles. Cyrus Field bet on the first transatlantic cable. David Ogilvy recognized the potential of advertising, and William McGowan of MCI was prepared for the deregulation of the telephone industry. Walter Wriston of Citibank showed foresight when he incorporated mass-production techniques into the bank's back-office operations. Ray Kroc used it in building McDonald's into a national institution that launched the fast-food industry. These men had foresight plus the courage to act upon it. Each of them committed significant resources to his vision in order to make it a reality.

Foresight isn't only for the geniuses and the wealthy, however; it starts with ordinary folks. *How have you demonstrated your foresight? Can you spot a good value?* It takes foresight to buy when things are at the bottom, whether you are acquiring real estate, securities, a patent, or a business. It takes foresight to create a product, introduce it, and watch it succeed as market forces evolve in the way you projected they would. It requires foresight to conceive a policy, act on it, and guide the results.

Who has demonstrated foresight in your industry? Did he have any special information? How can you gain the foresight you need? Whether or not others feel you have foresight depends upon what you have done in the past and plan to do in the future. To build your reputation, state your case when you feel that you have a unique approach. Put yourself on the line in discussions. You might be surprised by the comments you receive as well as the new opportunities that are offered to you.

Can You Handle Risk?

○ Are you excited by risk?

○ Have you taken risks and succeeded?

○ Are you more risk-oriented than people perceive you to be?

○ Conversely, do your actions look more risky than they really are?

○ Do others have confidence in your handling of the risks you undertake?

Separating risk and foresight is nearly impossible when you look ahead; but with hindsight, a distinction can be made and a track record seen. Foresight involves identifying trends; risk involves taking action based on this vision, whether or not the idea is yours. *Do you have both foresight and the ability to handle risks? Do you have the confidence to act on your convictions?* If so, you are dynamite.

A friend of mine has always relished risk. He loved it in business when he built a $250-million company from nothing, and he loves it in sports when he races large sailboats in awesome weather in all parts of the world. He thrives on challenge and is supremely confident.

Another acquaintance made his mark by handling progressively greater risks. He recently took a company out of bankruptcy, treading the fine line between success and failure. He tells me how tough it is, but he stays with it. He is cautious and persistent, and knows that calculated risks can pay off.

Decade to decade it is the new companies that add 80 to 90 percent of new employment, but taking risks is scary. We don't hear about the hundreds of companies that fail, but think where we would be without those ventures that are tried and do succeed—and the people who built them.

Have you tested your ability to handle risk? How much risk are you comfortable with? Business risk has always been with us, but now its importance is recognized. *Fortune* magazine's six leaders of 1986 were called "master risk-takers." Risk taking is becoming more common and the results more likely to be noticed. You need to know and develop your capacity for risk, since taking some risks is necessary for success at any level.

If you possess irreverence, you may be successful at taking a special kind of risk. Combined with imagination, energy, confidence, and spontaneity, wholehearted irreverence can capture the mood of a group and create a moment of good fellowship among unequals. It vaporizes the boundaries of decorum and triggers those all-too-infrequent surges of humorous appreciation. The opportunities are fleeting and timing is crucial, but the results can be spectacular. The wild ducks of corporate legend often possess irreverence, but using it requires the keenest skill and craftiness.

Thomas Watson, Jr., the former chairman of IBM, once said during a sales convention, "I love the wild duck"—to which a muffled voice from the audience replied, "Yeah, but most of them get shot down!" Wild ducks can be sitting ducks because they challenge the rules, buck the system, and raise havoc in the organization. They often antagonize established department heads who are skeptical of the unconventional. They can accomplish miracles or make colossal mistakes.

Recently, a chairman told me of his company president in Europe who consistently takes more authority than is his but just as consistently outperforms his domestic counterparts. The chairman looked serious, albeit with a grin on his face, as he explained how hard it was to deny the European president's requests. The chairman is not about to shoot this wild duck—at least, not yet. He likes the results. The guy is taking a risk and stepping outside his boundaries, but he is winning and sending the profits home.

What About Your Use of Humor?
○ Can you make others laugh?
○ Can you use humor to your advantage, both one-on-one and in groups?

○ Do people comment on your jokes—either favorably or unfavorably?
○ Are you known for putting others at ease with your humor?
○ Are you *sure* your humor is effective?
○ Do you unintentionally offend with your sense of humor?

Humor is a delicate but powerful tool. Like pepper or caffeine, a certain amount is great and too much is disastrous.

A sense of humor, though not essential for success, can be a strong ingredient. Judiciously used, it makes people comfortable around you. *Are you perceived as lively and entertaining? Does your humor play upon situations rather than personalities?* Humor in business is not the raucous I'm-going-to-make-you-laugh type. It's a turn of phrase, an observation, a contrived remark or analogy, a self-deprecating comment. It's sophisticated in its own way, and not cornball.

Humor can be most effective when you least expect it. It can defuse a tense situation or produce relief from periods of concentrated thought. A well-timed remark can make a group come to life, and attention focuses momentarily on you, the catalyst and provider of the humor. The pause might last a few seconds or a few minutes, but during that time, you are controlling the scene.

Humor and a good sense of comic timing can get you over a chasm that is impassable any other way. Even if a sense of humor is not one of your striking assets, perhaps you have charisma, the ability to make people smile and feel better because you are there. Humor comes in degrees.

I have a Danish friend who has been in the United States for 40 years and has only the slightest accent. You would hardly pick him out in a crowd. He is an engineer at heart and doesn't make waves—that is, until he is at the podium. There he pulls out an accent and wraps his English into the most entertaining double meanings, often contradictory and interspersed with contrived mispronunciations, and he delivers it all absolutely deadpan. He never breaks. He's fabulous. What appears to be spontaneous, however, has really been carefully thought out in advance.

He knows the value of humor, works at it, and succeeds—to everyone's enjoyment.

Can you spontaneously mix humor with business to your advantage? There is a place for humor during many business meetings, but only you as a participant will know when, if, or how much is appropriate. If someone else is creating most of the humor, see if you can't contribute some. Watch for opportunities, give it a try, and—most important—observe the effect.

COULD THIS BE YOU?

Bill was in a horse race, and he knew it. The vice-president of manufacturing was due to retire in less than a year. Bill and two colleagues were in contention for the job, and Bill could almost taste it.

Bill's dream was to run his own manufacturing operation, and he had invested 12 years with the company to that end. He saw himself as a hands-on manager with more experience on the floor than his two M.B.A. rivals. He thought they were lightweights—but he sensed they were edging him out. He had to do something.

Rocking back in his chair, Bill took stock of the situation. He had thought things were going well, but recently he'd been picking up little comments about his being a "diamond in the rough" or other phrases that could be taken as compliments but seemed to be sending a different message. He'd never worried much about being slick—he'd been too busy, and besides, his operations were among the company's best managed.

"If one person tells you that you have a tail," one of his managers had once said, "you think he's crazy. But if three people tell you that you have a tail, you'd better look over your shoulder." Well, Bill was beginning to look over his shoulder—not for a tail, but for indications of his roughness.

It was getting late. He and two engineers had been working practically around the clock on a new design. He was damn proud of the job they were doing, but as he looked at his reflection in the darkened window of his office, he didn't like what he saw.

Who was that rumpled-looking guy in shirt-sleeves surrounded by clutter and old Styrofoam cups of cold coffee?

Bill glanced at his sports jacket hanging on the back of his door. He'd stopped buying suits when he found he always wore out the pants first. His people didn't care whether or not he wore a suit—but then, they weren't in charge of promotions around this place.

Suddenly it became clear to Bill that in all these years of concentrating on substance, he had totally forgotten about presentation and style. He'd concentrated on his products and figured his career would take care of itself. For a while, it had—but he now realized that at his level, other factors were being taken into account. He'd gotten too gruff, too dug in.

It occurred to Bill that he had been selling himself short. Management liked the smooth-talking M.B.A.'s. By setting himself up in a rival camp, Bill was actually making them look better—and making it easier for management to focus more on his rough edges than on his track record.

He pulled an invitation to speak from his drawer and decided to accept. Public speaking had never really been his thing, but he could handle it. He needed the exposure.

His mind wandered to the staff meeting tomorrow. Usually, he just stuck to the facts, allowing them to speak for themselves. This time he would put more bounce in his report, more interpretation. He would add some visuals, put together some flip-charts. His senior managers liked that kind of thing. And he would wear a suit.

Bill was certain he had what it would take to be vice-president. Now he had to make sure management saw this, too.

PULLING IT TOGETHER

How others perceive you depends on how well they know you. The glance across the room takes in only your appearance and body language. A brief conversation adds voice, and a longer conversation or extended contact will uncover some of your other qualities. It's especially important to find out whether or not others are failing to see good qualities you know you have.

This chapter is not all-inclusive. Missing here is any discussion of your political astuteness or leadership ability, but these are discussed elsewhere. *What other notable characteristics do you have? What do you look for in others?* You may be ruthless or kind, sloppy or dependable, arrogant or friendly, stodgy or spacey. You may possess unusual willpower, ambition, courage, or integrity. All of these attributes make profound impressions on people, and everyone has his favorites when judging others.

Evaluating how others perceive you is difficult, but the signals will be there. If you're aware of how you are perceived by others on an ongoing basis, you'll avoid learning about a problem only when a decision hangs in the balance.

Take a moment to review the main points in this chapter by flipping back through the headings. *How do others perceive you with respect to these points, and how do you perceive yourself?* Where there's a difference, you might need to do some work. Note the points that are strong in your case and those that are not. Don't limit yourself to the qualities mentioned in the headings if there are others that are important to you. *How can you leverage your strong points and improve the weak ones?* Make a note or two about things to do.

5

How Well Do You Know Yourself?

While it's an issue you don't often address, knowing yourself is critical to your success. It's easy to get so caught up in corporate priorities that you lose touch with your own. Use this chapter to make sure you haven't lost track of what it is you truly want to achieve.

I've found that most people get in touch with their personal priorities only when they are faced with a decision, a job offer, an unusual promotion, or a big problem. Then they suddenly try to figure out what they want when their minds are clouded with anxiety, anger, or possibly infatuation—absolutely the wrong time! Why not ask yourself once a year what your underlying feelings, desires, and goals are, and see if they are in sync with what you are doing and where you are going? Make this check when nothing is at stake and you can be honest with yourself.

Looking after your priorities is something no one else can do for you. You are a complex mixture of talent, drive, personality, dreams, and ego—a mixture so extraordinary and so private that it defies even the most sophisticated management techniques. No one else has exactly the same priorities and inclinations you do. No one else can tell you whether or not you are pursuing a course that is right for you, and once you're on the job, no one else really cares. Your boss may have an interest in your future, but he will want you to do what suits him, not what suits you. What's exactly right for his purposes could be dead wrong for you.

Your priorities will change as you grow and achieve and as opportunities open up to you. You will recognize this best if you tune out corporate objectives every once in a while, all the plans and strategies that are laid upon you, and listen quietly to your own feelings and desires.

Your goals may be impossible to attain right now, but with planning, what is impossible now may be attainable in a year. And when you are working in the same direction as your own best interests, your strength and conviction complement your best efforts for your company.

What Are Your Natural Inclinations?

O Can you distinguish between what you are able to do, what you want to do, and what others expect you to do?

O Which of the above are you doing?

O What important personal values would you like to incorporate in your work?

O How do you spend your personal time?

O What's your idea of the perfect job?

The luckiest people in the world are those who are driven to goals that coincide with their natural inclinations.

Differentiating what you want to do from what you can do is not an easy task, particularly for people who can do a number of things reasonably well and of whom much is expected. But if you don't find out where your natural interests lie, you place your long-term success at risk. If you have a job that doesn't coincide with what you naturally want to do, you are likely to be shot down by someone who truly enjoys that job—thinks about it all weekend, lives the job as well as works it. He does naturally what you do with effort. And because it is so easy for him, he ends up doing more.

What do you truly enjoy doing? Which aspects of your work do you enjoy so much that time passes without your realizing it? Let's assume that you are not one who at age 14 decided that you wanted to be an oceanographer, astronaut, doctor, or chef. You didn't grow up with any one burning desire, but you are a competent person, good at what you apply yourself to doing, and dedicated to your own values. It may be five or ten years, if ever, before you receive the jolt that tells you what you're doing isn't your natural inclination or happiest way to live. What a waste to then recognize that you haven't really known yourself and that you've misdirected years of effort.

People with tremendous drive often end up pursuing goals that don't match their intellectual and physical capabilities. I am thinking of John, who was bright, good-looking, determined, and hardworking but rarely happy. He was too busy, too involved with attaining the next level. He wanted to be company president, and there was a lot of competition.

Twenty-one years later, John achieved his goal and was well recognized, but he hadn't changed. He was still unhappy. He developed stomach pains as the psychological and egotistical rewards he'd always expected failed to materialize. His performance deteriorated, and after a period he left for a lesser job in another company. A friend who knew him well said that John was always striving for a goal that wasn't his, but that he was convinced should be his.

Are you pursuing goals you feel are expected of you? Separating society's goals from those you might choose for yourself is not easy and requires considerable private reflection. If you had your way, what would you be doing? Popular belief holds that everyone should grab for the brass ring on the carousel, but a job that looks like corporate nirvana to your peers may be one you have to fight to face every day.

Your personal values deserve special attention because, for many people, well-being has become more important than material success. The more you emphasize certain values in your life, the more demanding you will be of your career. Where you draw the line is up to you, but your career takes up too much of your waking existence for you not to try to incorporate into your work those values that are important to you.

How well do you know yourself? So many people think they know themselves when in fact they do not. Some people know themselves innately, and happiness seems natural to them. Others spend many years, even a lifetime, attempting to know themselves to their own satisfaction. My purpose is not to suggest any particular approach for getting to know yourself but to emphasize the importance of letting the "inner you" run free.

Consider Your Private Goals

- ○ What personal achievements are you proud of?
- ○ What kind of life-style is important to you?
- ○ Why do you work so hard?
- ○ What are you trying to build for yourself?
- ○ Have you shaped your personal priorities into a goal?
- ○ How are you progressing toward that goal?

Over and above your natural inclinations are your personal priorities. Recognizing and fulfilling your private goals is an essential part of your happiness and success. Admit your preferences now, for they will come out sooner or later.

Private goals are those which lie outside the stated objectives of your job. You're probably already working as hard as you can to accumulate money, but the steps you need to take to fulfill your private objectives are different. These goals may be strictly for your personal enjoyment or edification, or they may ultimately reshape your work life, but they arise out of what you want for yourself, not what your immediate job demands.

For some, geography is a major priority. Maybe your dream is to live in Denver, or San Diego, or own a beach house. Perhaps you want to have a baby, or have enough time to read, paint, or write. Maybe you want to create a collection of fine art, or stay in one location long enough to finish some coursework, or see your spouse do so. *What is your private game plan? What steps will it require?*

It is conceivable that you are doing a good job for your company but that you are not growing as a person. *Have you acquired any new skills in the last year or two? What accomplishments would you like to claim next year?*

If you appreciate certain factors in your life-style, you'll sorely miss them if your job takes you away from them. Achieving or protecting a life-style you enjoy is a viable priority.

Are you well matched to the life-style your job demands? In some industries, you're expected to put in 100-hour workweeks, including socializing with other members of your industry and dedicating a fair portion of each weekend to keeping up with industry developments. Some people thrive on this; some don't.

It's trendy now for executives to have their own private locker rooms at the office, indicating that they work all hours and sometimes all night. A designer bathroom becomes a symbol of their 24-hour commitment to their job.

A high-strung cadre of employees at Data General Corporation once undertook a crash effort to develop a computer the company needed. As you can read in *The Soul of a New Machine,* they worked 15-hour days and weekends, lived and slept this project for close to a year. Outside activities ceased. Families broke apart under the strain. The machine came out and Data General prospered, but at great human cost. *Would you give a job top priority in your life?*

Your company's plans for you may be at odds with your personal goals. Many people set their private objectives aside while they concentrate on playing by the company's rules. Only you can decide to what extent you are willing to do this and for how long. If you must postpone your private goals, at least keep track of what they are. Most people don't derive complete fulfillment from their work over the entire span of their careers, so at some point it's a good idea to start working toward what you want. You may even be able to get your company to help you.

Bring your private priorities to the fore, so you don't stifle them and cause them to erupt unexpectedly later on.

Assess Your Personality

○ Do you recognize that there are personality types that are vividly different?

○ Do you know your own personality type?

○ Can you accept that there is no right or wrong type of personality?

○ Can you work effectively with other personality types?

○ Do you give others credit for being strong where you are weak?

People are different in how they go about doing the same thing. They find things out differently, arrive at conclusions differently, and vary in their speed of decision making.

It does matter if your personality is unlike that of the person for whom you work or with whom you are negotiating. The issue is not whose approach is better, but how to achieve the best results given your different personalities. Some idiosyncracies you will have to put up with, but they're easier to tolerate if you recognize that differences will occur and that other personality types can balance your own shortcomings.

Do you recognize your own strongest personality traits? No one personality type is best, but it isn't unusual for one type to be dominant in a certain area, and it makes sense for you to choose a job that suits you. If you are naturally reserved, for example, a job in sales will always be an effort for you.

Much has been written about personality types, and many different personality inventories—systems that indicate what kind of person you are—have been established. One example is the Myers-Briggs Type Indicator, which has been refined for over 25 years and is based on four continuums, shown in the accompanying illustration. Each continuum is divided in the middle, and a letter designation is given to each end. Your personality type is a combination of four letters, depending on where you fall on each spectrum.

(E) Extraversion	. . . . Introversion (I)
(S) Sensing	. . . . Intuition (N)
(T) Thinking	. . . . Feeling (F)
(J) Judgment	. . . . Perception (P)

My wife of 25 years and I are near opposites on the Myers-Briggs scale. Take the simple example of my asking my wife what time it is. She responds, "We're late." I repeat, "What time is it?" She replies, "We have to go!" I say, with absolute frustration, "Would you please give me the hour and minutes," to which she mutters, "Oh, what's the difference?" She is working in her time frame and I in mine.

This is amusing in terms of husbands and wives, but it can raise havoc in the workplace. Imagine a critical countdown procedure during which a technician says, "We're late," rather than, "Eight minutes, five seconds and counting." This technician is in the wrong job. He is going to make a lot of people, including himself, unhappy.

What About Your Sense of Loyalty?

○ To whom are you loyal?
○ From whom do you expect loyalty?
○ Is your loyalty misplaced?
○ Is it being exploited?
○ Is your loyalty to your company giving you a false sense of security?

I feel as if I'm treading on motherhood when I bring up loyalty, but if the subject hasn't bothered you by now, it will when you begin to examine your company closely in Part II.

We all want to be regarded as dependable, faithful, and unswerving in allegiance—but to what? Not too long ago loyalty was given to things that generally were regarded as constant: a university, a hometown, a religion, a political party, a spouse, an employer. Today nothing is forever, particularly in the workplace. It may be expedient for you to change jobs often, or your employer may be restructured around you at a moment's notice by a merger, takeover, or downsizing.

At home or at work, you give loyalty in proportion to the stability you perceive. I still see loyalty being given to employers, but more often I see people giving their loyalty to individuals, industry groups, or career goals—attachments that can continue even if an employment relationship changes.

Loyalty is emotional, not rational. You want to feel loyal to your employer, but consider how much loyalty it is wise to give and how dependent upon your employer you should become. *Are you being blinded by your sense of loyalty?*

Your company expects loyalty from you and may go to great lengths to encourage it, but you may not be rewarded appropriately in return. Instead, the company may take more out of you than it should. It's not unusual for management to give a loyal employee pats on the back and a more impressive title— but little in the way of a raise or increased responsibilities. I've seen loyal executives take on tedious tasks and work crazy schedules that other valuable but more pragmatic employees would not tolerate.

Only you can determine whether or not your loyalty is misplaced. Your need both to be loyal and to see yourself as being loyal could actually be working against you. As one human resources executive said to me, "All we can guarantee is a fair day's pay for a fair day's work." And he worked for a telephone company, a former bastion of stability!

If you are loyal to your company and you accept the jobs that are assigned to you and turn down offers from other companies, all for the long-term benefits you hope to receive from your company, you must ask yourself whether the company will still be there when you expect to collect and, if so, whether or not the company will keep you that long. Tough questions.

What Is Your Area of Expertise?
○ Do you have a special expertise in your company?
○ What strengths are attributed to you?
○ Would you describe your track as narrow or broad?
○ Are you overspecialized?
○ Do you like what you are doing?

People categorize and label. It's a way of keeping track. While you may not identify yourself strongly with your job, others will. This is fine if you like what you are doing and if your job has the future you want, but it can work against you if you've been miscast, if your specialty is too narrow, or if your reputation is different from what you'd like it to be.

Are you sensitive to how others label you? You are more likely to have problems with overspecializing if you work in finance, manufacturing, administration, or other fields where the natural urge is to move to a greater responsibility for the whole. As the pyramid narrows, recognition and compensation increase—and responsibilities broaden. You want to be capable of handling those responsibilities, and you want others to see that you are.

Have you been typecast? If so, you receive too much recognition for one specific thing. While it's good to be outstanding, being typecast can work against you if it builds a reputation you don't want. There's no clear line beyond which specialized becomes overspecialized. The important thing is to find out how others see you and to determine whether your career objectives are being compromised. If you've been typecast, are you doing what's necessary to be seen as you want to be seen?

Have you taken steps to broaden your expertise? What these steps are will depend on your field and long-term interests. In some instances, "broadening" will actually mean acquiring a greater concentration of knowledge in one specific area. Your expertise is what you make it. Look carefully at the moves others with a similar background have made. If you like where they are headed, see whether you are doing all that is necessary to move after them.

Perhaps you've done a tough job in one company and want to do the same again on a larger scale. If you are the kind of person who loves risk and constant challenge and hates maintaining the status quo, these moves will come more easily to you. A more cautious route is to participate in company and industry events and build the relationships that will be helpful to you as you move ahead. The idea is to move into positions that will enhance your expertise without jeopardizing your career progress.

Once you have categorized the expertise you have and the skills you want to gain, you are ready to move to the next point:

determining your career goals and the steps necessary to achieve them.

Determine Your Career Goals

○ Have you defined any short-term career goals?
○ What is your long-term goal?
○ How often do you update your objectives?
○ What new developments may cause you to change your goals?
○ How do you see the next five years with your company?

Setting forth your career objectives can be either an overwhelming chore or a relatively painless task, depending on how well you know yourself and how much attention you've given to your career. If you haven't set any career goals, spend an evening with *What Color Is Your Parachute?* by Richard Bolles, particularly his chapter "Only You Can Decide: What Do You Want to Do?" It's a quick, impressive assortment of exercises and comments to get you on your way.

Your career progress can be compared to getting in shape physically: You are conditioning yourself to assume greater tasks. In business, you need to take on bigger responsibilities with more visibility, more challenge, and greater compensation. Your expertise grows. Years of effort and the attainment of short-term goals have a cumulative effect: Ultimately you reach your destination.

Your career goals may be directly in line with what you are already doing, or they may lie outside the immediate parameters of your job. Getting an M.B.A. may be a priority, or building expertise in another area, or moving into a different industry. You may want to cultivate more recognition or participate more in industry events. Maybe you want to leapfrog your boss and get his boss's job, or run your own company.

Maybe you've had a revelation. You find that you really want to do something else, something outside all the training your company has given you. You're with a hot bunch on a hot track, but your heart isn't in it. You're embarrassed. *Have you tried opening up to your boss?* Try him out. See if he will get you an interview in the department you want. Sure he'll be disappointed, but the company is saving a dedicated and informed employee.

Today's giant companies have all sorts of specialized departments within them, one of which may be right for you. Transferring within your firm is tough on the ego because you must admit you changed your mind, and corporate types aren't supposed to do that. But you can preserve all your knowledge of people, products, and practices, and even more important, you can protect any financial stake you've accrued. If you're strong enough in your conviction, your performance will reestablish your credentials.

Occasionally, career progress is not progress at all, for in moving up, you are actually moving further away from what you enjoy doing and where you find greatest satisfaction. The prospect of advancement and greater responsibility is seductive, but there is also the danger of being promoted to your "level of incompetence" or to a level of discontent. Your ideal career objective may not be the same as the next promotion. *Does management's next step for you fit in with your long-term plans?*

Ask yourself periodically, perhaps once a year, if your objectives have changed. You'll need to make adjustments as you are able to claim more accomplishments and as opportunities are presented to you.

Continually refining your career goals is the only way to make sure your career is going the way you want it to. Remember why you are working, what it is you're after, and what it is you want out of life. You cannot afford to get so wrapped up in the problems and challenges of your current job that you neglect to think about your long-term prospects.

Take Steps to Achieve Your Career Goals

- O Do you recognize the necessity of career planning, even if you hate doing it?
- O Have you defined the steps needed to achieve your career goals?

○ Do you have alternate plans in case the main plan crashes?

○ When was the last time you checked your real career progress?

Your career is bigger than any one job or the attainment of any one private goal. Here we're looking at the long haul—what you hope to attain by means of both short-term tactics and long-term strategies over the course of your working life.

Thirty years ago, joining a big company and riding with it was more important than setting goals for yourself. Today even the biggest and best companies change direction or hit turbulence, and your employment is not assured. There are also other reasons why your company may let you go, even if you're doing a good job. The higher you progress, for example, the less room there is; someone has to fall by the wayside. In addition, your wishes for your progress will seldom exactly match management's plans for you.

How many companies have you seen change direction? How many friends of yours have been caught in the process? You must plan where you want to go, how to get there, and how you might change jobs—even if you hope you never have to do so. This is basic career management, a way of protecting your business viability and making sure you will achieve everything from your working life that you can reasonably expect. And while there is no manual of procedures to guide you, you need not act helpless.

The key to accomplishing a career goal lies in defining the steps needed to get there and in recognizing just what factors make each step important. Without a plan, your career progress is likely to be haphazard.

Can you integrate your career goals with the annual objectives your boss sets for you? Try starting with short-term goals, ones you can achieve in increments of 6 to 12 months. Steps that take too long to achieve are dangerous because you can forget where you're supposed to be going. Steps that are too rapid can make you obsessive about accomplishing them in an unreasonably short amount of time—and discouraged when you fail.

Remember, too, that some steps will be knocked out from under you, forcing you to rely on alternatives. It's extremely helpful to have fallback plans established just in case you need them.

Your career objectives can be achieved only by continuous and sensitive management, but doing your homework pays off. It doesn't take much time, and you will reap potentially vast rewards. The alternative, which is all too easy, is to keep looking back instead of forward—and to end up in a situation you don't like.

So You Want to Be President

○ Do you really want to be president?
○ Of your present company or any company?
○ Why?
○ What exceptional attributes do you have that make you suited to the job?
○ What will happen if you fail?

There is something special about being president. From my earliest years I remember the feeling I had upon hearing, "He's the president." Being president has been a shining accomplishment to us for so long that it's no wonder so many of the résumés I receive say, "I want to be president of a medium-sized company." This isn't necessarily something I want to hear. Many of these hopefuls are not, in fact, cut out to be president. Are you?

What makes you think you're different? Ask yourself if you can simultaneously direct today's operations and conceptualize tomorrow; if you are exceptional at delegating; if general management appeals to you; if you would enjoy dealing not only with employees but also with the media, Wall Street, and stockholders. What's your natural energy level? How much guidance do you need?

It's difficult to see the breadth of a president's responsibilities until you get there, and difficult to know if you will really be suited to the job. *Do you need to base your decisions on facts and precedents?* Presidents are often called upon to make intuitive decisions, to look behind simple situations for surprising answers, shades of meaning, or hints of conflict or latent problems. *How do you feel about risk?* As president, you may have to make some extremely risky choices, and the consequences are your responsibility alone.

The idea of running your own show does have a lot of appeal. Having the opportunity to exercise your own discretion with some degree of freedom sounds so intoxicating that many people don't consider the whole picture. *Do you want to risk getting into a mess that needs sorting out?* I've found that a search for a new president usually indicates the existence of a problem. Solid and secure presidencies are uncommon. Often new leadership is sought when growth or profitability or both have fallen off. This can be a great challenge and opportunity, but if you can't solve the problems, you may be out of a job quicker than you think.

Being president is fun for all the reasons you know so well, but you are also at the end of the diving board. If something goes wrong, you can't return to the line and say you'll take your turn again later. You're out. Presidents get fired. Lack of job security goes with the territory.

Rising to become president is very different from swapping one presidential job for another. If you're seeking your first presidency, ask yourself whether you are really the man for the job. If you already have experience and confidence as a company president, ask yourself whether the job is the right one for you. *What is the potential reward if you succeed—and what do you risk if you fail?*

The track is free for those who want to run on it, but there aren't that many top spots. By all means be president, but don't let the aura of the position blind you to its realities.

So You Want to Be an Entrepreneur
○ Do you have a driving entrepreneurial passion?
○ Are you utterly determined to succeed against all odds?
○ Can you thrive amid chaos?
○ Do you like running with little counsel and much responsibility?

    ○ Have you had experience building a business?
    ○ Can you make coffee, sweep the floor, and cajole the
       bankers?

The temptation to become an entrepreneur abounds these days as executives find themselves out of work or sick of their jobs. Enticed by the huge amounts of risk capital available from those who want to share in the high winnings, they decide to try something on their own. To be an entrepreneur—build a product, capture a market, shape a company—is dazzling, but it is also tough and lonely. Your chances of failure far outweigh your chances of success. But if you win—nirvana!

I see a trend now as major companies downsize and release middle-aged employees with sizable lump-sum severance packages. Many of them try to buy their way into entrepreneuring. Often they lose a lot of money simply in the negotiations. You'd be surprised at how many gaps I see on résumés for this reason.

Do you have the entrepreneurial personality? Entrepreneurs are driven, inexhaustible, confident, and competitive. They're opinionated and unconventional, but they all have enough charisma to get those around them to pick up the pieces they invariably leave half-finished. They are not perfect executives; their skills are skewed. *Are you too perfect an executive to be an entrepreneur?* You may be extremely adept at what you do, but this does not make you a natural entrepreneur.

There is danger in clinging to an unrealistic goal. If you've been telling yourself that someday you're going to quit your job and run your own business, now may be the time to decide whether you really mean it. If you are biding your time in order to gain more expertise, that's fine, but if you are halfheartedly putting in the hours until you break free, think again. You could be shooting yourself in both feet: You're doing nothing either for your alternative career or for your existing one.

Being an entrepreneur is not a road to privacy or a way to chuck organizational frustrations. You need the right contacts, and those contacts want direct access to you. You are the hub at the center of the wheel. *Are you ready and willing to be in on everything?*

Being an entrepreneur is the soul of America, but that doesn't mean it's easy.

COULD THIS BE YOU?

Jerry dipped his paintbrush into some phthalo blue. He loved seeing the vivid colors all lined up on his palette, loved the sensation of smearing paint on canvas. His picture was looking a little strange, but he was happy. Too bad he hadn't discovered painting until he was over 50. What a waste of years.

Jerry's father, an artist, had died when Jerry was two, and his stepfather, an engineer, hadn't thought much of what he regarded as artsy-craftsy pursuits. From an early age Jerry had accommodated his stepfather's emphasis on the technical rather than the creative. He'd become reasonably proficient at calculating and fixing; he'd scored well on mechanical aptitude tests; he'd admired engineers and disdained those in liberal arts or business school programs right up to the time he himself went to college, fought to be an engineer, and lost the battle.

He graduated with a degree in industrial psychology but still hadn't learned his real lesson. In the army he worked with radar; after that he went into manufacturing, then computers, and finally banking.

Over the years, Jerry made many plans and set many goals, but he could see now that he'd been halfhearted. He'd been responding to the pressure he felt to make something of himself. He'd tried—oh, how he'd tried! He'd gone through the motions, but without conviction. He was supposed to want to achieve certain things, so he said that he wanted to do so.

Jerry was smart, attractive, and sociable. He met with success in each role he took on, but the more successful he became, the easier it was for him to almost completely ignore his innermost drives. Almost.

One evening, a week or so before his 49th birthday, it hit Jerry full force that only sheer willpower was getting him through each workday. This realization disturbed him terribly. The next morning he found he couldn't bear to get out of bed. Things had reached a crisis point.

Jerry went to his current job at the bank that afternoon and quit. The president was astounded, especially when he learned that Jerry had no better job waiting, not even a plan. "I don't *know* what I'm going to do, Phil," Jerry said. "All I know is that I have to do something different. It isn't you, it isn't the bank . . . it's me."

Jerry entered a difficult period. It was a transition, but into what he didn't know. His family was appalled; his former colleagues were mystified; he thought maybe his neighbors were snickering at him. He had no label to affix to his life. He'd always been a go-getter; suddenly he was idle. He'd always scorned the idea of "finding yourself," but now that was exactly what he needed to do.

Jerry had thought he was doing all the right things. He'd certainly been working hard, but by failing to recognize his natural inclinations, he'd missed the mark, and this had diluted all his efforts.

He stepped back from his canvas. The phthalo blue was working out O.K. Jerry reflected that after his fourth industry switch—now he was in advertising—he felt he'd finally found his niche. Only recently had he started to feel the extraordinary confidence of knowing he was good at something and could dig deep to do the unexpected if he had to. Jerry recognized that he was playing a little catch-up ball, but he knew—and liked—where he was going.

PULLING IT TOGETHER

If you're perfectly suited to your job, you need never return to this chapter, but few are so fortunate. It's more likely that at a certain level—maybe subliminal, maybe not—things eat at you, and every once in a while you need to sit down and sort them out. Here's your chance.

Think of the great effort that is expended on business objectives: Strategies are devised, tactics implemented, meetings held, plans monitored, and corrective actions taken, all to make sure that the results are on target. Rarely is this same level of energy and awareness applied to your personal career.

Take a moment to review the chapter's headings, and as you consider these main points, stop to see how in touch you are with your priorities and how closely your career reflects them. Don't hurry. Leave yourself open to insights that may lead to other insights, levels of yourself that you've never acknowledged. You may be pleasantly surprised.

Part II

Taking Stock:
Checking Out
the Company

Now you come face to face with your company, which has as much impact on your career as you do. You entrust your career to the company in which you work, but if the company isn't healthy, neither is your job. Is your company in the right place, doing the right thing at the right time? Are you in the right place at the right time within it? Part II will help you evaluate the environment in which you've chosen to work. What your company does and how it does it either complements or inhibits your good work. You want to know which.

My background makes me particularly sensitive to this concern. I've been an executive recruiter for 14 years, as you know, which has given me the overall perspective for this book. Before that, however, I worked in advertising and on Wall Street. Both of these industries do painstaking research into the factors that are pivotal for their purposes. Advertising agencies analyze products and markets before huge amounts of money are spent on advertising campaigns; brokerage firms use the best financial and management research available to guide their investments. What I've tried to do is draw the best insights from these three sources and present them to you.

Some of the following points will require a little research of your own. For those that relate to the confidential operations of your company, you'll have to make your best estimates. You will never know as much as management, but you can learn enough to prepare yourself for developments that, to others, will come as complete surprises.

Your boss can be a valuable source of information, but don't expect him to supply all your answers. He doesn't have to tell you everything he knows. For his own reasons, he may deliberately play down certain kinds of information. And if you think a company that's good enough for your boss is good enough for you, think again. Unless your boss has performed his own career checkup, he's probably overlooking some important factors—and what suits him may be exactly wrong for you. You'll never know what his real reasons are for staying with your company. You could be following him into career suicide.

In some instances, the more difficult it is to find information, the more alert you want to be to unfavorable facts and potential problems. The company may not want you to hear the bad news—but your career may be on the line. There are ways of finding out what you need to know.

If you find that your company checks out unfavorably with respect to most of the following points, run, don't walk, to the nearest exit! That company has problems. Probably you'll find only a few points that are problematic, but bear in mind that the weak points could be entirely different 12 months from now.

I've tried to provide a tight screen. If you take Chapters 7, 9, and 10 together—products and markets, top management, and the financials— you have a crisis manager's check. What's that? It's the fast review a crisis manager performs when he undertakes a new assignment with a troubled company. Should you be any less thorough?

6

What Makes the Company Tick?

Like a person, a company has an image it projects, a certain operating style, and a private set of priorities tucked away inside that makes it tick. Call it corporate culture, but don't expect your boss to tell you a lot about it. He's probably adapted to your company's culture so closely that it has become an integral part of him. Chances are he's lost his sensitivity to what that culture is and how it could be different.

Corporate operations and priorities vary tremendously. You want to choose a company that is vigorous, that has values in tune with your own, and that will accommodate the way you personally want to operate. Is your company's culture one in which you can flourish? If not, what are your alternatives?

Even companies that are not too dissimilar on the outside can be fundamentally different within. I once recruited a vice-president for a $10-million company in which the executive vice-president read every incoming letter and telex first, and every outgoing letter to customers. Not everyone could live with that. Another company of the same size in the same industry has a congenial atmosphere and few operating formalities. What a difference! But most employees at each company are content, and both companies are prospering.

It is not realistic to hope that your company will change its style and priorities just because you are on board. Corporations develop habits, and you know how difficult it is to get someone to give up an ingrained way of thinking or behaving. If you discover that you and your company have fundamentally different objectives, that's a problem, since compromise is unlikely. You and management may both want growth and stability for the company, but if your emphasis is long-term and management's short-term, look out.

This chapter will help you start looking behind your company's image and media releases for signs of its general viability. You'll get a feel for the essence of the company—what makes it tick, how well it runs, what could disrupt its operations. You want to identify the company's driving force and where it may be headed. It's fine for a company to say where it wants to go, but does your common sense agree that the resources and enthusiasm needed to get there are available?

In later chapters you'll fine-tune your understanding of your company by concentrating on one area of its operations at a time. For now, go for the overview, a gut-level feeling for what kind of place your company really is and whether or not you belong there.

Take Stock of Your Company's Image and First Impression

○ Does the company have a good reputation?
○ Does it make a favorable first impression?
○ What substance is behind the image?
○ Do you feel good describing your company to your friends?
○ Do they buy your enthusiasm?

You've got to feel comfortable facing your company each day—comfortable with what it stands for and its position in the community as well as comfortable working there.

Corporate images and first impressions can be misleading. Companies are self-serving; they use public relations and advertising campaigns to project profiles that can be very different from reality. Even highly visible companies with well-known corporate cultures can hand out surprises behind the facade.

A good corporate reputation is a favorable sign, but a reputation can be out of date. You may be inclined to place your faith in the image of a corporation, in the architectural distinction of its offices, its art collection, or the socially desirable programs it sponsors. That is the public image of a corporation, and it's tremendously important that it be consistent and laudable. However, to protect yourself from misconceptions and the resulting disappointments, don't stop with a first impression, whether you're evaluating a *Fortune* 500 company, a smaller organization, or a division within your own company. Management wants you to see things in a certain way and to make favorable assumptions when you don't have the facts. *What assumptions have you made? What discrepancies do you see?*

Consider Your Company's Personality
○ Does a sense of achievement and purpose prevail?
○ Are rules and schedules important?
○ What are the company traditions?
○ Are they put forward with pride?
○ Do you find people in the company candid, open?
○ Do you like what you see around you?

Each company has its own atmosphere. Carefully selecting the company personality that's right for you will determine in large part how much success you can expect. It's hard to succeed when you don't fit in.

Company personality comes through as you walk the halls, speak to employees, watch them working and talking, watch managers interact with their people, glance at the company bulletin board, and read the company handbook. Company personality is what can make an otherwise tolerable existence stimulating, challenging, and rewarding—all of which allow you to run harder and be more productive.

Most companies have a credo or mission statement set forth by early management clarifying their values and goals. Founders are opinionated. When they feel strongly about something, those who work for them had better feel the same way. *Who are the company heroes?*

A large part of a company's atmosphere is determined by its operating style. *Is your company formal or informal?* When I joined an investment banking firm that had been founded in

1845, I once addressed the chairman by his first name as we stood by the ticker tape. He stiffened. Clearly, that wasn't done. In contrast, not long ago when I put in a call to Jim Treybig, the president of Tandem Computers, I asked the receptionist how to correctly pronounce his last name. She didn't know. "We all call him Jimmy!" she said, and her enthusiasm told me a great deal about Tandem.

Some companies love the stimulus of new ideas and welcome a challenge to the accepted way of doing things. In others, the process for putting forth new ideas is so cumbersome that few make the effort to contribute. *Does your company have the capacity to adapt and stay current? Is management receptive to new ideas?*

In the garment industry, where changing fashions can make or break a company, the pace is frantic. In an "old-line" law firm, decorum and demeanor are important. In a regional utility company, Little League and local activities tend to yank people away at five o'clock sharp. There is no "right" style, but there is a style that's right (or wrong) for you.

Do you know the atmosphere in which you are most comfortable? Where are you going to find it? It is possible to locate good companies that do things the way you do. If you are a suit-jacket type in Atlanta, Coca-Cola would make you comfortable, but if you prefer shirt-sleeves at all times, Delta Airlines in the same city would be more to your liking.

Sometimes it is insufficient to be merely neutral when management demands that you be an active supporter of its policies. Whatever the work style management expects, it's up to you to recognize it, do it, and enjoy it—or acknowledge to yourself that by not doing it, you are laying the groundwork for problems. Incompatibility is a ground for divorce.

Pinpoint Your Company's Driving Force

○ What keeps your company energized?
○ How effective is your president or CEO?
○ Do you sense an intensity that's unusual?

○ Do you contribute to the momentum?
○ What might change your company's driving force?
○ If it has been lost, how might it be regained?

The best driving force generates enthusiasm, energy, and pride within the company. It builds intensity, whether it is a person, product, or ideal. In a smoothly running company, the driving force may simply be inertia: Things continue to go well and build their own momentum.

If your company has a sense of energy, you'll feel proud of your contribution, which in turn, builds more intensity and determination. A company without dynamism is in danger.

Have you figured out who or what is the driving force behind your company, or whether one actually exists among a variety of strong factors? What you're trying to identify is that extra force that truly makes a difference. It could be an innovative leader, a project or new product that has captured the spirit of the employees, or commitment to a particular goal.

Often an entrepreneur drives his company, usually with great effort and frequently at great risk. A powerful individual can persuade employees and customers alike of his vision; his dynamism fuels his entire organization. When a company's driving force is an individual, however, there is risk, since he is virtually irreplaceable after he moves on.

How Well Is Information Distributed?

○ Is your company open- or close-mouthed?
○ Does management communicate openly with employees, stockholders, investment analysts, and the media?
○ Are interdepartmental communications efficient?
○ Do you feel up-to-date on operations and procedures in your department?
○ Is informal news provided in a timely manner?

Information is hot now. Getting it, slicing it, and delivering it fast where it is needed is a growing and healthy industry. How information moves within your company is totally under management's control. It's part of the style and personality of your company.

If your company is a public corporation, look first at the way in which it makes investment information available. If it communicates well with investors, it is proud of the story it has to tell. Investors want to hear all the news, both good and bad, and so do you, so look at your company's annual and quarterly reports. *Are reports open and clear in addition to just looking good? Are meaningful data included?* Follow newspaper reports and what investment analysts are saying about your company. You should get an idea of whether or not the corporation is forthright in providing information. If corporate communications are veiled, it may not necessarily indicate that management is hiding something, but you should wonder why the firm is being so circumspect.

On a daily basis, internal communications mean more to you. *Does your company have up-to-date internal communications systems? Does it get to the heart of matters and not burden you with paper?* Newsletters, voice mail, electronic mail, and video hookups all contribute to the smooth and rapid exchange of information. These systems need to be constantly monitored and adjusted in response to new developments.

Does your company encourage communication between all locations and all levels of employees? Jim Treybig of Tandem— "Jimmy," as we now know—founded his company in 1974, a year of doldrums for the computer industry. To seek every advantage in competing against the established giants, Treybig emphasized internal communications. He eliminated all information barriers and kept everyone talking and sharing ideas. Today Tandem is a $750-million company, and the information is still flowing, now with teleconferencing, electronic mail terminals on all desks, and a quarterly journal that includes well-written articles about the company's achievements, goals, and aspirations. At Tandem there is also an open-door policy that includes a sign-up schedule posted outside the door of each executive. You want to talk with someone, you just sign up, no questions asked. The company also holds Friday beer busts that encourage employees to meet and share their ideas regardless of their levels within the company. Tandem says that it has a "common fate" environment and everybody must talk with each other. Sometimes something good comes from talking with the "wrong" person. You get an insight you hadn't expected.

What kind of information does your company make available internally? How soon do you hear of new developments and procedures? News of company awards and achievements as well as personal news and notices of company job openings can be a great boon to morale. If your company does not keep this kind of information flowing, ask yourself why management has not made internal communications a priority.

How Much Cooperation Is Encouraged?
○ Is there a sense of teamwork in your company?
○ Do managers of different departments meet together?
○ Does this happen frequently?
○ Do people at various levels meet regularly?
○ Does a spirit of harmony focus everyone on the same goal?

Communication, cooperation, and coordination within a company lead to teamwork, and that harmony is important to find. Without it, you have inefficiency at best, chaos and combativeness at worst.

Traditional rivalries exist between departments. Engineering wants to sell product A because it's the best. Marketing wants to push product B because of certain demographics. Sales reports that customers really want a combination of A and B, and finance says the company has already exceeded its research and development budget.

Ford Motor Company tackled this problem head-on with the Taurus/Sable automobile. In 1980, it brought together representatives from design, engineering, manufacturing, marketing, finance, and sales to solicit suggestions and to provide immediate feedback on how one department's proposal would affect the others. The project was successful and benefited everyone. Taurus, brought out in 1985, was a leader for Ford.

Do you sense cooperation around you? The Japanese value teamwork so highly that they purposely transfer people laterally so they can learn the operations of other departments and work with the people in them. They claim this broad familiarity with operations, as well as a true inclination to cooperate, enables them to make changes quickly.

Some companies take pride in pitting departments against each other, even to the point where personal gain becomes paramount. While the heavy-hitters may get a thrill out of watching others fail, this kind of competition seriously undermines a company and is destructive to its long-term goals.

Assess Your Company's Work Environment and People Programs

○ Does your company do something extra for your well-being?
○ Does management sponsor extracurricular activities?
○ Does it make facilities available?
○ Is the company responsive to the interests of its employees?
○ Does it make your work environment pleasant?

Some companies go out of their way to keep people animated and satisfied. This is part benevolence and part good business: Happy employees are productive employees.

Many programs are not the ideas of management but of employees who start something that is then endorsed by the company. Employees participate, and the company provides the environment or other support. You've seen this in sports teams, company-sponsored volunteer activities, and corporate support for local causes. These programs cost the company little other than concern.

Providing lunchrooms, lounges, fitness centers, and medical facilities can be expensive, but a good work environment is greatly stimulating to employee morale. Corporate benevolence also shows up in traditional ways, such as company-sponsored get-togethers or programs to provide matching grants and in innovations such as flexible hours or on-site day care.

A company has many opportunities to show its concern for the well-being of its employees. In Chapter 8, you'll have a chance to rate your company on how well it develops its people professionally, and in Chapter 12, you'll evaluate the benefits and perks your company offers. Here you want to see whether your company demonstrates on a day-to-day basis that it cares— or couldn't care less.

Awards programs are simple but effective ways to keep people motivated. Ogilvy & Mather has a unique way of bringing smiles to its employees: Management gives surprise bonuses in the halls for jobs well done.

At Levi Strauss, management allows the sewing machine operators to determine how they want company charitable funds distributed locally. Committees of workers determine who gets what and then present the checks from the Levi Strauss Foundation to the local charities. This gives the production-line people a chance to interact with the leaders of the community on behalf of their company. That to me is imagination.

Does your company bring out the best in you and your associates?

How Is Your Company Structured?

○ How is your company organized?
○ Is its structure one of the most efficient in your industry?
○ Is it stable?
○ Is authority centralized or decentralized?
○ Does the organization of your company aid or impede your getting things done?
○ Where will you end up in your company's structure?

How your company is organized will affect how much you can participate, be seen, and be promoted. Your company's structure can work for or against you.

Companies can be organized by function, product, line of business, geography, or in a matrix. Some companies have hundreds of business units, some have few. Some are highly centralized, some are aggressively decentralized. Some seem to be in a constant state of flux.

Is your company's organization the best for the business? Is it likely to remain as it is? If you see a company with a better organization in your field, examine the trade-offs. You might try suggesting that company's approach to your company or incorporating it in your own operation.

The best organization is that which works best for your company at its stage of development. But your progress, and what you'll need to do to get where you want to go, will depend upon the type of organization your company has. *Does your company's structure suit your ambitions?*

If you want to run a business, it's easier to do so in a large corporation made up of integrated businesses, but if you want to head up a huge sales operation, you're better off in a company organized by function. If you're at a junior level, you can make an impact faster in a decentralized operation. In some companies, specialists can gain greater recognition and compensation than managers; in others, the opposite holds true.

Frequent organizational change is not always a bad sign. A human resources executive at American Express once joked to me about the "every-18-months shuffle." For him it was a lot of work, but for the company it seems to have been a path to success. If you are in this kind of company, you have to be more alert to the relative benefits of core business versus new ventures and see where your skills fit in. *Given your company's structure, how are you going to get as much responsibility and involvement as you want?*

Look at Manufacturing and Production

- ○ Are your company's manufacturing facilities advantageously located?
- ○ Are they clean and organized?
- ○ Are state-of-the-art tools being used?
- ○ Is your company a low-cost producer?
- ○ Can facilities be expanded as needed?
- ○ Are shipments going out on schedule?

Even if you're the advertising manager, you need to at least glimpse at your company's manufacturing facilities. Manufacturing eats up capital; it either makes money with its operations or wastes it. The quality of your product and how speedily it's delivered can make customers happy or mad; whatever part of the company you're in, this will affect you.

In Chapter 7 you'll be looking carefully at the strengths of your company's products and markets. For now, just concern yourself with production. If you're in a professional or service company, you may skip this section—but don't skip the next chapter!

I've found that cleanliness and orderliness correlate with success. The front office can look great, but boxes piled helter-skelter in the plant imply lack of control. And more than one analyst has noted from the condition of the rest rooms that a company may be in trouble.

If your company is a low-cost producer relative to others in the industry, you can take comfort that major expenditures have already been made that your competitors still have to face. That's an advantage. So is having land or facilities to expand into as your company grows and new markets open up. If you're not a manufacturing person, ask someone who is about these issues and see whether he's enthusiastic or defensive. You'll know.

Ask about inventories. Concern for inventories is ongoing. Inventories are money, and generally the less you have sitting around the better—as long as the company is meeting shipment dates. *Do you see any buildup of inventory?* Rust or dust on materials in the plant will cause you to ask more questions. *Does the company have a materials requirements system to optimize inventories?* Misjudging the market can cause inventory problems that hurt.

If your company's manufacturing operation is responsive and flexible, you can use its capabilities strategically. A brief surge in production, for example, could allow you to push a particular item, and an occasional rush schedule that can be accommodated smoothly can give you an edge over a competitor. *All in all, how do you really feel about the production facilities of your company? Are they equal to, or possibly better than, those of your competitors?*

Consider Research and Development (R&D)

○ Do companies in your industry invest in R&D?
○ What is the R&D budget of your company?
○ How does it compare with others in your industry?
○ Does the R&D group have a record of bringing forth successful new products?
○ Does it keep existing products up-to-date?
○ Is R&D a prestige operation within your company?

Service companies and suppliers of commodity products have little need for R&D, while companies in the forefront of industries such as electronics or pharmaceuticals have a tremendous need for it. In industries where R&D is a matter of survival, the effectiveness of your R&D group can determine the prospects for your company and your career.

Is your company putting enough into, and getting enough out of, its R&D investment? Back in 1980, Mostek was on top of the world with a 16k chip. In electronics, however, product cycles are short, and price-performance ratios are constantly improving. Mostek was eclipsed in only a couple of years by the Japanese with a 64k chip—technology moves that fast. Mostek's R&D group was not alert to industry developments, and the company lost out.

Are R&D funds going where they will help you most? I don't mean to suggest that you know corporate objectives better than management, but if R&D funds are going to a new project in a different division while your projects languish, that R&D effort is useless to you. It also implies that your company's priorities are in another direction. Questioning what those funds are doing doesn't make you greedy; it makes you realistic.

Some companies treat R&D like maintenance, deferring the costs in bad times and supporting them in good times. This isn't good enough. R&D involves imagination and persistence. You get and keep the best R&D people in your group if it has prestige and independence within the company. Your company does not have to be a Bell Laboratories, but it should provide a stimulating environment for those people to whom you look for answers that others in the industry have not found.

What About Environmental Considerations?

○ Does your company pollute air, water, or land?
○ Is air or water purified before it is discharged?
○ Are any company personnel exposed to toxic chemicals or extreme noise, air, or water pollution?
○ Has the company used toxic waste dumps in the past?
○ Is there any record of environmental problems?

Polluting the environment and endangering people with pollution is not only reprehensible but also against the law—and what used to be legal may not be legal now. If your company gets hit with an environmental problem, management gets distracted, funds get diverted, and your job progress could be jeopardized.

A client of mine heading a rust-belt company negotiated the sale of his company to a large corporation that could use his accumulated losses for tax reasons. Shortly before the papers were finalized, toxic waste dumps were found that the company had used many years before. It was estimated that the cost of cleaning the dumps could run as high as $100 million. The buyer walked away, and the company may be facing liquidation. A blunt surprise to my client and his employees from the environmental side.

Does your company have someone trained in environmental concerns monitoring its operations? Beyond waste dumps and otherwise polluting the outside environment is the issue of endangering employees. Monitoring inside a company is relatively easy, and precautions can be taken. Respirators and masks are commonplace now, and you see ear protectors on baggage handlers at all airports. Failing to provide such protection can result in a class-action suit with additional claims from former employees. These lawsuits divert management's attention from running the business and can have serious financial ramifications.

Is your company aware of environmental considerations and on top of them? If so, this point is simply one more to file away in the back of your mind until something comes up to cause you to ask a question.

Beyond the pragmatic business concerns, there is a moral side to protecting people and the environment. Good programs reflect well on management. If your company is responsible regarding environmental considerations, it may be enlightened in other areas, as well.

Examine International Operations

○ Does your company depend on international operations?
○ How vulnerable is the company to exchange-rate fluctuations?
○ How financially sound are the countries in which your company has its major operations?
○ How politically stable are those countries?
○ How does your company treat people on their return from international assignments?

International operations can run into all manner of problems, from social unrest to political gamesmanship. In turn, operational problems have a direct effect on you.

A client of mine bought a company in Europe in 1980 when the U.S. dollar was weak. He saw opportunity for growth and counted on a strong earnings stream to pay off the debts he incurred. But the dollar then strengthened to the point where it took twice as many repatriated dollars to equal his projections based on 1980 dollars. This was the corporation's first move offshore, and it consumed management's time for several years. Result: A formerly super-high-growth company stalled out.

"International" is not just another department within your company. It comprises specialists from each of the countries with which your company does business, and each specialist monitors his specific variables. Countries can be very different from one another. Countries are also sovereign, remember. They possess absolute power to make laws and change them as they see fit.

They can change social values or imprison people, and there is no higher authority to which to appeal. *Where does your company do business? What risks do you see? Can they be hedged?*

On a personal level, you want to know how your company views its international operations and the people who venture far away to run them. If an international assignment could be part of your career, see what the long-term trade-offs may be. Some companies value international experience and regard it as a necessary step before assuming general management responsibilities. Others offer you the glamour and perks of an international posting but let you take your chances when you return—a problem if you've gotten out of touch. Major companies often have consulting groups that give returning employees a chance to be seen by the domestic operations as well as a chance to look around, both inside and outside the company. Be alert to these possibilities if an international posting comes your way.

COULD THIS BE YOU?

Ian Postlethwaite hung up the phone and walked over to his office window. He looked at the typically British scene below and idly followed the red double-decker buses as they plowed along through the rain. His company had just asked him to come to U.S. headquarters and head the international marketing division. The offer sounded good, but he wanted to make sure.

Ian's ancestors came from the Lake District of England. Ian looked British and worked in London, but in fact he'd been born and raised in Detroit. Early in his career Ian had gone international with a posting in Hong Kong, and since then he'd run the foreign offices of three different companies.

Ian enjoyed his international assignments and had thought that they were good for his children while they were young. But the kids were preparing for college now. Maybe it was time to move on.

Ian was undecided. While he liked its reputation, he hadn't grown up with this company, and he really knew only the international people. He would need to make sure that the company's fine public image was matched by its private priorities.

Ian knew his strengths and recognized that the move would take him away from them; however, it should set the scene for advancement. Before accepting the job, however, he needed to do some research.

During the next few days, Ian made a number of phone calls to people he knew well in the company, and he even called some friends who had left the company. He was gathering information about what made the company as a whole tick. He knew his own operation inside out, but returning to headquarters would place him in a new arena.

On the evening before the president's arrival in London, Ian reviewed his notes in his library at home. His family said they would ride with him either way; it was purely his business decision. He was trying to be systematic and unemotional.

One of Ian's first concerns had been how international people were integrated back into the company. His calls had put his mind to rest on that one. International was regarded as the big market for the company; he would have no trouble stepping directly into the international marketing position and would not lose prestige by doing so.

The next concern on Ian's list was teamwork, and here again things looked positive. All his information pointed to good cooperation and an absence of sharp political divisions within the company. At any one point, a number of large project teams would be working together; the constant interaction of personnel had a unifying effect.

But where was the company going? The answer to that lay in the president, who was also CEO. He was the driving force behind the company. He'd made a number of acquisitions, many in the international field, and the company was stronger for them. Ian agreed with what the president was doing and had picked up few complaints from his contacts. He'd had just two meetings with the president, both of which had been quite formal. He had no problems with the president personally, although he hadn't seen enough of him to say he liked him.

Ian had never thought much about the domestic production facilities, but he knew that outdated or limited facilities could hurt. He reviewed the comments he'd solicited. Again the president got high marks; he'd sold some of the old operations, and most of the remaining facilities were modern, with room to expand. Cutting back as markets contracted would not be easy, but all in all, Ian thought the production side looked positive.

Research and development didn't look as strong. The R&D budget gave Ian some concern because he would have liked to see more investment there. However, the costs of restructuring the company had been high. Maybe R&D would be a priority in the future. He made a note to ask the president about it.

Ian's wife entered the library just as Ian made his final notes. "I think the Postlethwaites are going home, Alice," he said. "I've got a couple of questions for the president tomorrow, but if he says what I expect he will, we're off."

PULLING IT TOGETHER

The culture of your company—what makes it tick—determines whether or not you're going to be happy. Whatever the company, there are practices, habits, and traditions that you should recognize and feel comfortable with. These are the things that will come through to you daily, that will be reflected in every activity of the company, and that will either reinforce or detract from your efforts.

Take a moment to quickly review the chapter's main points. *Does everything hang together, make sense?* Make notes to indicate problems or strengths, and list the points you want to come back to another time.

7

How Strong Are the Products and Markets?

A company can't succeed without good products, priced favorably, and customers willing to pay for them. Whether your company's products are tangible (toasters, microchips) or intangible (financial advice, consulting), you need to know if they can really make a dent in the marketplace, both now and in the future. Without this assurance, your job is in jeopardy.

Products and markets change fast. Is your company keeping up? Is it holding its position against others in the industry? Does management have the muscle to keep your products competitive and your company healthy? Before jumping to conclusions, review the sections in this chapter. Keep the expansion or contraction of your industry in mind, since on a longer-term basis, even the best of companies in a declining market will have problems.

To make the most of your company's products and markets, you need to correct weaknesses and exploit strengths. You can't afford to get caught by a time bomb you overlooked or blindsided by your own complacence.

True marketing—analyzing the demographics, customers, competition, product characteristics, and so forth—is enjoying a renaissance. As the saying goes, companies are learning to "sell the dog what he wants to eat," not what the technicians want to make. If your company doesn't sell what the customer wants, someone else will notice the gap and fill it. And that will hurt.

Advertising agencies and marketing people do tremendously valuable studies on products and markets on which major marketing plans are based. But these studies are confidential. What you have to do in this chapter is try to project the same kind of data and then put your own best judgments to work.

Product cycles are becoming shorter because the forces of technological change and competition are becoming stronger. The manufacturers of such products as Kleenex brand facial tissues or Gillette razor blades may imply that their products don't have cycles, but in fact they do, and even the most firmly established companies spend vast sums on advertising and R&D to maintain their positions. For most, the product cycle is a fact of life—or more correctly, a matter of life and death.

The following pages will put the dominant marketing concerns in perspective. You won't come out of this chapter a marketing whiz, but you will know the questions to ask and will be more sensitive to the factors that make a difference.

Take a Look at Your Company's Products

- ○ Why do people buy your product?
- ○ Is it up-to-date?
- ○ What advantage does your product offer over others?
- ○ Is your company doing enough to hold that advantage?
- ○ What is your product's greatest weakness?
- ○ Where is your product in its cycle?

A healthy company requires healthy products to prosper. To be secure in your present position, you need to know why your products are strong and why they're likely to stay that way.

What's special about your product? A proprietary advantage, patent, special ingredient, unique design, or strong reputation can all weigh heavily in your company's favor. So can a feeling on the part of your customers that your company has the muscle and the smarts to take care of them.

Once you've pinpointed your product's particular strengths, ask yourself what other companies in your industry are doing. *Why is your competition allowing you to keep your advantage? How long can it last?* If your company doesn't continue to deliver, your customers will switch to the competition—fast.

Is it likely that your company will change its product orientation? Companies change directions for many reasons, some of which are planned and some are not. Depending on your position, these changes may or may not enhance your career, but the important thing is to be sensitive to new developments and to assess the impact they may have on your plans. Change is fine as long as you anticipate it and position yourself so that it is in your favor.

Niche products are popular now and can be highly successful as companies fit new products between the lines of established giants. Discount brokerage houses, for example, did this to the long-established full-service houses, and the Hyundai and Yugo automobiles have done it to the auto industry. *If yours is a niche product, will the big companies try to recover the ground they lost to you?*

Attempting to displace an established leader means initiating head-to-head competition. This requires the right price point, strong advertising, efficient distribution, and more. It's tough and expensive. *Can your product take the heat?* If you're the leader, unexpected competition drains resources and revenues. *Has your company been good at anticipating competition?*

Having an advanced product usually gives you an edge. There are exceptions, however. Sometimes a space-age idea simply doesn't catch on, and conversely, certain products can stay in service and remain profitable long after they've become obsolete. Once you know your product's life cycle, check for vital signs. *Are unit sales on your product growing or declining?*

Are you comfortable with your company's products? The more specific points that follow may help you with your answer.

Consider Product Quality

○ Does management emphasize the highest standards of quality?
○ Is your product's quality good for the price?
○ Is your product's quality consistent?
○ Are product liability suits a potential problem?
○ How are consumer grievances handled?

Quality is related to price. For any product, whether it's a wrench or a will, the customer knows the range of prices and the relative range of quality he can expect. It is imperative that your product meet or exceed customer expectations. The expected level of quality must be there in order for your company's product to succeed.

Quality starts early, in the design or planning stage, and follows right through to execution. It's more than an inspection or an occasional threatening letter from management. If your product's quality is inconsistent in any way, your company's reputation and revenues will suffer. Bad news travels very fast among consumers. Uniformly high performance is difficult to achieve, but worth the effort.

It's easier to evaluate the quality of a can opener than the expertise of an attorney, but even with intangible products, quality is related to price and reputation. If you're in a service company, review the credentials of the people who are rendering the advice, writing the reports, or completing the returns. See how heavily you rely on their "products" and how good their performance has been.

There is always the possibility that something will go wrong with your product. An intangible product may be incomplete or insufficient; a tangible product may be defective, break down, or be abused by the consumer. *What recourse does your company offer disgruntled customers?* You can't please everyone all of the time, but your company must stand by its product. What kinds of guarantees or conditions does your company offer?

Service is becoming more complex as products become more sophisticated and owners can't make repairs themselves. In many cases, products are now used as part of a system, and only someone who understands the entire system can isolate and correct a problem. *Is service for your products readily available? Can repairs be made easily?* Servicing your products can bring in good revenues, but too much servicing can signal customer dissatisfaction.

If something goes seriously wrong with a product, your company could end up in court. Product liability suits are not unusual these days and can wreak corporate havoc. *Is there an aspect of your product that could lead to liability? Have there been such suits in the past?*

You want to be assured that your company's products are satisfactory and that your company stands behind them. Quality and service are the twin columns that support good products. *Do you feel assured?*

What Are the Markets for Your Company's Products?

- ○ What are the markets for your company's products?
- ○ How are they defined by demographics?
- ○ Are your markets growing, holding steady, or contracting?
- ○ How long have they been showing that trend?
- ○ How long is that trend likely to continue?
- ○ What might change it?

If no one is interested in your product, you're out of business. Your concern is to know your market, the forces that shape it, and how it is changing. You don't have to be a market analyst to do this; just use your common sense.

Ford's market is automobile buyers, but market segments exist within that overall market. Those who buy Lincolns are different from those who buy Escorts. The same principle applies to different market segments for a single product. Your company should address the biggest market possible, but it has to hit the hot button of each market segment.

What's happening in your markets? Is your company prepared? Markets are always in a state of flux. If your company is selling into a particular market but hasn't adjusted to market changes, you're likely to get hurt. The baby-boomers, for example, are becoming middle-aged, and their buying habits have changed. This is changing the size of many markets. But the baby-boomers are only one demographic force. People are staying healthy longer, working longer, and living longer, all of which creates new markets for a range of products.

Sometimes a company will address a market it believes should be there but isn't. I can think of several magazine attempts, including a multimillion-dollar videotext venture, that were spectacular flops. Despite all kinds of optimistic market predictions, the buyers simply weren't there.

If your company can continue to refine your product and tailor it to specific needs, you should be able to open up new markets even as existing ones change. *What is it that gives you the confidence that the market for your products will remain strong?*

What Is Your Company's Market Share?

○ What company dominates your market?
○ What company is moving up fast?
○ Where does your company fit in?
○ Is your company gaining or losing its share of the market?

In business, competition is not polite, and you can get hurt if you're not part of the winning team. The object in business is to dominate a market by gaining the leading market share. That is regarded as success. Your company gets to be "No. 1" by taking another company's share, moving ahead in the rankings, and possibly putting your competitor out of business.

Many companies will remain only in markets where they can be a leader. Emerson Electric Company, for example, comprises 62 businesses; of these, 82 percent rank either No. 1 or No. 2 in their markets. Charles F. Knight, chairman of Emerson, feels this position of market leadership is essential if the company is to maintain its record performance. A market leader has not only pricing flexibility but also a large pool of loyal customers who can make things happen.

A rising share of an expanding market is the magic combination. Companies in this position can broaden product lines where appropriate and introduce new products where openings occur. It's a comfort if your company has this sort of record, but it's also difficult to maintain.

Everybody wants a bigger market share, and many companies buy and sell businesses to gain the share they can't build internally. You have to know how your company stacks up against the leaders in your industry and have some idea of how and why your company is going to succeed.

Share statistics may not be discussed much in your industry, but market share tells a story. Look at your industry and see how close your company is to being a leader. *Would a conservative investor want to buy stock in your company?*

Assess Pricing Strategy

○ How much flexibility does your company have in its pricing policy?
○ Does management encourage "creative" pricing to get the order?
○ Is this in compliance with the Robinson-Patman Act?
○ What is the best price point for your product?
○ What price are you asking?
○ Are price changes made in an orderly and timely manner?

Pricing is the front line of your company's contact with the consumer. The price points your company chooses relative to the quality of your product send a message. You want your price to be perceived as current and fair, whether you are selling toothpaste or tax advice. Charging less than your competitors for a product of comparable quality is wasteful; charging more is chancy.

Creative pricing is fine within limits. The risk is that you might engage in discriminatory pricing, thereby violating the Robinson-Patman Act. For this you can be sent to jail, not just for what you personally have done, but for what those responsible to you have done—yes, even if you didn't know about it. There is a reason for well-defined prices, and if your company pushes you to negotiate beyond those limits, you should see a red flag. Ask questions to make sure you're on firm legal ground.

Customers resent companies that change prices frequently or without notice. *Are your company's prices consistent?* In most industries, price is a matter of trust: The consumer expects a fair profit to be taken in exchange for value given. Price fluctuations can break that trust and turn a good customer into a doubting one.

You're looking for reassurance that your company responds to market forces by changing its price accordingly, with appropriate notice, thereby demonstrating leadership. Price increases or decreases that "stick" will show strength and a willingness to compete.

Examine Profit Margins

- ○ Are your company's profit margins fat or skinny?
- ○ Which way are they moving?
- ○ If they're fat, are you providing an umbrella for your competitors?
- ○ If skinny, is there enough to pay for advertising and R&D?
- ○ What could change your profit margins?
- ○ How wide are the profit margins of the market leader?

A profit margin is net sales minus costs of raw materials and production. It tells you what your company has left for marketing, R&D, overhead, and a net profit. Profit margins determine how much money your company has to work with. Grocery products typically have skinny profit margins but are sold in high volume. The profit margins of luxury items are generally fat, but fewer units are sold. In between is a wide range.

Fat profit margins are a joy to have, but only if your company can protect its position. Xerox, for example, used to own its market with innovative products, but it had such wide margins that big competitors were able to successfully move into its territory. Watch out for this situation, for market leadership is hard to regain.

Healthy margins that are realistic provide enough income for good resources, marketing flexibility, and enthusiastic bonuses. Deteriorating margins send warning signals and focus attention more narrowly. Loss of income tears a company apart, forces traditions to be broken, requires that loyal but unimaginative people be fired, and leads to the hiring of change agents. These measures are roughest on those companies that have long been successful and where traditions are considered to be set in concrete. Still, it's the law of the bottom line. The old, cherished ways have ceased to work and must change.

Most profit margins are not exceptional, since most companies are constrained by competition. Check to make sure that your company's margins are favorable, are meeting projections, and are holding firm. *Do your company's profit margins compare favorably with those of your competitors?*

Margin information is normally confidential, but subtle questioning will give you an idea, and if you prove yourself responsible, you may be given better numbers. Be sensitive to profit margins because their effects are so broad.

What About Advertising and Promotion?

- ○ Is your company's advertising budget in line with that of your competitors?
- ○ Is your advertising reaching the right audience?
- ○ Is it persuasive?
- ○ Is there enough of it?
- ○ How effective is your company in promoting its products?

It's often said that 50 percent of all advertising is wasted, but nobody knows which 50 percent. You will recognize a good advertising campaign, though, because it will walk ahead of you in the marketplace, creating an image for your company and differentiating your products from those of your competitors. For a professional or service firm that doesn't "advertise," public relations achieves much the same thing.

Reach and frequency are the bywords of advertising. *How many people see or hear your messages, and how often?* Corporate advertising improves a company's image in the community, and product advertising hits each product specifically. At either level, good advertising can be powerful. *Is your company's advertising well regarded within your industry? Is it effective? Is it telling the right story?*

Are advertising people or technical people in charge of your advertising? Some technical companies still think that advertising consists of listing specifications rather than describing benefits and solutions. Solution selling is in. If your advertising isn't working, it can always be changed—*if* management understands the need.

Sales promotion works more intimately with potential buyers. Promotional efforts vary by industry but include supermarket demonstrations, department store giveaways, distributing samples through the mail, and participating in trade shows. Working a trade show is expensive for a company, but it puts your products in front of your buyers and alongside those of your competitors. It gives the buyer a chance to compare products and gives you, the selling company, a chance to make relationships, demonstrate your product, and sell. *Does your company participate actively in trade shows?*

Advertising and promotion can do good things for your company. Together they can bring in new business and make products move. Identifying and catering to the reasons people buy is a subtle art. If your company does this well, take pride in it. Good things will follow.

Consider Packaging

○ How does your company package itself?
○ Does the packaging of your company's product look and feel good?
○ Does it enhance the product?
○ Is it unique, imaginative?
○ Is it efficient for distribution and selling?
○ Which competitors have a better package?

The packaging you're concerned with here is the kind the customer sees—that which helps sell your company's product. Boxes and bottles come immediately to mind, but packaging is also a matter of how your company presents itself.

Service companies present an image through their offices, logo, stationery, and the manner in which they conduct business and convey expertise. As a consultant, I am known not only by the correctness of my recommendations but also by the appearance of my reports as they sit on people's desks or are handed out for review. My letterhead is as much a packaging concern for me as the right bag is for a cookie company.

Does the packaging of your company's product do the most that it can? I once recruited a president to set up a U.S. operation for kitchen knives being imported from Australia. One of the first things he did was change the packaging. The old boxes were blue and gray on white, with diagrams showing how the knives were sharpened—nice, clean, and boring. The new packages had luscious photographs of freshly sliced tomatoes in full color on a glossy stock that made you hungry to look at them. You felt good picking them up because they looked so good.

Photography is only the graphic aspect of packaging. What about the shape of the container itself? Factor in the commercial considerations of stackability and handling. *What could make the difference for your products?*

How Are Sales and Distribution Handled?

O Does your company have its own sales force?

O If not, whose salespeople does it use?

O Are the salespeople motivated and well trained?

O Are your company's products distributed to customers quickly?

O Is the distribution system up-to-date?

Your concerns are whether or not sales are being made in the best way possible and whether or not your products are being delivered on schedule. Weakness in either area hurts your company. *Do you have confidence in both your company's sales and distribution systems?*

The best product from the best company can languish if the field sales force can't take care of the customers. For example, at the height of the personal computer boom, I was unable to get a salesperson from a certain computer company to return my telephone calls—so I wound up buying from another manufacturer.

Keeping a sales force trained and motivated is no easy task. It's expensive, whether it's done in-house or by outside professionals, but it's essential. The sales force not only gets the revenues but also, to a very large extent, sets the image of your company with your customers.

Direct sales by your company's own employees is ideal, but between the manufacturer and the customer it isn't unusual to find distributors, wholesalers, or jobbers, each negotiating for his own best profit margins. The challenge is to motivate those middlemen to give your product first priority.

Distribution keeps the promises of the salespeople and gets the product to the customer. Delays and snafus are extremely irritating to your customers, but every method of moving goods has its drawbacks. *How vulnerable is your system? Do you have alternatives?* A system that is archaic or in chaos will undermine even the best sales effort.

While you're still thinking about distribution, consider what other products your system could carry to the same customers. *What new products could you add easily?* Some companies are flexible and eager for new items; others are limited. Management should already be thinking along these lines, and any outsiders who may want to acquire your company certainly will be looking for such untapped strengths.

Take a Look at Your Company's Customers
○ Are customer relationships with your company typically long- or short-term?
○ Does your company have the prestige customers within your industry?
○ Has your company lost any major clients lately?
○ Does your company have many customers, or do two or three dominate?
○ Do existing accounts buy more and more of your company's products?
○ Does your company continue to attract new clients?

In Chapter 3, you evaluated your personal relationships with your clients or customers, whoever they are for you and whichever you call them. This chapter asks you to examine something different. Here you want to see with whom your company is doing business.

The easiest way for a firm to do business is with one huge customer, but it's a dangerous approach. That one dominant customer could leave. Even having two or three customers can make a company vulnerable. The most reliable approach is to maintain a range of customers, some old, some new; some big, some small, and some growing. This way the company is covered when the inevitable defections occur.

You want your company to have the best accounts in your industry, of course, whether you're selling to individual consumers in your city or to the biggest companies in the country. Your company is known by its customers. Good customers are not only good business but also good advertising. *Is your company's list of prestige clients growing?*

Customer relationships change, and tracking these relationships can tell you a great deal about the success and acceptance of your products. Watching this whole pattern of what customers your company has, which are coming on, and which are leaving can give you a good idea of how your company is doing and whether the quality of its customers is going up or down.

Your company's customers are comparing your products daily with those of your competitors. Their actions are your early warning system.

COULD THIS BE YOU?

Morgan was a lawyer with a medium-sized consumer products company. His specialty was tax, and he'd been evaluating the effect the new tax law would have on his company's various subsidiaries as well as on the corporation's consolidated return. Some of the numbers he ran across surprised him, and although he was no expert in sales or marketing, he decided to do some probing.

Morgan's company manufactured various lines of household products, and although it didn't have a proprietary advantage, it consistently ranked third or fourth in its markets. Morgan didn't know where to start, but he knew the marketing people down the hall, so he went out to lunch with them.

Not the type to make a frontal assault, Morgan asked casual questions and came to the conclusion that the company's pricing strategy wasn't aggressive. Apparently, one executive vice-president held tight control, and the field people felt they had little leeway when trying to bring in sales. On the positive side, however, Morgan learned that the company's market share was steady. Furthermore, favorable demographics were likely to improve it.

A week later Morgan asked a few questions about profit margins. He could tell they'd been trending down, but he had no idea why. He learned that there had been an unusual price increase in one of the basic raw materials but that this cost was expected to come back into line shortly.

Morgan was beginning to enjoy building this broader understanding of his company. He decided to look into advertising and promotion. Some throwaway lines from the marketing people had intrigued him. He'd always felt that the company's advertising was tasteful, but he soon learned that it was written mostly by the company's own engineers. Morgan examined some of the packaging in the company store. Utilitarian, he thought, but nothing captivating. This disturbed him because many of the company's products could be impulse buys—*if* they caught a consumer's attention.

Morgan was building his picture. He didn't have to ask anyone about sales because he knew from his numbers that they were concentrated in the East and mainly in department stores. When he stopped to think about it, Morgan realized that discount stores must be cutting into his company's sales. He also figured that the real growth of the company was not in the East but in other parts of the country. Why, then, were the sales managers all located in New York, when they should be living and entertaining in their regions? What a waste of social opportunities and travel time.

By now Morgan had come a long way from his original concern about profit margins. The company was in fine shape, but there was room for a lot of improvement. Morgan thought the key lay in the company's two senior officers, who were now near retirement. Probably they were just doing what they had always done and hesitated to fix something that wasn't broken. Morgan did not pretend to understand all of his company's workings, but he did feel better for his review, better about his company, and better about his potential in it.

PULLING IT TOGETHER

If your company's products or markets are going down, your company is sure to follow, as is your job. However, that's not likely to happen if you and your colleagues take an interest in your company's products and sales efforts. This is an area in which you can make things happen, but first, you must know what's going on.

You want to feel comfortable with the positioning of your company's products relative to those of your competitors, with your company's advertising and marketing support, and with the products themselves. This should all combine into a powerful strategy. *Is your company doing the right things to achieve customer satisfaction and keep the company healthy?*

If after reading this chapter you find that your company's position is tenuous, you'll have a good idea of where to direct your energy in order to make the best of your situation. Making a move is your last resort, but if push comes to shove, at least you'll be ahead of the others. You make your best move from a strong company before everyone knows it's on the ropes, and you do it when your talent is scarce, not when your associates are flooding their résumés on top of yours.

Do your company's products really stand out in the marketplace? Can your company follow through on all the potential for success that you see? Review each of this chapter's sections again quickly. Consider what your company could be doing better and see how much you know about what your competitors are doing. Determine your answers and note what points you'd like to keep in mind.

8

How Good Are the People and How Well Does the Company Develop Them?

Companies differ dramatically in their attitude toward people. Some are benevolent, some brutal; some build the talent they need on a long-term basis, others buy what they need when they need it to meet short-term goals. Whether your company is a developer of people or a user of talent will make a difference to your career.

You want to be with a company that recognizes the importance of keeping its people up-to-date and motivated. In the right atmosphere, people are allowed to grow. They generate ideas, suggestions, and spirit. They drive an organization. People who are valued and who value each other make things happen and take pride in being part of a powerful team. And as you may have experienced, the opposite also holds true: People who feel exploited become closed and bitter, and who can blame them?

The signals you're looking for start with your company's hiring process. Try to gauge the importance management places on this front end of the company, from college recruiting to direct hiring to the way your company handles applicants. Getting the right people makes a difference. American Express says its policy is to "attract and retain the best and the brightest."

Electronic Data Systems claimed to hire eagles, seeking them out one by one—a grand idea.

Bringing good people on board is only the beginning. Even the best hires don't stay that way without training. They can't. If a company doesn't have programs to keep them at the top of their profession and give them new dimensions, they lose their competitive edge. Four or six years of college don't spread over a forty-year career.

The higher you go, the more sophisticated you need to be, in terms of both your professional expertise and your general skills such as negotiating, planning, communicating, and creative thinking. You need these strengths to compete internally and externally. With them you serve both yourself and your company well. You need training on a continuing basis, and the points in this chapter will help you determine what your company provides and how valuable it is to you.

Evaluations and succession planning are your next concerns as you think about where you want to go and how you are going to get ahead. You want to know how carefully your company monitors talent and takes your goals into consideration. Is the process formal or informal? It could be a discussion at the coffee maker followed by notes on the back of an envelope, or an elaborate procedure with interviews, forms, and review meetings at various levels. It costs money to maintain a sensitive evaluation system. If your company does so, you should feel better.

The United States is known as the land of opportunity, and our cowboy hiring and firing practices reflect that. We are unrestrained by social classes; all may run at their best speed and free in spirit. But the transient nature of our employer/employee relationships cuts both ways. You can move freely, but you can also *be* moved.

This brings up the last consideration: how a company separates its people. Firing people is never pleasant, but some companies make more of an effort than others to get released employees off and running in a new direction. Of course, you don't plan to let this happen to you, but if you get derailed, it's good to know how your company has handled others in the past.

It's the hiring-development-separation life cycle of employment that you want to keep in mind as you read this chapter. Good companies attend to all phases.

Consider Your Company's Hiring Process

○ How many people usually interview a candidate?
○ How many levels get involved?
○ Does the candidate get to meet his prospective peers?
○ Is the hiring process rushed or careful?
○ Does your company do its best for both itself and the candidate during the hiring process?

How your company hires new employees says a lot about management's concern for people. Companies that hire quickly often fire quickly. It all relates to handling people, a treasured asset to most—but not all—companies.

Let's look at how a lot of hiring is done. You're a candidate, and your first interview is with someone in the human resources department. You survive that cut and are passed along to the hiring manager for another interview. After these two meetings, you're offered the job. You're happy, and you accept.

But wait a minute. It occurs to you that the process was rather rushed. You've lost much of what you should gain from the hiring process: a chance to evaluate the company even as it is evaluating you. Management has made a decision about you, but you have lost your chance to find out more about management. This is a big decision for you. *Isn't it an important decision for them, too?*

The only time your boss's boss will look at you purely as an individual is during the hiring process. Before you are hired, you can ask questions of him that may be awkward after you've come on board. You want your boss's boss to know you and to be familiar with what you're being hired to do. You need to make sure he is as committed to your role as your prospective boss is. It's better for both sides if certain issues are ironed out before a candidate is hired.

Let's assume you have an interview with your boss's boss after all. That's still just three people you've met within the company. *Wouldn't you also want to meet two or three of your prospective peers?* You're going to be interacting with these people, and you'll all be reporting to the same boss. *What about the key subordinates with whom you would be working closely?* If their interests are different from your own, you're better off finding this out ahead of time.

Skills don't work together; people do. As a candidate, you want to make sure you fit on the team. As an established member of the team, you want to know that management selects newcomers carefully.

Does your company use psychological tests? I never use them, but a number of my clients do. I feel they are most useful when others in the hiring company have been given the same test so a basis of comparison has been established. I have not seen any psychological tests to be feared, but the question is how relevant they are.

Do you admire the people your company hires? Ask yourself if your company hires top people you enjoy working with. *Is there a general hiring philosophy?* Some companies make a point of encouraging managers to hire people potentially better than they are; others prefer people with some experience; and still others seek those straight out of school.

When you are hiring, can you get the people you want? To advance and grow, you must be able to bring in people under you who can do your job and free you up to move. This won't happen if smart prospects shy away from your company's hiring process.

How you are hired tells you a lot about how much your company values its people. Within reason, the more elaborate the process, the better it is for you.

Is College Recruiting Effective?

○ Does your company recruit at specific colleges?
○ Annually?
○ How qualified are the people who do the recruiting?
○ Do good students join your company?

○ Are special programs provided for college recruits?
○ Do they stay long enough to make a contribution?

College recruiting, handled well, holds great potential for your company. It's not a necessity, but neither is it something to handle casually. To be effective, recruiting requires long-standing relationships with college placement directors, who want to know that they can count on your company considering their graduates in good years as well as bad. To get the best students, you need placement directors who think well of your company and who will direct good students to you.

There's another level to college recruiting. Your company should be familiar with the heads of the departments from which you take the most students. You want their recommendations, and ideally you want them to be familiar with your operations. These relationships, too, should be continuous.

Who does your company's college recruiting? Some law firms send junior partners. Young fast-trackers make an impact because students identify with them. The more usual procedure is to have a human resources person make the first cut. Whom your company sends may depend upon the urgency with which it is seeking particular talents.

Does your company choose colleges for their image—Harvard or Stanford, for instance—or for the quality of students relevant to its needs? Ask yourself whether the match is right. *Do college recruits stay and progress?* You want them to feel a partnership with the company and to stay for a period of years in exchange for the training they receive. Big companies that give formal training are asking this directly of their student recruits. The effectiveness of your company's program depends on how well young trainees progress through the company; if people come to you for training and leave shortly thereafter, your company isn't getting what it should from the recruiting expense.

What About Outside Hiring?
○ Does your company often hire from the outside?
○ Are these outside hires strong?
○ Do they prosper in the company?

○ Are they accepted by the long-term employees?
○ Is there a healthy mix of homegrown and newly
  recruited talent?

You want to make sure your company strikes a balance between encouraging talent from within and hiring strong people from outside when necessary. A consistent but limited dose of outside talent is desirable and healthy. It prevents inbred complacency and the not-invented-here syndrome.

Does your company assimilate outside hires? In some companies, newcomers are rejected, isolated, and made largely ineffective. That mentality is destructive for everyone. Be ready to greet a newcomer to your company and help him—you never can tell when you may be one yourself.

Where does your company get its new leaders? Sure, the ideal is to keep people on board and move them along as positions open up, but not everyone can handle increased responsibilities. Some people stagnate. Some become followers, which helps nobody. This happens in even the most successful companies, but it doesn't show up until the success wears thin and irreverent creativity is needed. Xerox, Polaroid, and Kodak have all suffered a bout with this disease.

Traditionally, companies have maintained deep staffs to draw from, but this is no longer considered the most efficient use of financial or human assets. You don't want to be an understudy, you want the leading role—and your company can't afford to bankroll a lot of extras.

To stay current, top-ranking consulting companies need a constant flow of experienced experts. These are "up or out" companies—and by necessity, more out than up. At the other extreme are industrial companies in which long tenure is often associated with capability, or at least the right to a job. In this kind of company, newcomers are resented—a danger you want to avoid. *Could you bring in subordinates from outside today if you had good reason?*

If you are being courted by a company with few outside hires, it's imperative that you speak with one or two of them. Ask them how they were received. If the company is reluctant to make them available, that alone sends a message.

How Effective Is In-House Training?

○ Does your company keep you up-to-date professionally?
○ Are in-house courses provided?
○ What kinds of courses are available?
○ Who attends them?
○ How many hours or days of training do you receive per year?

You know in-house training is important. Your concern is what training your company provides as standard company practice and how you get it. If this training is set up in-house, you know the commitment of management is strong. So much depends on your company's attitude, as well as on your level and potential. The message here is that you need continuous training to stay effective, and if your company doesn't recognize this, you have a problem.

Companies know the benefits of training their people. According to the best estimates of the American Society for Training and Development, companies annually spend $30 billion on formal, budgeted training programs and $180 billion on unbudgeted but informal on-the-job training, for a total of $210 billion. IBM alone spends more than $700 million on training operations. That's big dollars. Many employees are sharpening their skills, and you will be at a disadvantage if you don't get your share of training during the course of your career. You don't want to be with a company that uses and drains employees for ten years, then fires them and hires new ones.

What in-house trainee programs are available to new recruits? A good trainee program benefits you if you're in it and benefits the company if it turns out capable people. *Who is picked from your company to get in-house training?* Probably that authority rests with the operating unit. Although you may request special training, your manager has to approve it, pay for it out of his budget, and justify it with recent appraisals of your work and what can be expected of you—another reason to have a good relationship with your manager.

Who sets the curriculum for in-house training? Companies with distinctively different operating divisions may let the divisions initiate the training that's appropriate for their needs. The Travel Related Services Division of American Express, for example, has one standard course that is delivered in 33 countries and in 8 languages.

Are courses provided to broaden your managerial and related skills? Some companies require that managers take so many hours of people-management training each year. Other employees may be kept up-to-date on technical subjects. Salespeople often receive the most intensive training, as they are on the front lines.

Does your company have centralized educational facilities? Today many companies maintain their own "campuses." Near me in Connecticut, GTE took over a monastery with extensive grounds and created a beautiful education center. This campus trend is growing. According to Harold Lazarus, professor of management at New York's Hofstra University, 25 companies now have such campuslike centers at costs averaging $20 million each. Lazarus found that primarily companies in telecommunications, finance, and computers recognize the need to keep their people up-to-date so the companies can prosper. Locating these centers near headquarters allows senior executives to make themselves available more often.

Many companies don't have centralized facilities but do have standardized programs. *Are courses available on videotape?* Participating in in-house training programs is a boost to you professionally. It's also a necessity if your company offers such programs and you want to progress within your company. Conversely, if you're not invited to participate, that's a vivid signal that something is wrong.

Your concern is to use all the training available to you, whatever the level of sophistication in your company. *Is your company committed to keeping you in top form? Does it do so?*

Consider Your Company's Use of Outside Training

○ Does your company encourage you to get outside training?
○ Is this in addition to in-house training?

○ Is a broad array of courses made available to you?
○ Are university programs included?
○ Does your company have a tuition refund program?
○ Are funds available for you to attend seminars?

The bottom line of all training is your company's dedication to keeping its people up-to-date. If your company's in-house offerings are limited, outside programs are your alternative. Today these are proliferating, and the subjects are becoming more specific, part of the boom in information distribution.

Pursuing outside training ranges from attending a one-shot seminar to getting an advanced degree. What subjects you want to pursue depends upon your profession and abilities; the offerings are limitless.

One advantage of outside training is the variety of people attending the programs. People with different backgrounds from different companies participate together. More ideas come forth, you broaden your network, and you grow socially as well as professionally. You can meet leaders in your field while you learn.

One of the first things you should do to maintain a high profile in your industry is get on the mailing lists for seminars and other training programs. Each industry has its own providers of specialized information whom you should know about. Whatever your company policy, you can't attend these programs if you don't know about them.

What outside programs are available to you? Executive programs at universities continue to be popular, and their range has been expanded. There are also other routes to take.

- Bell Communications Research offers a range of courses, open to all, in telecommunications operations and management.
- Quality College, founded in 1966 by Phil Crosby, offers courses on product quality. The program has been expanded from its original Florida location to six other locations in Europe and the Far East.
- Kepner-Trego, Inc. first offered its five-day course "Problem Solving and Decision Making" 30 years ago. It remains

the firm's flagship offering, supported by a wide range of other courses.

- The American Management Association has provided training since the 1940s. Courses are divided along 11 divisional lines (finance, marketing, and so on) and range from the level of executive secretary to president. This $100-million international organization will also conduct courses at your company.
- The Forum Corporation in Boston provides a wide range of courses.
- Wilson Learning in Minneapolis, a subsidiary of the publisher John Wiley & Sons, is another broad-based organization.
- The American Society for Training and Development (headquartered in Alexandria, Virginia), an association of people involved in training, provides its members with a data base of available courses. However, it does no training itself.

Is your company willing to help you gain a formal education? A basic perk to investigate is your company's tuition refund plan. Most companies encourage you to pursue "related" education in outside institutions. Digital Equipment pays full tuition and salary to engineers pursuing advanced degrees, and there are variations on this theme. The absence of any such program should make you cautious. Remember, your bottom line is staying up-to-date.

Examine the Evaluation Procedures

O Does your company have a definite program of evaluations?
O How frequently are evaluations conducted?
O Do they provide healthy give-and-take?
O Are your comments recorded?
O Does your boss's boss review your evaluation?
O Do managers take the process seriously?

Formal evaluations are a two-way street. Your boss tells you where he thinks you are (a judgment you attack, defend, or graciously accept), and you tell him where you want to go.

Evaluation techniques are becoming more elaborate, and companies are conducting evaluations more frequently as they try to nurture their good workers. They want to identify early on your potential for success. They want to know whom to invest in for the greatest return as much as you do.

In Chapter 1, I spoke of your boss and his inclination to evaluate you constructively. Now, move beyond this and consider how important the evaluation procedure itself is in your company. Evaluations can be tough and take time, but they are the best way for you to learn what management thinks of you and for you to tell management what's on your mind. *Is your company's evaluation process effective?*

How many people read your evaluation? It's not unusual for your boss's boss to review your evaluation; this way he can monitor up-and-coming talent. The human resources executive for your division may also review your evaluation before it goes into your personnel file. If you're doing well and want to get ahead, these skip-level reviews will work in your favor.

Is there a formal evaluation procedure in your company? General Electric's approach is to give an evaluation every 12 months, which purposely does not coincide with salary review time. The process starts with the employee's making a self-appraisal of strengths and weaknesses that he submits to his manager. There is give-and-take in the process, and the results are recorded on a form that contains all the reviews that the employee has had. The evaluation concludes with the manager's giving his expectations for the next period.

There is also an annual manpower review at GE, a part of succession planning that determines each person's next career move. The employee uses one side of a single page to record what he wants to do next, and the other side contains the manager's appraisal of whether or not he feels these goals are realistic.

Have you taken a look at your company's hiring form lately? Very often these forms provide checklists of qualities and aptitudes. You've already been hired, of course, but you can still take a moment to review the factors on which you are rating prospective employees. Would you be hired tomorrow?

A good evaluation process is dedicated to improving your performance. The more constructive criticism you receive, the better.

Take a Look at Succession Planning

○ How formal is succession planning in your company?
○ What must you do to show up well in your company's succession plans?
○ Have you moved as you expected?
○ If so, do you believe you will continue to do so?
○ Does the company try to accommodate your interests?
○ Who is in charge of the succession-planning process?

Good succession planning works. A by-product is a list of stars, a group that the company protects, challenges, counsels, and compensates to keep as happy as possible. It's a list to be on if you can.

To get a grip on succession planning in your company, look at how people have moved and see what you can expect for yourself. *How broad are your opportunities? How do you see the next five years with your company?*

In entry-level and training programs, succession planning is highly competitive, but you generally know the rules. Performance is the main determinant. In middle and upper management, however, the game changes. Now management skills and creativity come into play, as do contacts inside and outside the company. In this nebulous area, knowing how your company's succession-planning program works becomes important. *Who is measuring what?*

In your company, succession planning may be formal or nonexistent. Either extreme can work against you. I know of one company where succession planning is based strictly on the annual evaluation form, and a low rating in certain areas keeps your name off the list of fast-trackers. That's pretty rigid. On the other hand, Continental Can Corporation discourages formal succession plans, having found that it doesn't pay to tag people too early for positions two to three years out. The designation invariably gets out and demoralizes others, and besides, things change too fast. Continental Can's solution: "Train the hell out of everybody, test them in a number of situations, and keep them current."

Do you know where you're headed? A good boss or human resources executive will always advise you of your next expected step, but there are no guarantees. Be sensitive to what you need to do to rank high in your group.

Is There a Good System for Posting Job Opportunities?

○ Are internal job openings posted?
○ Are they up-to-date?
○ Are the plums posted as well as the prunes?
○ Are you encouraged to investigate those openings for which you're qualified?
○ Does your company make an effort to save employees?

Again, you're looking for a good balance. A company that posts job opportunities is making an extra effort for its employees—a nice thing to know. But if the company goes to extreme lengths to promote from within, it may become inbred. The optimum situation is a human resources group that is both pragmatic and innovative, that reviews inside candidates in weeks—not months—and then, if necessary, goes outside for the skills required.

Big companies have a problem coordinating all the employment needs in all divisions. Often you feel that even as employees are being let go out the back door, very similar people are being welcomed in through the front door. People at Tandem Computer told me that their company's solution is to post most jobs and make an extra effort to give them to "interested and reasonably qualified" employees. It will even accept a little shortfall in experience from an employee that management believes in. That's more than fair. *Will your company allow you to stretch?*

I was once told by a new vice-president of a company in transition that he would be needing three critically important specialized assistants and that I would probably have to search for them. Before I started, however, the big company had to check all its divisions. This took three months, and in the end no one came forward. A lot of time was wasted, and the company's zeal to promote from within slowed the performance of the vice-president.

If your company doesn't post job opportunities, let your human resources executive know what you want. He will know where the openings are, and you want your name to come up.

How Are Firing and Separation Handled?

○ Is your job in danger?
○ What would happen to you if you were fired?
○ How many people has your company let go lately?
○ How have they been treated?
○ Does the company make an effort to help?
○ Are exit interviews important?

I'm not talking here about being fired for cause, but about all those other separations that can occur. You've heard lots of variations. Someone leaves for health or personal reasons, or resigns by mutual agreement, or decides to pursue other endeavors. It all comes down to leaving at your company's wish, not your own. How your company handles these separations and the frequency with which they occur is worth noting.

People get fired for all kinds of reasons, some of which make sense and some of which don't. Hundreds of thousands of people have been fired in the last few years as companies have slimmed down and gotten competitive. Placing blame is not the issue here; what you want to check out is the process your company uses.

A company that separates well shows concern for its employees. *How considerate is your company?* Separations do not have to be acrimonious. If the process is handled well, the employee will appreciate and remember it, and a reservoir of goodwill remains.

Some difficult situations can be salvaged if management can alleviate a problem or transfer an employee elsewhere. *If your company can't or won't save your job, what will it do for you instead?* Some companies provide offices and secretarial services for a number of months, counseling and guidance in preparing résumés, and medical benefits until you are resettled. Others provide the services of an outplacement firm, whose "client" you then become. These firms often have their own offices, extensive libraries, and counseling services to point you in the right direction. What assistance does your company provide?

When a valued employee leaves voluntarily, a well-conducted exit interview can help both sides. It shows concern for the employee and is the time for the company to emphasize "staying in touch" if the other offer doesn't work out. More companies are now recognizing the value of getting good employees back after they've checked out the neighbor's greener pastures. The exit interview can also provide the company with insightful information and may reveal situations of which management was not aware. By changing these situations, the firm may be able to deter other valuable employees from leaving.

Does your company have a full-employment policy? Some companies go to great lengths to avoid laying off employees. This policy works in growth companies and when times are good, but when the economic cycle turns down and stays down for a while, employees may be asked to produce more or to do things they've never done before. This may be good or bad for you, depending upon your alternatives.

How a company separates its people is a telling point. If you're uneasy asking your boss about your company's procedures, ask a former employee how he was handled. Or ask your boss what benefits you could give one of your people if you had to let him go.

COULD THIS BE YOU?

As Connie walked to her office, she felt exhilarated. She'd just had a breakfast meeting with her prospective boss, a vice-president from a rival consulting company, and he'd finally offered her the job. After five interviews, she thought it was about time management made up its mind—but then, that was its style.

Connie hadn't actually been looking for work elsewhere, but she thought she would accept the offer. She was doing well where she was, but the new position was very attractive. She also felt she'd had her eyes opened a bit. The other company had very different ways of doing things, and on reflection its approach made more sense than she'd ever realized.

Connie recognized that the privately owned consulting firm she was with could be regarded as austere. She had always believed that the seriousness of her company made it superior, but now she wasn't sure. Without question the other company was happier and brighter, right down to the design of its offices, and she was beginning to see that she might thrive in that environment.

Connie was a seasoned executive and knew her ground. She could play hardball if she had to—which in her present company she often did—and she'd learned how to lobby on her own behalf to get the industry exposure she needed. After so many years of sink-or-swim management, she'd gotten pretty resourceful. Her boss was taciturn, but Connie did well on her annual evaluations, and since she was still there, she figured she was well regarded. Heaven knows the company didn't hesitate to cut deadweight.

The other company was so different. The people seemed rah-rah by comparison. There was a gung ho attitude that Connie associated with war movies. Could she operate in that environment? How would she come off? These thoughts had occupied her mind as she had asked questions, and she'd been taken aback by the openness of the answers she'd received. She was pleased that the company wanted a number of people to talk with her, because she wanted to talk with them. Apparently, management wanted new people to feel as comfortable as possible before they came on board rather than finding surprises later. Of course, she wouldn't know how well this worked until afterward.

Prepared to do battle, Connie had hit the hot button and asked about an issue that frustrated her in her present company, the opportunity to attend seminars and conferences—not only to wave the company flag but also for her own benefit. To her surprise, she hadn't had to sell her prospective boss on the idea. He recognized that in order to be effective, Connie would need to meet her colleagues in other companies, stay up-to-date on industry developments, and periodically sharpen her skills. Just thinking about these new opportunities lightened her spirit.

Connie had also inquired about the kind of staff she would be allowed to hire. Her interviewers asked her not to come in thinking of hiring but to work for a while with the talent that was already on board. They didn't think she would have to hire anyone, but they seemed reasonable. She also knew that if she had to hire, it would be easy for her to attract good people into that environment—something that did not hold true in her present position.

The new company, she'd learned, was informal. Sure, somebody was watching who did what, but you didn't feel it on a daily basis. Cooperation and general enthusiasm seemed to take precedence over who got credit for what. She'd been told that the hierarchy was meant to be flat and that how she functioned would earn her more respect than any title. The more she thought about it, the more confident Connie felt that she could make things happen.

She'd even asked about how they fired people. Connie smiled as she recalled the surprise on her prospective boss's face. "Quickly when there's cause," he'd said, "but carefully if there's an interpersonal problem or a cutback in operations." The company had asked outplacement firms to help a number of people get resettled. Certainly an improvement over her present firm, where employees seemingly ceased to exist after they were fired.

Connie would be doing roughly the same kind of work in the new company as she was doing now, but she felt her career was opening up. She liked the idea that her new employer was willing to put some energy into her career and realized now that her present firm, although successful, was unnecessarily brutal.

Stepping into her office, Connie immediately wondered how she would feel to leave it. Sure, there were some things she would miss, but all in all, there was a great deal to look forward to.

PULLING IT TOGETHER

The life cycle of employment—hiring, development, and separation—is what you're looking at here. You want to know how important this cycle is to your company, for it *is* a cycle, and an ever more frequent one.

A careful hiring process is the key to getting employees who not only are good but also work well together. Think how much you enjoy being with stimulating colleagues. Sharing and building with people you respect is a great experience, but it doesn't happen often, and it doesn't happen by chance. There has to be a careful selection process.

The company's next step is developing its people—guiding, training, and evaluating them. You depend upon the opportunities your company gives you, and you want to avoid any company that simply draws down your present bank of experience without replenishing it in return. *Is your company giving you a chance to grow? At your present rate, how long can you continue to contribute?*

Even in the best companies you must determine what you need to stay competitive and ask for it. Don't sit back and assume that someone else will know what you need better than you. It's not likely. *What should you be doing to stay current?*

Your company's separation process may suddenly become extremely important to you. Check it out in advance. Even if you personally aren't let go, you can learn something about your company from the manner in which others have been fired.

Take that extra minute as you have at the end of the previous chapters to review the topics quickly. See what's strong and what's weak.

9

Who's in Charge Here?

"The longer I'm in business, the more I recognize the importance of the CEO. He sets the tone, tempo, and objectives, and everyone else imitates him."

The speaker, a vice-president in a multibillion-dollar company, was a candidate in a search I was conducting, and he was grilling me about my client's senior executives. He had learned to look first at the top. Even if you have no contact with your company's chief executive officer (CEO) and the senior managers seem remote to you, don't underestimate their importance to your career. Your company is only as good as they are.

Most companies maintain an image of integrity, and while you may expect this image to be a reflection of a company's inner workings, what really goes on in-house is more akin to football linemen skirmishing while everyone watches the graceful pass downfield. The CEO and his senior executives play a tough game in-house and save the graceful passes for the media. You want to know how tough—and how good—the in-house game is.

Management's games can cost you your job. If your senior managers take a big gamble and their judgment is poor, the result can be fatal. U.S. Lines, for example, spent a billion dollars on container ships, only to see freight rates fall; the company was forced into Chapter 11 bankruptcy protection. Do you have faith in the good judgment of your company's top management?

Some managements play "we bet your company" and tell you about it later. If you're not part of the top team, it's difficult to know what risks are being taken, and your vote isn't solicited. "We bet your company" isn't necessarily a bad game, but you should know the stakes if your career is being put on the line.

With a sensitivity to what's going on, you may be able to get some idea of the potential risks and rewards, and of the impact an outcome may have on you. The bottom line, however, is the good sense of your company's management.

Some senior executives have impressive accomplishments, and you'll want to run with them because of their prior track record. Others manipulate companies for their own benefit at the expense of employees and stockholders, and those you want to avoid. Your challenge is to differentiate between the two types.

If examining your senior managers makes you feel somehow disloyal, consider this. If they're good, don't you think they're dying to have you know how good they are? And won't you perform better and tougher if you're convinced of their ethics and capabilities? I think you will, and I think if they're good, they'll want you to know it. Loyalty is not the issue here. The idea is to get good, solid information upon which you can base your career.

These days more CEOs recognize that they must be aggressive and do the unconventional. Corporate survival can't be taken for granted. This has led to what Steven Prokesch, in a *New York Times* article on "Remaking the American CEO" (January 25, 1987), calls "a generation of ruthless management." Do you consider your company's top management ruthless or simply responsive to the times?

If you accept that it is management's responsibility to maximize values, you won't be surprised to see a business sold once a "magic price" is put on the table. It may be impossible for you to anticipate these kinds of transactions, but sensing the priorities of your top executives can help you be prepared.

A subtle point to keep in mind as you go about evaluating your company's top management is the difference between owners and professional managers. The former can be the latter, but never vice versa. In general, an owner has the long-term good of the company as his goal, while the professional manager has been hired for short-term performance. If he doesn't produce financial results, he may be out of a job; if he doesn't get the price of the company's stock up, he may lose much of his incentive compensation as well as some of the executives he brought on board with high expectations. Owners aren't better than professional managers, but there is a difference.

This is your opportunity to see what your senior executives have done in the past, to anticipate what they may do in the future, and to project the effect this may have on you. Since your CEO holds the reins, that's the place to start.

Examine Your Company's Chief Executive Officer

○ How long has your company's CEO held that position?
○ Is the company stronger because of his efforts?
○ Do you have confidence in him?
○ Does he attract and build strong managers?
○ Does he delegate responsibility?
○ Does he have a broadly recognized reputation?

If you don't agree with your CEO's priorities, you're in trouble. Whether you work for a small company or a big one, your career is directly affected by your CEO. Knowing his direction allows you to evaluate your own.

For the next few minutes, examine your CEO objectively. Strip away your natural deference and look at his style and what he has done. Try thinking like an investment analyst. You are, after all, investing in your career. Or try imagining that you left the company a year ago and are now reminiscing with a former colleague. *How have your CEO's actions affected your company? Your career?*

A CEO who attracts and develops strong executives will not only build strength within the company but will also have a ready supply of high-quality people wanting to work for him. You'll have a stimulating environment in which to grow, plus access to good people when you need them.

Some CEOs retain more than a reasonable amount of control. This can have a demoralizing effect on a developing manager. I know of one successful company in which the CEO involves himself in so many decisions that divisional managers seldom stay longer than a couple of years. The company is healthy, well regarded on Wall Street, a good place to learn the business—but a poor place to become an executive. This is a situation you want to see ahead of time. *Does your company's CEO monopolize too much authority?*

Can you take pride in your CEO's reputation? If not, be wary. His reputation, for better or worse, will be reflected upon you. By knowing his reputation, you will know the way many people regard your company and, by association, you. If the CEO's reputation is impressive, there's bound to be some rub-off on you, and broader opportunities will be presented to you.

What is your CEO's management style? Some CEOs are exciting and make headlines; some are quiet, steadying forces; some are talented but unstable. Whatever your CEO's style—and anything is possible—it generally permeates the company as other managers emulate him. It's far easier for you to prosper within the company if you share the CEOs priorities. Be careful if you don't like what you see at the top.

The CEO is like the conductor of an orchestra: He has complete control. If you watch closely, you can see his interpretation; where he puts emphasis, where he goes for subtle yet telling effects, what he ignores. *Where do you sit in your CEO's orchestra?*

Consider Your Company's Owners/ Controlling Interests

○ What role do the owners/controlling interests play?
○ If involved, what do they like to do?
○ What do they do best?
○ Are you handling a pet project?
○ How strong is any one controlling interest?
○ How and when will ownership be passed on?

Owners and controlling interests can do as they please, and what they do isn't always best for the company or for you. That owners have this latitude is nothing new, but controlling interests introduce a new dimension. They are often investors in for a quick turn without any fundamental interest in the business. Their ideas of how to reap the most from your company may be advantageous to them but downright destructive for you. Find out if there is a controlling interest in your company and what it has done in the past. You may be surprised.

A friend of mine received five W-2 forms for one year, and he never changed jobs; the ownership of his company had changed under him. A few years ago only small investment bankers bought and sold companies as you might handle a portfolio, but now the major Wall Street investment houses are doing the same. The game has become too rich to miss out on, and you and your career are in the middle of it. *What are the intentions of your company's controlling interests?*

An owner who is actively involved in running his company is apt to be stubborn about his beliefs and practices, particularly if he founded the company. Some owners only want to pursue certain types of business, regardless of the profit potential of related lines, just because that is where they are most comfortable. I've seen instances in which owners who didn't need money ran marginally profitable companies and saw no reason to change. It's pretty clear that while some owners can steer a company to great success, others can hold a company back—and your career along with it.

Is your CEO a founder of the company? Successful founders have strong egos. They've gone through the fanatical dedication of entrepreneurs, been tested, been frustrated, and are now on top. They're opinionated and used to having their opinions respected. A founder knows how he made his way and may feel just as strongly about how you should make yours—something you want to know ahead of time if at all possible.

Be alert to the real intentions of your company's owners/controlling interests. *Do their actions make good business sense? Do they bode well for you personally?*

What Is the Track Record of Top Executives?

○ Have your company's senior executives been successful in the past?

○ Why?

○ Do they have good reputations in the industry?

○ Is their emphasis on financial wizardry or responding to markets?
○ Are they short- or long-term oriented?
○ Are company successes the result of well-planned effort or luck?

Let your curiosity run as you find out how your company's senior managers got where they are. It's not enough to look at the places these managers have been and the titles they've held. See what they did and how they did it. *Have they been truly creative? Or did they ride on someone else's plans?*

I once attended a lecture by Mortimer Feinberg, a professor with a strong consulting practice who put forward another measure to keep in mind. He felt that any senior manager should have the experience of working himself out of a major problem or mistake before taking on top responsibilities. He added that those who are moved before they can find a solution can be severely damaged.

Learning how and what your top executives have already done gives you a better idea of what to expect from them in the future. Someone who has used a particular approach up to this point isn't likely to change now. *Are the skills of your company's top managers in tune with the needs of the company?*

Check Out the Ethics of Senior Management

○ Do you have any qualms about the ethics of your company's top managers?
○ Are they aggressive yet ethical?
○ Have you ever been encouraged to overstep legal boundaries?
○ Are you proud of the ethics of your company?
○ Has anyone from your company been convicted for ill-conceived business practices?

You know that senior managers are being sent to jail. You've seen Wall Street executives in handcuffs, have read of banks accused of laundering money, have heard about major corporations accused of cheating on defense contracts, and have seen public officials toppled for taking payoffs. A new awareness of ethics has taken hold, if only because laws have new and harsher teeth. This isn't ice hockey, where you sit in the penalty box for two minutes for a foul.

Back in 1981 *Business Week* ran an "Executive Guide: Preparing for a Day in Court." White collar crime is not new, but the jail sentences are, and you can be held responsible for something you knew nothing about. The best preventive action is to scrutinize the behavior of your company's senior executives and to set firm ethical boundaries for yourself—if necessary until you are able to move into an environment where you feel comfortable. Business practices are set by your company's top managers, and unless they are sincere and consistent in their commitment to high ethical standards, such standards are not likely to radiate throughout the company. *What is your gut feeling about the standards of top management?*

Corporate lawyers try to protect executives, but think for a moment what you say most of the time to your in-house counsel. Isn't it usually, "Tell me how I can do it, not how I can't"? You're eager. You want to win—and so does your competition. That's why ethical standards have to be clearly understood.

If you have a bad impression of the ethics of your top management, be wary. Sure, greed still exists, but a move is growing to play fair and slap hard those who cheat. The consequences of poor ethics can be dire. Once tarnished, your reputation will never regain its original luster. You may be fined or sent to jail—which brings us to litigation, the next point.

What About Litigation?

○ Does your company have a history of heavy litigation?
○ Is it currently sustaining big litigation expenses?
○ Regarding one large matter or several smaller ones?
○ What are your company's chances of winning?
○ Could the dollar liability be devastating?
○ Is management distracted?

Litigation can starve a company. It preoccupies management and drains financial resources. A company's very existence can be at stake.

When your company is in litigation, charges have been filed. Management has gone beyond the preventive phase of high ethics and is now involved in the sport of courtroom spectaculars, a new kind of drama with high-priced lawyers, withering barrages of questions, and shocking revelations.

Litigation is expensive and monopolizes top management's time, energy, and imagination. If your company is tied up in major litigation, your career prospects can be at risk, even if you're not directly involved. And if you are personally involved, the damage can be irreparable.

Are your own business practices above reproach? When a wrong move is made, or appears to have been made, it hits the papers. Opinions are formed early. You begin compiling records, focusing on how to defend your past actions instead of looking ahead. You fill out depositions for the opposing lawyers and possibly sit and answer more questions for those lawyers. You worry. Your own lawyers must be paid. All the while you try to keep your work from suffering and to take advantage of opportunities, as an executive must. You try to protect your family as you protect yourself, but it's tough. There's hardly enough time.

Are any of your company's senior executives presently involved in litigation? In the midseventies, the CEO of Xerox spent 32 days giving testimony over a period of 14 months. That's more than 6 weeks of workdays spent in court, plus time spent in preparation. Think how much this must have distracted the CEO and his staff.

I'm not telling you to cut and run if your company gets involved in litigation or to steer clear of any company with litigation problems. But if you can't play a role in solving the problems, or if they are going to hurt your career, think carefully about how you can best serve yourself and your family.

Some litigation—what I call "home run" litigation—involves huge claims brought by small companies against giants. If the small company wins, and sometimes it does, it's a bonanza. If you're with a small company in this situation, your uneasiness over the litigation need not be as great, unless the giants have destroyed, or are in the process of destroying, your market.

Sometimes the giants go against each other, and the stakes can be very high. For example, Polaroid sued Eastman Kodak for patent infringement, and Kodak had to remove a line of instant cameras from the shelves and cease production. Kodak had to wrestle with appeasing early purchasers of those cameras.

Excessive litigation is a warning sign. Look at the issues and try to determine if your company is doing things it shouldn't. *Why are others attacking your company? What is your personal exposure likely to be?*

Assess the Goals of Senior Management

○ Where does management want to take the company?
○ Are these goals reasonable?
○ Are they likely to be achieved?
○ Is senior management taking enough risks?
○ How well are corporate goals communicated throughout the company?

On a racing sailboat, the skipper has an afterguard with whom he discusses tactics. Diverse opinions must come up, but so must a mutually agreed upon course of action. A boat can't go in two directions at once, and sailing with the middle of the fleet guarantees a mediocre finish. In your company, you want to know that diverse opinions are present, but you also want to feel in agreement with the chosen goals.

The smaller the company, the more relevant this issue is, but whatever the size of your corporation, you need to feel management's goals are reasonable and achievable. You can't put your full energies toward goals you see as futile. *How do you feel about management's goals?* If management has communicated its mission statement and solicited and received support for its strategic plan, you should be in an enthusiastic environment with everyone pulling together. A common goal, a unified team—it should be exciting. On the other hand, if corporate goals are poorly communicated, you have cause for concern. You need to find out whether there is a plan that just wasn't made clear or whether momentum is keeping things going without leadership.

What will attaining management's goals mean to you? You want to know where your operation fits in the game plan. The point is to anticipate, give yourself time to get into the right place at the right time as often as possible. Put everything you can into your present job, but also give lightning a chance to strike.

Are your company's senior managers in touch with operations and markets, or are they insulated from reality by elaborate entourages, perks, and privileges? Hopefully, you will feel that management is inspiring you as it challenges you to meet goals that excite you—a bit of nirvana, but not impossible.

Take a Look at the Age Spread in Senior Management

○ How young is the youngest senior executive?
○ What's the overall age spread in top management?
○ Which seems more respected, performance or age?
○ Will a number of retirements occur simultaneously?
○ Are your prospects favored by the age spread?

It's illegal to talk about age. The issue is like a little bug called a "no-see-um"—you don't see it, but it sure can bite. Age discrimination isn't the point here, but rather the spread of ages in your company's senior management. *What are the implications for your advancement?*

It used to be that executives evolved into senior managers after they'd proved themselves in various predetermined roles. Consequently, senior executives were older, if not just plain old. But that was when companies were stable, when the organization man was king, and when Japan made shoddy products. Today younger people are invited into management, and in better companies their ideas are respected. *Is your management open to young ideas?*

It appears to me that more corporate presidents are taking the reins in their forties. They have the experience required as well as the skill, energy, and determination. Younger CEOs often rely more on their staffs, since they haven't sat in all the chairs, but that can build an atmosphere of cooperation.

Are you older than your company's top executives? First, be complimented because you must have something they want. Next, be careful. You've got to keep current, keep making yourself needed. Do you? Even if your performance is good, you may be regarded as an outsider. As a recruiter, I feel I've lost out on two searches because I was 15 years older than the senior executives giving out the assignments. I hadn't faced that before.

If several older executives are clustered at the top of your senior management group, it means that a number of changes will occur in a short time frame, generating both opportunities and confusion. *How vulnerable is your company to a group of simultaneous retirements?* Competition will ensue, provided the natural successors have not already drifted away out of frustration.

Read the age signs early and see what problems they may pose for you.

Does Senior Management Share a Similar Background?

○ Do your company's top executives have a common background?
○ What is it?
○ Does your boss have it?
○ Do you?
○ Do valuable people without this experience leave?
○ Are there some renegades who shake things up?

The most typical example of senior executives with similar backgrounds is the stable company where all the top executives have grown up in that company. Acceptance into senior management can get more selective if the top ranks are only from certain colleges, or share a certain experience, or progressed along a particular route. In some companies, you can see how the doors begin to close as you move up. *Is your senior management group homogeneous? What are the implications for you?*

Sometimes a new CEO brings in his own team. It's a natural preference: He wants people around him with whom he's comfortable and in whom he has complete confidence. This will cut some people off from advancement possibilities, but others will use the new routes.

A different bias exists in the company where the top executives have always come from one discipline (say, finance) or one subsidiary of the corporation. That background is the common proving ground. You may not agree with the usefulness of this tradition, but if it exists, you should recognize it sooner rather than later. *Do you see any barriers to your advancing?* If there is an "inner circle" and you're not a part of it, you're at a severe disadvantage.

Performance is being recognized more and more as the main determinant of executive potential, but you would be wise to be alert to commonalities in the backgrounds of your company's top executives. *What's the situation in your company? Is there a good spread of backgrounds and experience in your senior management group?*

Consider the Turnover in Senior Management

○ How much turnover has occurred in senior management?
○ Has there been too much or too little?
○ Why has it occurred?
○ Is it continuing?
○ Are good people coming in, or leaving?

Turnover is an indicator of change and is not necessarily good or bad. It depends on the situation. In a moribund company or in one coming out of reorganization, turnover is good. It means someone is trying. In a company with a high reputation for consistent performance, it indicates unrest. The existence of turnover, however, presents you with a reason to probe further.

Is turnover a sign of turmoil in your company? Generally, only CEOs and presidents make headlines when they move, but the story beneath the headline can be even larger. More can be going on than is apparent. So and so was the eighth president in eight years, or the fifth to be discarded by a legendary chairman, who is now on his sixth. So and so's resignation was accompanied by those of 17 other division presidents and senior managers. Remember, too, that any untimely resignation of a top executive leaves vulnerable those who were faithful to him and depended upon him, possibly leading to more turnover.

Proceed cautiously in the presence of a high rate of turnover, but try to put it in perspective. *What has been accomplished as a result of the turnover? Is the company stronger or weaker?*

Some companies have a reputation for high turnover but have high compensations to go with it. You know what to expect in such a company. In the company where turnover is unusual, however, its presence is unsettling. Something new has been added, and you want to know why.

What if no turnover has occurred? This may or may not be a problem, depending upon the dynamism and success of the company. If the team is winning, why change it? But if it's losing and still no changes occur, watch out.

Study Your Company's Board of Directors

○ Is your company's board of directors active?
○ Do you think the members are well selected?
○ Why—or why not?
○ Are a variety of skills represented?
○ Did one CEO bring in most of the board members?

You may think I'm really asking you to stretch too far in examining your company's board of directors, but the pros and the analysts do, so why don't you? There is nothing you can do about your company's board, but you can determine how comfortable you are with its members.

You know the traditional role of the board of directors. As the story goes, on the organization chart the board sits above the company's CEO and below the stockholders. The board members are highly respected individuals who counsel the company through monthly meetings with the CEO. They hold or have held high positions in industry, government, or academia; receive roughly $30,000 plus expenses and perks for their services; and conduct their nonconfrontational meetings in an elaborately appointed boardroom dedicated to their use.

So much for tradition. Today you're just as likely to find discord as conflicts of interest arise between the president and the stockholders, with the board of directors in the middle. The CEO selects most if not all the board members, but the stockholders expect the board to protect their interests. If its members fail to do so, stockholders initiate lawsuits against the board for dereliction of duty.

An example: The president of Mellon Bank resigned in 1987 after a major drop in earnings, whereupon it was revealed that only four meetings of the board of directors had been held in 1985 and only five in 1986. A closer monitoring of the bank's lending policies might have signaled earlier that trouble was brewing. Stockholders, feeling that the members of the board of directors should have seen this, initiated lawsuits. They felt the board of directors wasn't doing its job.

Insurance companies are now walking away from issuing liability insurance for corporate officers and directors, finding it too risky to underwrite. When they do write such policies, the premiums can double or triple for less coverage. You desperately want good directors, but the good ones are afraid of the liability associated with the job. Quite a conundrum.

Considering all of the above, and your own knowledge of the directors of your company, would sitting in on a meeting of your board provide a most stimulating exchange of ideas? Or do you think it would be a forum to acknowledge your CEO's wishes? Or something else entirely?

How much do your directors participate in running the company? It's hardly reasonable to expect them to be able to second-guess management based on the pristine reports management prepares and hands to them as they enter the boardroom, even given the three hours of preparation time for each hour of board meeting that many directors say are necessary. And it's unlikely that the directors will be openly critical of the CEO's policies during those meetings. Still, you want your company's board to be more than a figurehead.

Are your company's board members really able to help? Do they do so? Ask yourself if they are more than just good friends of the CEO. Are they prudent managers of risk? Are you pleased that they are on board? To help you decide, review each of the directors against the points in this chapter. You may find some interesting results.

In his book *Managing,* Harold Geneen suggests that diligent boards of directors should address the key issue: not what the company earned last year or this year but what it should have earned. He is quick to add that this is difficult to assess, given the one-way flow of information to the board, but he then suggests that if each director had a considerable personal investment in the company, probing questions would be asked. Geneen feels that if activist boards like this became the norm in this country, we'd see a great boost in productivity.

Is your company's board of directors coaxing the best productivity out of your company?

What Can You Learn from the Chairman's Toys?

○ Does your CEO have an intense hobby?
○ Does he take business time to pursue it?
○ Are company employees used to support it?
○ Are company assets used?
○ Is this use of time, staff, and assets significant?

The chairman's toys are unproductive assets carried on the company's books primarily for the enjoyment of the CEO and occasionally a few other top executives.

I first heard the term "chairman's toys" from a bankruptcy consultant who discovers them as he looks at problem companies, often on the edge of liquidation. The first place he looks is the transportation account. To date he's found aircraft, yachts, and limousines, of course, but also collections of antique automobiles and even racehorses. In addition, he's found condos and guest lodges in the south or in ski or hunting areas, depending upon the interest of the CEO. Considering that each of these companies was facing reorganization and that these indulgences were still on the books, you can see how great a CEO's dedication to his toys can be and the interest they may have held for him in healthier times under less scrutiny. *Does this bring any indulgences of your CEO to mind?*

Companies are becoming more sensitive to this point. I know of one CEO who is an avid polo player; his company was preparing to sell a polo club, part of its real estate holdings, in order to focus on the company's core business. I also know an East Coast CEO who acquired a company of only modest value in the Northwest, and interestingly enough, he loves to vacation in that area. These aren't flagrant misuses of company funds, but they are questionable. Too many instances like this and you may see a second line of priorities in your company.

Companies have long put offices where their senior executives like to be, but make sure there is no unusual drain on company assets or the CEO's time. You don't want the chairman's toys to distract him from pursuing the main strategy of the company. The smaller the company, the closer you are to potentially being hurt by this point. Your role is not to play watchdog, but the presence of such toys could have a bearing on your long-term decisions.

COULD THIS BE YOU?

Terry was concerned about his company and his future within it. Things had changed. He'd noticed that the group executives were playing a more active role in setting policy. That wasn't inappropriate, but along with this latitude came a lot more political maneuvering and competing for power. More energy was being expended on short-term goals because no long-term strategy was evident. The CEO was still the same and no significant changes had occurred in top management, but Terry was bothered by this new turn of events. He thought back as he searched for an explanation.

Terry had joined the company seven years ago because a new CEO had just come on board whose track record Terry knew and respected. The CEO was a star. Terry wanted to ride with him, and ride he did. He moved up to vice-president as the company surged ahead. The CEO had made a tremendous impact, and Terry had often congratulated himself on his own good timing.

Terry recalled those exciting first four years. He'd never thought anything could go wrong, and apparently it had taken him another three years to recognize that something had. Now he was surprised that he could have been so unquestioning for so long, because whatever had occurred certainly hadn't happened overnight.

He thought back to his first annual management meeting four years ago. He remembered that some of the older officers had grumbled quietly about the CEO's involvement in the national elections that year. Terry hadn't minded the man's being involved in politics; to him it seemed a great thing for a CEO of a large company to do. It hadn't occurred to him that the grumbling of the senior officers only advertised that a gulf existed between the CEO and his top team—a gulf so wide that it left his staff insensitive to what they said in the presence of junior officers.

In the course of the next year, Terry had learned that the CEO was chairing a businessmen's group and that he was still active in politics. Terry now realized there had been signs that the CEO's attitude had changed. He'd become more cavalier, more aggressive in challenging his own officers, and quicker to grab the spotlight. The gulf between the CEO and his staff had widened. Just as disturbing, none of the senior officers had been accomplishing anything special. Although the business continued, much of the fire in the company was gone. The senior managers, many of whom had been vigorous hotshots, were getting lethargic.

Two years ago, the CEO had been quoted in the press as saying, "Once you've been president of a company like this one, you've seen the best of the corporate world." At the time Terry had thought this sounded loyal, but now he drew a different conclusion. His idol, the CEO, was bored. He was distracted by other activities and creating a vacuum where his leadership had once been. That vacuum was resulting in infighting, and in turn, the power plays were affecting Terry. The company had split behind two strong leaders, and Terry's inclination to play both sides wasn't working in this atmosphere.

Terry thought further. The company had missed some changes in consumer preferences lately. It had stuck with its old models instead of responding to the demand for something new. That wouldn't have happened seven years ago, or even four years ago, Terry thought. Moreover, just this last year the CEO had been in the media a lot, but little of his exposure had to do with the company. He was heavily involved in politics and national policy groups and seemed to be traveling constantly, but still he held onto his role as CEO. Even in absentia he protected his position aggressively—some might say abusively.

This company has a problem, Terry thought, and so do I. I've got guys on both sides of the fence taking potshots at me, and I have to make a move soon to one side or the other or go elsewhere. Damn. I didn't want to get into a mess like this—but at least my eyes are finally open.

PULLING IT TOGETHER

You should not hesitate to look carefully at your CEO and top executive group. All the major business publications often carry stories of what CEOs did, could have done, or didn't do and hold them up for scrutiny. A new book, *Unstable at the Top: Inside the Troubled Organization,* by Manfred F. R. Kets de Vries and Danny Miller, gives numerous examples of trouble initiated at the top and the consequences pushed down through the organization.

How you handle what you find out about your senior management depends upon where you are and where you want to go. Maybe you've found warts, but they're the kind you can live with. Maybe top management has an unusual style, but it suits your own. Or maybe you've found a situation you don't like and with which you don't want to be associated. Now you have a better feeling for the ground rules.

Run back through the chapter's main points and make a note of those that trouble you.

10

How Good Is Your Company's Financial Health?

You can't know the real health of a company until you understand its financials. Your company may have the best management, the biggest buildings, the highest reputation, and products and people without equal, but if its financial results aren't good, you could be in for a shock. This chapter will give you a quick but tough check on the financial health of your company. It will either set your mind at ease or cause you to look deeper.

"But I'm not an accountant!" you might say. "Besides, all I need to know is sales and earnings, and those are quoted in the newspaper." My reply is that you don't have to be an accountant to look at the financials and that you're burying your head in the sand if you don't look beyond the obvious. Think how you'd feel if you suddenly learned your company was filing for bankruptcy. It happens, even to the most prestigious corporations—Penn Central, W. T. Grant, Continental Illinois Bank, International Harvester, and the list goes on.

The numbers you need to see are readily available from a variety of sources, and with a little sleuthing you can obtain some additional data to interpret. The data originate with your company, so start with the big three: your company's balance sheet, profit and loss statement, and consolidated statement of changes in financial position (sources and uses of funds).[1] These

[1] If the financial terms in this chapter are unfamiliar to you, I suggest you get

statements are in every annual report and most quarterly reports, and—along with the footnotes pertaining to them—hold all the keys to the performance of your company.

In addition to these three statements is your company's 10K, a form it files annually with the Securities and Exchange Commission (SEC) describing its operations, and a quarterly 10Q. These forms have a standard format that can make your analysis easier, and they are available from either your company or the SEC.

In the last few years, companies have been volunteering more financial information, recognizing that they can hide little from the explosion of data bases and from the aficionados who rummage through them for submerged tidbits. Growth companies are particularly forthcoming, with data and performance ratios prepared for you. Without getting into the realm of the investment analyst, there are sources outside your company you can go to for information:

- Financial services—such as Moody's, Standard & Poor's, and Bests—that rate companies.
- Brokerage houses, either national or regional, that follow your industry and company.
- Industry publications and reports.
- Research firms that serve your industry.
- Insider-trading reports to the SEC. Officers are required to report purchases or sales of stock in their own companies.
- Networking in the industry.
- General business press and television coverage.
- Your stockbroker. If you have an account with a full-service broker, you can ask him about your own company and others.

If you are with a private company or are considering joining one, you can only *ask* for the information mentioned in this

a brochure from a major brokerage house or a book that explains the interpretation of financial reports. I have attempted to keep jargon to a minimum, however, and let the major concepts dominate.

chapter. A private company is under no obligation to share financial information, nor is it regulated by the SEC. Asking, however, shows you care, and how management responds or doesn't respond can be revealing.

A senior vice-president of a prominent investment firm once said to me after interviewing a candidate, "I've never been asked such questions before!" He was shocked. The firm was privately owned, and the candidate, an M.B.A., had questioned its financial strength. The senior vice-president wasn't accustomed to such questions, which seemed to him like heresy. He wouldn't have dreamed of asking them himself. Three years later the firm was merged out of business!

Some financial experts maintain that you can't rely completely upon company data because management wants to put things in the best possible light. I believe you can trust management, but you must be sensitive to its position. If management has problems, it no doubt plays them down because its job is to get rid of problems and find success. Management wants to buy time to fix the problems and wants to maintain the good reputation of the company during difficult periods. It wants to project confidence. That's not being untrustworthy, but it does mean you have to go to the footnotes to find some of the dicey data in company reports.

Some also say you can't trust the "big eight" accounting firms, which I think is ridiculous. Just don't expect of them what they can't do. They are professionals in accounting practice and procedures, not corporate investigators or business prognosticators. They make sure a company reports its data according to accepted practices. These firms do protect the services of their ever growing number of departments, and yes, they do compete for clients and get fired by CEOs who don't like the opinion given, but I still say they are trustworthy.

You may also have heard that the analysts with the major investment companies are more concerned about protecting their relationships with the managements of the companies they follow than they are with writing critical reports when necessary. There is something to this claim, but then you have to understand the jargon the analysts use. "Buy" means everything is great, and anything other than "buy" means look twice. Remember, analysts live and die by their analyses, and good analysts live very, very well. The best in 66 industry categories are chosen each October for the All American Research Team by *Industrial Investor* magazine, the authority on ranking analysts. Their work has been carefully scrutinized for value. Make an effort to see reports of this nature on a continuing basis. They cover a lot of territory, often including your competitors.

The hard information is available, but you have to put it together and interpret it according to your industry as well as your personal comfort level when it comes to risk. The sections that follow will help you put your company's financials in perspective.

What Are the Company's Revenues?

- ○ Has a major change in revenues occurred lately?
- ○ Why?
- ○ What has been the five-year trend?
- ○ What customer or foreign country is the biggest contributor?
- ○ How much of your company's revenues are nonoperating/nonrecurring?
- ○ How much is due to exchange-rate fluctuations or changes in accounting?

You don't want to join a company without a strong revenue stream. It's too dangerous. If you're already on board, you want to keep track along with management and make sure you're not surprised.

Revenues are the starting point, income from which your company progressively deducts expenses to determine its gross profit margins, earnings before taxes, and finally, earnings after taxes. The more revenues coming in, the more dollars your company has to work with. Some analysts feel that an aggressively growing revenue stream is more important than the costs, since once revenues are provided, you can always control costs. Many variables affect this generalization, but I think there's something to it.

Have there been any sharp increases or decreases in company revenues lately? If so, find the reason. Decreases are obviously unsettling, but sharp increases can also be cause for concern. If an increase in revenues is due to gaining market share—say, by sales of a new product—good, but if the increase is due only to higher prices, that's potentially dangerous. Management could be milking a product for short-term goals; over the longer term, the company may actually lose market share.

How vulnerable are your company's sources of revenues? You considered vulnerabilities already in Chapter 6, where you took a look at international and environmental concerns, and in Chapter 7, where you checked your company's markets. One major customer or dominant foreign country may be a blessing when things are going well, but if problems develop, you could be in the soup. Is there a good spread of customers providing revenues?

Nonoperating and nonrecurring (NO/NR) revenues are generally lumped together even though they are quite different. Nonoperating revenues come from outside the company's mainstream operations—for example, office rents received by a company whose primary business is manufacturing widgets. Nonrecurring revenues derive from any one-time situation, such as the sale of a business, plant, or excess inventory. Your challenge is to determine what you consider to be NO/NR and see if you agree with management. This often requires a careful reading of the footnotes in the annual report.

Some CEOs include the revenues from selling companies under operating revenues, the rationale being that the corporation sells companies all the time. This financial sleight of hand can make operating revenues look better than they really are. I find this practice a little hard to accept, especially knowing that abuses occur in reporting these types of transactions. If revenues from selling companies show up under "operating," make sure selling companies really is a recurring part of operating income and that the dollar volume for this kind of revenues is roughly the same from year to year.

How do your company's revenues compare with those of your competitors? Obviously, many factors have to be taken into account, but if you compare the trend lines, you may learn something interesting.

What Are the Company's Earnings?

○ Are your company's earnings keeping pace with revenues?
○ If not, why not?
○ What has been the five-year trend in earnings?
○ How does this compare to industry norms?
○ Are the figures based on fully diluted earnings?
○ How much of your company's earnings are nonrecurring?

Earnings are profits. If a business doesn't turn a profit, its investors would do better to put their money in the bank. Still, there's more to analyzing your company's earnings than looking at the bottom of its P&L, and an earnings trend by itself does not reflect the company's complete financial health. Read behind the numbers and learn to recognize some of the variables to determine how healthy your company really is and how secure your job may be.

A nice increase in reported earnings can even be misleading. For example, earnings could be increasing while revenues stay flat. Increased earnings can't be squeezed out of flat revenues for very long, even if management is making tough moves. You've got to have increasing revenues to prosper over the longer term.

Another factor to consider is dilution. *Are the reported earnings fully diluted?* Warrants, convertible preferred stock, and convertible debentures, issued when the stock is low, can all potentially be converted when the stock rises. Their conversion dilutes the impact of the earnings growth (the earnings must now be spread more widely), diminishing the earnings trend you may have become accustomed to.

Does your company have a lot of convertible securities outstanding? If these are in the hands of a few holders, conversion could change the ownership balance of your company. Is that possible?

The issues you considered with regard to revenues also apply to earnings. Look at your company's earnings trend. *Have there been any sharp increases or decreases? Are increases the result of bigger share or price increases?* See if deviations from the trend line seem logical to you. Compare the trend of revenues with that of earnings and try to determine what accounts for any differences you find.

What nonoperating and nonrecurring earnings do you see? One-time payments are even more important here than they were with revenues because decisions are based more frequently on earnings data than on revenues data. Check those footnotes. Make sure you agree with management about what constitutes recurring earnings.

You've already considered what vulnerabilities might affect your company's revenues. Now check for factors that could cut unexpectedly into earnings. *What costs or expenses could suddenly increase?*

Inflation makes earnings look healthier than they really are. It reduces the impact of depreciation charges as prices and revenues rise. Depreciation deductions for replacing equipment are no longer sufficient.

Many variables exist, and you can't expect to be smarter than the professionals who prepare your company's data. Still, you want to find a minimum of vulnerabilities as you check your company's earnings, and you hope to find reasonable explanations for anything disturbing.

What Is the Company's Cash Flow?

○ What was the company's cash flow last year?
○ Was it significantly more than earnings?
○ If so, why?
○ Was cash flow possibly negative?
○ How does your company's cash flow compare with that of your competitors?

There's nothing like cold, hard cash. It takes cash to pay salaries and bills and to buy raw materials. Your job is in jeopardy if your company doesn't have cash, regardless of what it reports for earnings and revenues.

Cash flow is generally earnings plus depreciation (see your company's consolidated statement of changes in financial position). Depreciation deductions represent monies set aside to replace old equipment, but regardless of the purpose, depreciation is dollars that can be spent, and it can have a tremendous impact on cash flow. Corporations with expensive assets—buildings, for example, or ships—can claim high amounts of depreciation; even with negative earnings, these assets have the potential to generate high cash flow. *How does depreciation affect your company's cash flow?*

The best cash flow comes from a high stream of earnings, of course, but other sources of cash include deferred taxes, sale of equity, long-term borrowings, and sale of plants or assets. These additional sources are important because today companies change their capital structure more frequently, often to generate cash.

Once you accept that your company must have cash to operate, it becomes a test of how much cash your company has or doesn't have. If your company has high cash flow plus good earnings, you can be confident about its health. Of course, you may want to compare your company's cash flow with that of your competitors to put it in perspective.

Beatrice Companies was running a cash flow twice earnings in the mid-1980s. At the other end of the spectrum was W. T. Grant, where cash flow actually turned negative while earnings rose. Those who were watching closely were not surprised when W. T. Grant filed for protection from creditors. It couldn't pay its bills!.

Cash flow can be influenced in a big way by changes in your company's investment in inventory and receivables (unpaid bills outstanding). These bear watching, because when they increase, they eat up cash. Even decent profits can be offset by a negative cash flow due to big inventory increases' consuming cash.

There are many ways to measure a company, but cash flow gets to the guts of a company quickly. *How does your company look?*

What Is the Company's Debt Picture?

○ How much short-term debt appears on your company's balance sheet?

○ How much long-term debt appears?

○ Has the company's amount and type of debt changed significantly recently?

○ If so, why?

○ Does cash flow cover the payments of principal and interest?

○ Is the company's debt load normal for your industry?

If your company can't handle its debt repayment schedule comfortably, management will be distracted and the normal operations of the company will suffer—and so might your career. Heavy loads of debt can and do sink companies.

Is your company too deeply in debt? How much debt is too much depends on many factors: the amount of debt management is accustomed to servicing, the amount your competitors must service, your company's ability to raise prices, your company's ability to sell assets, new products about to be introduced, the terms of the debt, and the state of the economy. The point at which debt becomes destructive depends upon the mix of factors and what your company is doing and can do.

One way to get a handle on your company's debt picture is to determine its debt-to-equity ratio. Add the short-term and long-term debt as shown on the balance sheet and divide the total by the value of shareholders' equity. It's impossible to say what ratio is appropriate for any company, but no debt is best, and more debt than equity is less than ideal. Look carefully.

How much money does the company throw off to pay creditors? You want to know whether or not your company can cover the annual interest payments easily. One approach is to divide operating income by the total annual interest payment to see how many times the interest payment is covered. Finding the interest amount in the annual report isn't always easy; you may have to ask a financial type to help you dig this out.

Also look at the type of debt. Poorer-quality debt (that is, debt issued at higher interest rates) is cause for alarm, while converting poor-quality debt to high-quality is definitely a strong sign.

A new wrinkle—leveraged buyouts and the junk bonds with which many are financed—came into play in the early eighties, increasing the debt of many companies to what some consider dangerous levels. Those high levels of debt are always entered into with planned strategies for how the debt will be rectified— but the best of plans don't always work. If your company is involved in such a situation, see whether you agree that the debt can be satisfied without ruining your company. If you read the business press, you'll see many examples to put this in perspective.

Without getting too technical, you can just look at the debt line on the ten-year comparisons in your company's annual report. See whether the debt load is consistent and whether the total looks reasonable. If your company's debt seems high, ask questions. You want to know why it's high and whether or not your company can handle it. If debt is on management's mind, your boss won't be surprised that it's on yours, too.

What Unusual Financial Liabilities Exist?

Which of the following might exist in your company:
- Underfunded pension plan?
- Long-term benefits to retirees?
- Long-term leases?
- Other long-term commitments or contracts?
- Environmental costs?
- Litigation exposure?

Unexpected liabilities can hurt. You've already looked at your company's environmental concerns (Chapter 6) and thought about current or potential litigation (Chapter 7). Here is the place to fill in any additional financial liabilities that could mortally wound your company.

The unexpected often requires monumental decisions and the redirection of large amounts of money and effort. Texaco, for instance, took protection under the bankruptcy laws to protect itself from Pennzoil and an $11-billion judgment. Johns Manville sought similar protection to escape the pressure of mounting lawsuits over its asbestos products. These matters can dominate management's attention and slow or even stop the forward motion of a company until they are resolved. Depending upon where you are, your career could be stalled, as well. *Are any current or potential liabilities preoccupying management?*

The unexpected does happen in companies. This can be disappointing, but a little foresight can ease the shock. Contracts may be great when they are entered into, but if circumstances change markedly, they can become a millstone that can break a company. I'm sure Westinghouse felt great about its uranium contracts in the late sixties, but soon after, uranium definitely wasn't the place to be. With courts making environmental and product liability judgments in the millions as they have, it pays to keep an eye out for the long-term consequences of decisions that are made, or were made before you even came on board. It can be difficult to anticipate the results of arrangements made ten years ago, but be sensitive to what you hear, and if a hint of trouble comes up, ask additional questions.

What Undervalued Assets Exist?

Which of the following might be undervalued by your company:
- ○ Real estate owned?
- ○ Long-term property leases?
- ○ Overfunded pension plan?
- ○ A patent, royalty, or licensing arrangement?
- ○ Brand name recognition?
- ○ Inventories?
- ○ Manufacturing capacity?
- ○ Distribution system?

This is the plus side, and undervalued assets can be a big plus. They can also be a minus if they attract a takeover attempt.

It's not always easy to assign a dollar figure to what is undervalued by your company. Still, you want to recognize undervalued assets so your company can exploit them, and you want to know how others might be evaluating them. Articles have been written about the "breakup value" of companies, suggesting that this valuation, which reflects unrecognized assets, is more important than the traditional book value.

Southern Pacific Railroad, McDonald's, and Exxon. What do they have in common? Massive holdings in real estate that are hardly reflected in the basic business of each. Real estate can often be found on balance sheets at cost, while the actual value is many times higher. That big value exists, awaiting the appropriate way to exploit it. The unrecognized value of real estate is easy to determine, however, since appraisers who do "optimum use" studies are available.

What other hidden assets might your company have? Long-term leases can be very valuable, as can patents, inventories, or anything else your company possesses that would have a considerably higher value for another company. Brand names that have positive customer acceptance are now recognized as having big value—so big, for example, that Beatrice Companies was taken over when its shares already seemed to many to be fully priced.

Another unusual asset was the many millions of dollars that were channeled out of overfunded pension plans and into company operations as a result of the roaring stock market of 1986 and 1987. This is all perfectly legal. Although I disagree with the philosophy, it's certainly better to take funds out of a plan than to have to add funds to make up a shortfall.

Look at your company first to gauge its health, as a financial analyst might. Then take a second look as a takeover artist might, examining strictly the value of your company's assets. If a big difference exists, your company may be a tempting target for someone! In that case, you have to ask yourself what would happen to you and your operation in the event of a takeover. *Do any surprises come to mind?*

What Is the Company's Capital Structure?
○ How many classes of stock are listed?
○ What are the voting rights of each class?

○ Are all classes of stock equally in public hands?
○ Are any unusual issues of warrants, rights, or
   convertibles outstanding?

As soon as you see class A and class B stock reported in the financial tables, you immediately think to look into the differences. You wonder why the company found it necessary to issue two classes of stock and how the rights differ. A big company that is struggling may have to issue convertibles to sweeten the offering of various securities, but too many classes of stock in a small company makes me nervous.

I recently stayed away from an initial public offering of a company because the president, whom I knew, had set up a second class of stock purchased mostly by the former owners of the company. I thought this was unnecessary, just another thing to keep track of, and I avoided the whole situation.

I've never owned enough stock in any one company to worry about voting my shares, but I've never bought a stock where I couldn't vote if I wanted to. How a company's capital is structured can get complex, and at some point, you begin to wonder what the company is trying to do. *Is the capital structure of your company easy to understand, easy to invest in?*

I like to see one class of common stock. Then you know where you stand. (Public utilities with their multiple classes of stock are regulated and are therefore a separate issue for the purposes of this point.) A clear capital structure may make the stock of your company more attractive to investors, which may cause it to rise more easily—a benefit to both the investors and you.

The structuring of your company's capital provides another insight into management's thinking. A quick review of it is no waste of time.

Who Owns the Company's Stock?

○ How broadly are your company's voting shares held?
○ Who are the biggest holders?
○ Are they friendly to management?

○ Have they gained by holding your company's stock?
○ Have senior managers been buying or selling shares of company stock?

You already took a look at your company's owners/controlling interests in Chapter 9 from the standpoint of working for them. Now check who owns your company's stock from the standpoint of stability of the company. At the extreme, you might call it a takeover watch.

If your company has a good management team in place, you hope to find that they can run for their goals without having to worry about being second-guessed by their own investors as well as by their competitors. You also want to see senior officers owning stock, so they have a personal stake in how the company's stock performs. A healthy company with motivated management is a powerful combination.

In discussing stock ownership, takeovers immediately come to mind. It used to be that you could anticipate a takeover attempt if you saw stock starting to accumulate in various accounts, generally the "street name" of various banks or brokerage houses. Today raids can happen so fast that they are difficult to anticipate from stock ownership alone. Still, it's a point worth remembering.

Let me focus on what I consider the ideal situation, rather than on all the possibilities. Your company's stock is owned by a broad selection of individuals, funds, and pension accounts. The stock has potential, and its owners have no interest in selling. The senior managers hold enough stock so that the increased value of their equity will be significant to them. It's a good sign when management buys stock in your company. (Remember, this has to be reported to the SEC and is in turn reported in the major financial journals.) It's also nice to learn that senior executives have come on board with grants of large numbers of options. Sure, you may be envious, but they will be motivated to make the company do well. *Do your officers own reasonable amounts of the company's stock?*

Even if your company is private, you can form an opinion of the owners and the motivation they are evidencing. *Are you encouraged by what you see?*

What Is Wall Street Saying?

○ Do good investment firms follow your company?
○ Do they comment on your company frequently and thoroughly?
○ What are they saying?
○ Does your company provide good information to analysts?
○ Have analysts' reports identified problems you hadn't been aware of?

The research reports from investment banking firms are great sources of information. They run from one to 20 pages and are called "institutional reports" because they are given to the major banks, insurance companies, and managers of money. Commissions from trading securities are expected in return. Even given the biases analysts may have that I mentioned earlier, these reports are very valuable if you can find them. They are not confidential, but their distribution is restricted. *Do you know who follows your company?*

There's no easy way to get these reports, but a friend of a friend may be able to help you. To get hold of a report on your own company, ask someone in your financial department for a copy. See if you can get a "base" report plus the updates. To get a report on another company you're thinking of joining, call the vice-president of investor relations, say you're thinking about buying stock, and ask which investment firms have written about the company recently. Then ask him if he will send you a copy, but if he won't, take your chances and call those firms directly to ask for a copy of their report. This may or may not work, but it's worth a try. My opinion is that this information is as valuable to prospective employees as it is to prospective investors, and a way should be found to make it attractive to the investment firms to make the reports available. *Can you get copies of investment reports on your company?*

Once you have a report, don't expect to find blatant negatives. If the situation is that bad, there's no need to write a report. The fact that a report exists at all tells you that the investment firm thinks there is potential in the company and important info that should be read.

Most analysts stake their reputations on their reports. They don't waste words, but they do cover what they see as the pivotal points. You can pick up what they think of other divisions in your company, how your company is doing versus your competitors, what the takeover rumors are, the financial projections, and why the projections look the way they do.

I've heard CEOs say, "I don't give a damn what Wall Street thinks, we're going to do such and such . . ." They may be right for their purposes, unconventional though they are, but for your purposes, give those reports a read if you can.

COULD THIS BE YOU?

Martina was unsettled. She was beginning to see the name of her company in the business pages, and she wasn't accustomed to that. It alarmed her, in fact, as she thought of takeovers and leveraged buyouts and what happens to acquired companies.

Martina had been with this supplier of software for microcomputers for just 18 months, and things were going beautifully. She managed a programming team and was working as long and as hard as her body would allow, and her people were doing the same—yet everyone was happy. She'd left a consulting company to build her track record in management, and this position was everything she'd hoped it would be. There was a great sense of teamwork, management was accessible, the firm was growing— but those few articles in the press made her uneasy.

First she'd read about an international company that had acquired two smaller software companies. The writer had speculated about what companies might be next on its list, and Martina's was mentioned. Then there was the article about the importance of breakup value as opposed to book value, and Martina's company was one of the examples. Apparently, customer acceptance of her company's brand name was very high. The last article, a rather routine analysis of her company's earnings stream, had gotten to Martina. She didn't want her job destroyed by a corporate takeover. Sure the stock was moving nicely, but someone could be accumulating a stake and sitting, waiting to pounce. "Everyone else is tearing into the financials of this company," thought Martina. "Maybe I should do the same."

Like any smart former consultant, she knew the place to start was the balance sheet, because without strength there, everything else would be an uphill fight. She was pleased with what she found: no long-term debt, no buildup in receivables or inventories, and cash and receivables were twice current liabilities. The company was strong.

The second schedule Martina checked was profit and loss statement. Here she saw a continuing strong earnings trend and even a slightly increasing pretax profit margin. Good again.

The consolidated statement of changes in financial position was her third schedule, and again Martina was pleased to see that almost all earnings were from operations; there had been no sale of assets. She scoured the footnotes of the annual report and couldn't find any unusual liabilities. The only unusual asset she could come up with was the attention the company's brand name had gotten in the newspapers.

Martina was still restless. She called a friend in her former consulting firm who'd been an analyst on Wall Street and asked her to find out who was following the company and to see if she could get hold of the recent reports. It took a week, but eventually two reports arrived, one prepared by the firm that underwrote the company's stock and the other by a national investment firm. "Not bad coverage," Martina thought. Both reports were constructive, but that of the smaller firm was more opportunistic. She could sense that this report was talking about her company in a way that made it not only a hot stock but an acquisitions candidate as well. Apparently, management hadn't voted in any "poison pill" or "shark repellent" to prevent a takeover.

Martina was now less perplexed, but more disturbed. Here she was with a great and growing company, and it was almost too good—so good it was vulnerable to being taken over. The stock was already high, but Martina knew everything was relative.

Martina decided there was nothing she could do except keep her group as productive as possible and the company's stock as high as possible. She thought she'd better buy some stock herself—or better yet, talk to her boss about options, at least a grant in the event of a takeover. If he refused, so be it, but if he agreed, it could be very nice indeed. "I should have thought of this earlier," Martina mused, feeling much better for the exercise.

PULLING IT TOGETHER

This chapter started with revenues and went from there, but if you're going in to a treasurer or financial person, follow Martina's lead and start with the balance sheet, the profit and loss statement, and the consolidated statement of changes in financial position. The financial expert first wants to see a solid balance sheet, good equity and ratios, and then he moves on. If you follow the same sequence, it's a signal to the knowledgeable that you're in tune with them.

Now you have a feel for the financial health of your company. It may be strong—so strong that the company is at risk of a takeover—or it may be weak, but at least you know where you stand. *Can you build relationships with some people in finance? Can you get the investment reports about your company more frequently now that you know who puts them out?*

This quick review of your company's financials can't equal a full analysis by an investment firm, but it's comprehensive enough to turn up anything unusual that could be a problem for your company—and therefore for you, as well. I hope you found some things of importance that you hadn't been aware of.

Before you leave this chapter, let your eye run over the topics covered, and if a thought comes to mind, make a note of it.

Part III
Reviewing the Balance Sheet:
Putting It All in Perspective

The game continues. Now it's time to look at the big picture—the forest rather than the trees—and finally, to take charge.

You've walked through all those factors you bring to a job as well as all those issues controlled by your company. You should feel pretty good by now, regardless of the weaknesses you may have identified. You're aware of them, and that's half the battle. Now you're in a position to eliminate, mitigate, or possibly just sidestep them.

What remains is the crux of your career checkup. Is your job really doable considering the prevailing conditions? What are you getting for all that you give? How do things stack up? Is it possible that you should make a move?

Big questions, but important answers are waiting. You're in control as you draw this together.

11

Is the Job Doable?

"It's got to be doable if they offered it to me."
Wrong!

"It's got to be important if they want it done."
Sometimes.

"If I bust my ass, they've got to take care of me."
Don't count on it!

Is your job doable? Oh, if this were just a silly question—
but it isn't. Impossible jobs are assigned more often than you
think, sometimes intentionally but usually unintentionally. Your
boss may have handed you a job that has set you up for failure.
Some jobs just aren't doable (because of prevailing conditions),
even though management would dearly love to get them done.

I mentioned earlier that as I interview job candidates I hear
a lot of questions from people who have been around and been
burned. One dominant question is, "What do they *really* want
done?" These executives know the business school words. They
want to know about the touchy stuff behind the corporate job
description, such as having to close a plant, discontinue a product,
or remove people.

Being asked to challenge a tradition, or a power base, or
company inertia is not unusual, and it isn't "bad." It's just that
you should know in advance what you'll have to do to be
successful and whether or not you'll be able to get what you
need. Are any snakes buried in the woodpile?

Eager as you are to make an impression on management,
make sure you don't jump at an impossible task. Know what

has to be done, how it should be done, and whether you can do it. Just one point—something missing, something in the way—can stall the whole show. If you feel hesitant about asking too many questions, remember that some caution is appropriate even in the best of situations, if only to show that you are thoughtful and careful about what you undertake. Besides, you'll have to face all the questions sooner or later.

Don't allow yourself to be fooled because your boss has given you an assignment or because a plausible job has been structured and is being offered to you. That only means someone wants the job to be done, not that it's doable.

Today you must know more about any job you undertake. The days of the loyal follower who will be cared for because of his good intentions are gone. It's true that good companies will recognize exceptional efforts that don't succeed, but avoid these failure-prone situations if you can. You can win by losing only so many times.

What Are Your Specified Responsibilities?

○ What are you supposed to do?
○ How can your objective be measured?
○ Do you agree that it's the best objective to pursue?
○ Is there any hidden agenda?
○ To whom will your achievements be obvious?

The first step in getting a handle on the doability of your job is to define your responsibilities. After making sure you're the right person for the job, also make sure the job is the right one for you.

In Chapter 2 you reviewed your annual plan and how it is determined. This is different. Here you want to look at the overview. Explore what has to be done in your position on a long-term basis, why it wasn't done earlier, who wants it done, and how you might do it. If you've been offered a promotion or a new job, examine it in light of the other options available to you. You want to minimize the surprises that can come all too easily later on.

Are the job specifications complete? Do they reflect the prior-ities of current management? Be sure you're comfortable with the objectives underlying your responsibilities and certain they are in line with management's other goals. You may find that the job entails aiding a group that in the long run won't be helpful to you or that the position is less important than your boss suggests. Clear this up if you can.

Every position, unless it is very new, has its own momentum, a direction that the people involved have come to expect and accept. *Are you being asked to change the status quo?* Topping existing high standards is difficult enough, but refocusing a job presents new challenges. Where are the sacred cows? What will be the ramifications if you start making changes? How much change is reasonable?

Some kinds of jobs can be stimulating, particularly if you're asked to make new inroads and are expected to be aggressive and innovative. Handling a turnaround or penetrating a new market can be fun—if that's your style and if you have the support needed to play the game. But you may also be asked to wind down a dying subsidiary, to hold the fort until everyone is gone. That's a downer, no matter how many dollars are thrown at you. *Are you enthusiastic about your responsibilities?*

You might expect your boss to tell you everything you need to know about your job, since he's responsible and theoretically understands the position and wants you to succeed. With so much movement in corporations, however, he may not be familiar with all the subtleties of your job. If there are land mines that could give you problems, he may not be aware of them—or simply may not wish to discuss them with you until you're into the middle of the job. It's also possible that a hidden agenda may exist that your boss or his boss wants accomplished but that isn't told to you up front.

Get as much information about your responsibilities as you can from your boss, but don't expect him to tell you everything. *Have you talked to other people who are close to the situation?* Do some intelligence work, check the remaining points in this chapter, and use your intuition. Things are often not what they seem, and jobs are no exception.

Have You Got Enough Authority to Do the Job?

○ Who gave you the authority to do what needs to be done?
○ Was this authority within his power to give?
○ Is your authority adequate?
○ What might cause your authority to be lessened?
○ What additional authority would you like to have?

Here you want to explore the source of your authority as well as its limitations. If your company trusts you to accomplish an objective, you'd think there would be little question about giving you the appropriate authority. However, questions do develop, and without adequate authority, your hands are tied.

In what different areas must your authority be exercised? What boundary disputes might come up? So many people I recruit today are quickly given *responsibility,* but the *authority* they need is slower in coming. You're running the show; you must anticipate the authority you will need—top-down authority as well as the sideways latitude that may come into play as a project twists and turns.

Do you really have the authority you believe you do? Will others respect it? You don't want to go running back to your boss every time you hit static.

Authority is often enthusiastically given at the outset of an assignment while everyone is focusing on the proposed success of the project. As the project is executed, however, convolutions occur, particularly if you've been brought on board to bring about a change in a company that those already there haven't accomplished.

You can head off authority disputes with careful questioning in advance. It's worth some honest probing to try to avoid them. Abortive efforts don't earn merit badges—they only require tedious explanations.

Must You Infringe on Anyone's Turf?

○ Whose noses might you put out of joint as you do your job?

○ What will other people lose because of you?

○ What will they gain?

○ How much resistance do you anticipate?

Now that you've defined your responsibilities and the limits of your authority, look at those people who will be affected by your objective and over whom you have no control. If they're involved and you can't simply tell them what to do, you must find a way to cooperate with them. Your success here can make or break your objective.

Companies hire people who can protect their turf from competitors and outside factors. These people are often equally tenacious, however, about protecting their turf from intrusions on the inside, as well. If your job requires that you work through others and accomplish your objective on someone else's turf, the demands on you are higher. If you're aware of this and don't mind, no problem, but finding out about it unexpectedly can be fatal. *Have you scouted out all the people you'll be working with? Can you honestly expect their support?*

I once recruited a vice-president of manufacturing whose assignment was to introduce state-of-the-art operations. After taking the job, he discovered he had no actual authority over the division heads, who'd had a long tradition of autonomy. He couldn't flat out tell them what to do, and they weren't about to let themselves be persuaded. The guy was great, but he failed.

Staff positions require a special temperament, since your role is to advise, though you're measured on the extent to which your recommendations are implemented and how effective they are. Your personality makes a difference. The ease with which you get your job done also depends upon whether you're handling an expansion, which means more jobs and more assets, or a contraction, which means less of each. These two examples are at opposite ends of the spectrum, but you get the idea.

In seeking the cooperation of others, it helps if you and the other person know in advance what will be required and have time to plan. The central point, however, is who wins and who loses. If you can create the increasingly popular "win-win" situation, turf ceases to be an issue.

How Broad Is the Commitment to Your Job?

○ Who is as committed to your job as you are?
○ How many others have an interest in seeing you succeed?
○ Is your objective a high priority with management?
○ Does anyone above your boss have a direct concern in your project?

Back in Chapter 2 you took a look at the value of your performance and who stood to gain from your efforts. This is related, but the critical point here is who can be counted on to help you.

Start with your boss. *How committed is he to your work?* Without the support of your boss, you're as close to being a freestanding entrepreneur as you can get, but without the advantages.

On the other hand, it's disconcerting to find that you're doing something that benefits only your boss. *What about your boss's boss?* Support from both levels is valuable in helping you get things done and in solving problems as they develop. The higher the commitment to your job goes, the greater your comfort level.

Who gets excited about what you do? The more risky your undertaking, the more crucial it is that you have support—but the commitment you need will not always be there. If you feel you don't have enough support, try to find out why it's missing. Is your job so plain vanilla that you're taken for granted?

Do your peers have a stake in your success? If their success depends upon you, they'll be quick to assist you and involve themselves in your project. Also, you won't hesitate to ask them for help.

Has commitment to your job continued through the dull times as well as the peaks? You want the initial enthusiasm of others to be sustained. Frequent, brief meetings with your supporters are the best way to ensure their continuing commitment to you. Their body language will tell you more about their involvement than their words.

Are the Funds You Need Available?

○ How much new investment do you need to do the job?
○ How soon do you need it?
○ Can the company afford it easily?
○ Whom do you have to convince to get your funding?
○ Do you think you'll get it?

You buy a used car and you fix the brakes and add new tires to bring it up to your desired level of performance. When you take a new position, there are things you'll want and need to do your job. If your needs are inexpensive, you have no worries, but if you require a new plant or an expanded sales force, the funding you receive is more significant and your success more dependent upon it. The same holds true as you grow into your job and your responsibilities expand. The more you're trying to do, the more you'll need to spend.

Analyze your position carefully and project the investment you'll need to accomplish your objective. *Have you shaken out the surprises and added them to your total?* If there are any misunderstandings, now is the time to clear them up.

Whether you need a new desk or a new warehouse, you should determine how your requirements fit with the interests of the company. *What are management's priorities?* Whether you're in a cash-rich company or one in which funds evaporate before your eyes, look at where investments have been made recently and see how closely your needs compare. Depending on your project, you may have first call on funds or no call at all.

Who signs the checks? How easily can you get to that person to make your presentation—or plea? Recognize the route in your company that makes funds available. Investment funds tend to follow winners as management tries to increase the momentum already evident, so the best way to make your case is to demonstrate your effectiveness. How likely are you to get the dollars you need when you need them?

Do You Have Enough Time?

- ○ How much time have you been given to accomplish your objective?
- ○ Is this schedule realistic?
- ○ Who set it?
- ○ Why is it as it is?
- ○ Is this schedule one you wish to work within?
- ○ What might upset the timing?

With today's emphasis on results, time is as important a part of the job equation as your objective itself. Your first concern is whether or not it's possible to meet your objective within the time frame allotted. Secondarily you must decide whether or not you want to try. That's a call only you can make.

Start your analysis by finding out who set the schedule and what factors caused him to make it the way it is. Once you know these factors, you can keep an eye on them and anticipate changes in your deadline.

"Time" means, among other things, overtime. Putting in long hours can make the difference between winning and losing. You must get your army into place before your opponent does or you lose the battle. Working furiously is the dynamic in some corporations most of the time, and in others occasionally. David Ogilvy said that it builds spirit to work late a few nights a week, and many of his people did work late. What's the practice in your company? Once you recognize the norm, you'll be better able to judge what's expected of you. *How do you feel about the number of hours you'll be required to put in?* Go back to Chapter 5 and remind yourself about the kind of life-style you decided you want.

Some schedules can be extraordinarily demanding. Most are designed to meet a certain window of opportunity. You need to keep track of the progress you're making toward your goal. One of the more common approaches is to maintain a PERT (Performance Evaluation and Review Technique) chart, on which all procedures that contribute to the completion of a job are shown with start and end dates, plus those steps that can occur simultaneously and those that are contingent upon prior ones' being completed. Don't let your chart get so elaborate that it becomes incomprehensible. Put it on one sheet of paper or the back of an envelope and carry it with you. Make it your working record, not a presentation to the board.

Time. A deadline. An unrealistic schedule can tremendously complicate an otherwise straightforward project.

Have You Got the Right People?

- ○ What skills do you need in your group to accomplish your objective?
- ○ Which of them do you now have?
- ○ How many of your people are really strong?
- ○ How much latitude do you have in hiring?
- ○ Where will you find the people you need?

The right people make things happen—people with the right skills and the determination to get your job done. Before accepting a job, or before attempting to accomplish a particular goal, try to determine what skills you'll need and where the people who have them are located.

A new general manager I recruited said to me after his first month, "This place is like an Oreo cookie—great people on the top and bottom, but the middle is soft." He'd met all the top people in his interviews and was now seeing the softness. And it was giving him problems.

Where do you see strong people? As you seek them out, you're really on your own. Your predecessor probably had his favorites, but then you must improve upon his performance and do this in your own manner. Your boss can give you insights on people, but not the details you need.

Are you saddled with leftover "organization" men? You may be stuck with a low-performance group at a time when your operation needs rejuvenation and innovation. This often happens in companies that have topped out after long periods of growth and in family companies where people are retained for reasons unrelated to productivity.

How much new blood can you bring in? Do you have the authority and the budget to find and/or train the people you need? Make sure you can bring in "your people" if necessary, since without the right group, you will get nowhere.

Are There Attitude Problems in Your Group?

○ What attitudes are found in your group?
○ What outlook predominates?
○ How ingrained is it?
○ Is it widespread throughout the organization?
○ Do you need to make radical changes?

Attitudes are a special aspect of having the right people, since someone with the right skills but the wrong attitude can actually work against you. If you're going to have to change attitudes in your group, you have a major challenge.

Attitude problems can crop up in different ways. It's difficult to deal with a contrary individual, even more challenging to win over a suspicious group, and toughest of all to buck ingrained attitudes that have prevailed throughout a company for years. When AT&T was broken up, people who had long been accustomed to stability—those who had never felt the pain of a lost order, or the thrill of a new one—suddenly had to be introduced to competition and instability.

In another example, a company had been a sole source supplier to the government for 20 years, successful and profitable with the liberal benefits to employees that such profitability could support. However, new requirements that all contracts for the government be put up for competitive bidding have squeezed these profits, and put pressure on the employees to produce more, as they see some of their accustomed benefits erode. The attitude of these people requires—and deserves—more delicate handling.

Have people in your company always done things one way— and been successful? It's hard to persuade people to fix something they don't consider broken. If the old way has been profitable for a long time, you can anticipate resistance to a new way, even if change is absolutely necessary.

In Chapter 8 you took a look at your company's attitude toward newcomers. If your group welcomes new ideas from outside, you're in a position to make a strong contribution. If it doesn't, be prepared for a long and probably frustrating period of transition until you prove yourself—or are rejected by the system.

The difference between your success and failure can be lying quietly in the fabric of your company. Seek out those attitudes that might be a problem.

Does Your Operation Have the Productive Capacity You Need?

- ○ How much productive capacity do you need to attain your objective?
- ○ Do you have it?
- ○ If you have more than you need, what does the excess cost you?
- ○ If you have too little, can you add more?

This point sounds familiar because you already checked your company's manufacturing and production capabilities in Chapter 6. Here, however, you are taking a look at your own domain—your space, equipment, and overhead—since this is where bottlenecks and cost overruns can occur.

If you are an individual producer, your productive capacity is either within yourself or on your desktop. If you're a small-scale producer, check how much space and equipment you need and see whether you have too much or too little. This section will be most helpful, however, to those who use actual production facilities.

Your job isn't doable if you're limited by inadequate productive capacity or saddled with expensive excess capacity. You need an appropriate amount, plus the flexibility to expand or contract as market forces dictate.

Sometimes your production facilities are where you are, but often they're at a location you might not have examined closely or that you possibly even take for granted. *When was the last time you visited your production facilities?* Accumulations of inventory or inoperative equipment could be sitting there, waiting to drag you down. These are things that can diminish your flexibility and hurt you as business cycles change.

Walk the ground of your operation and sense the tempo, feel the equipment, watch the movement of the goods, and check the information system monitoring this movement. Note the positives and the negatives, the costs, what can go wrong.

In taking a good look at your productive capacity, you may also find opportunities. *What potential do you see? Does anyone else recognize it?* Compare your operation to others in your company and see whether yours is one of the better or poorer ones. *How far are you from your ideal productive situation?*

Is the Technology in Your Division Up-to-Date?

○ Does your operation employ state-of-the-art technology?
○ Is it proven technology?
○ Is a commitment to current technology evident in your products?
○ In your offices?
○ Who has more advanced technology than you do?

You considered your company's overall commitment to up-to-date technology back in Chapter 6. Now, examine the technology evident in your own operation in each of four areas: your products, your production facilities, your R&D, and administration. You want to assure yourself that each is current without being so new that it's experimental and therefore risky.

In most competitive industries, your products must equal or exceed the *product performance* of your competitors' products for you to stay in the game. You can't afford to be behind the power curve in your industry unless you're a "big blue" leader in whose lap everyone feels secure. *Is state-of-the-art technology reflected in your product?*

Success and profitability go to the low-cost producer, and often *productive efficiency* depends upon the technology employed. The U.S. auto industry, recognizing this, invested billions of dollars to retool and get its costs more in line with those of the Japanese. *Is your equipment up-to-date?* An ancillary problem is finding people with the advanced technological skills you need. The latest and best technology can be expensive, but it doesn't have to be bought. It can be licensed or even shared.

Technology in *research and development* is largely a matter of how much money is available, as you saw in Chapter 6. Even so, small companies frequently outflank big ones in product breakthroughs. *Are you confident that your company's R&D effort is adequate to your needs?* If not, find out now what this is likely to mean to you.

Data processing, voice mail, personal computers, video hook-ups, work stations, local area networks—in-house technology has changed, and continues to change fast. *Does your operation make good use of the latest communications and computer technology?* I'm not saying you have to have offices out of the twenty-first century, but neither should you hand a competitor an advantage on account of outdated methods.

Technology isn't just something for the other guy to worry about. It's important for you to know what you need, where you need it, and whether or not you have it.

Do You Have Assured Supplies of Raw Materials?

○ What raw materials do you need?
○ What are your sources?
○ What disruptions to the supply are possible?
○ Are substitute materials available?
○ Might crazy price fluctuations affect you?
○ Could international problems jeopardize your supply?

"Raw materials" means something different to everyone. Don't skip this section just because you aren't worried about where your next shipment of iron ore is going to come from. Whatever your line of business, there are raw materials you depend upon and expect to be there. Most times they are. It's what happens when they aren't that you want to investigate.

Where can you get hurt from the supply side? Wherever you work, you probably appreciate lights, the telephone, and heat or air conditioning. You require current data and information. Add to these your particular needs. Silicon Valley, for example, had its own brand of shortage when a new chip for the personal computer was in very short supply. Competition for these chips was so great that companies found their inventories stolen overnight.

Raw materials requirements become more apparent as you move into production facilities. A builder needs local woods; a cabinetmaker, imported and exotic woods. The latter is subject to more variables than the former. A car manufacturer has a wide variety of dependencies, from semiconductors to upholstery and steel, and not all of them come from domestic sources. The loss of any one piece can hold up your operation and, if it could have been avoided, take a chunk out of your reputation. *Can you anticipate scarcities and plan alternative sources?*

As you saw in Chapter 6, international situations can profoundly affect your operations. Look at the Middle East and petroleum, or Japan and currency reevaluations. You can't change the course of international events, but you can be alert to how they might disrupt your plans.

Water. It's an integral part of many operations, and though it seems simple enough, it's not something to take for granted. The Southwest transports water for crops through irrigation canals, and the Northwest needs it in massive amounts to run turbines for cheap hydroelectric power. The rest of us all use it in some way.

Let your mind wander. *What are the dependencies in your operation?*

What Has Been the Turnover in Your Position?

○ How long was your predecessor in your position?
○ What happened to him?

○ How long did his predecessors stay on the job?
○ Why did they leave?
○ Does it all sound normal?

Excessive turnover in a position signals a problem. You must find out whether it has existed in your position and, if it has, why. *Why will things go any differently for you? Has anything changed?* Get behind the platitudes on this one. It's important.

Normal job tours are two to three years in a big company and longer in a small company. Occasionally, a hotshot is promoted quickly, but this doesn't happen two or three times in a row in one position. Changes at that rate cause chaos.

Do you think you're special? Maybe you are, but don't be too quick to discredit your predecessors. If you respect their efforts, you may also be able to learn something that will make a big difference to you.

I once interviewed a candidate who had left a job as vice-president after only seven months. He was outstanding, but he'd found that the president wanted in on every decision—no, more than that, he'd wanted to make every one, and when one was made for him, he would countermand it. It developed that this president had run through three vice-presidents in two years. That kind of turnover is a bad sign.

If you can, talk with your predecessors. If necessary, search them out through former colleagues or their previous secretary and find out what happened. If you don't want to make waves yourself, have a friend call in to find out where they've gone.

If the situation is likely to get dicey soon after you arrive, you'll impress no one by being shy going in.

COULD THIS BE YOU?

Rocker wasn't happy. A job he'd started with the greatest enthusiasm wasn't working out. He felt strained and just couldn't get things moving. "Think time," he said to himself. "Time to analyze this thing and see what's gone wrong."

It had started so well. The initial meetings with the recruiter and the company had been full of promise. Management had seemed to know what it wanted done, and everyone had been in agreement—or so Rocker had thought. Looking back over his first year, he was beginning to wonder. He pulled out the original specifications given to him for the job, which in typical big-company formality ran two pages. They'd spelled out everything. Or had they?

Rocker was the chief engineer, and he had been charged with bringing out a telephone switch for a specialized market. His responsibilities and authority were all there in the specifications, but in reality they weren't so clear. Why was he having so much trouble?

Rocker remembered how he'd suggested to his boss that they use pulse code modulation technology for the switch. His boss had told him that wouldn't be necessary; audible signals in addition to flashing lights wouldn't be required. Rocker had felt then that he wasn't truly in control of the project, but the real irritation had come two months ago when his boss had asked for both of these features in a hurry. "That guy is afraid to let go," Rocker thought, "and he's making me look bad." But there was more.

Even Rocker's boss had approved the hiring of two more engineers, whom Rocker had said at the outset he'd need by now. But recently, word had come back that funding wasn't available, at least not this quarter. "Trying to do this on overtime is pushing things back further and further," thought Rocker. "And if we're too late, the project is dead." Oh, maybe not dead, but his company's competition would grab a position that would be nearly impossible to dislodge.

What else? A nervous boss, financial cutbacks of planned staff when they hurt most, a window of opportunity that was closing . . . and potential problems with manufacturing. Rocker wasn't sure manufacturing would be ready when his designs came out because his boss was handling those negotiations. He hadn't given much thought to manufacturing because it was still six to eight months away, but now he realized there could be more trouble from that front. What if the switch wasn't a priority for them? What had they been told?

Rocker began to see himself in a bind. If the situation didn't improve, he was going to be on the beach for failing to produce the switch in the two years he'd agreed to. He would have to pressure his boss for more freedom to talk with the financial types as well as the guys in manufacturing. To them, Rocker's project was just another problem.

Rocker thought carefully about his boss's strengths in the organization, and the more he thought, the more he could see that his boss was on the periphery. He wasn't really in the power structure, and he probably couldn't get a fair hearing. No wonder the guy was nervous. "All the more reason to push him," Rocker concluded. There was always the possibility that his boss would fire him on the spot, but Rocker felt confident that wouldn't happen. Considerable money had been spent to date on his project, and no one would want to hear that it was in jeopardy.

Rocker was beginning to plan an approach to his boss that would be heavy but might turn things around. In essence, he would imply that they both had a potential bomb on their hands. Rocker thought he could persuade—or scare—his boss into giving him the go-ahead to talk with finance and manufacturing and explain the demands of this project. It was an uncharacteristic move for him, but Rocker didn't know what else he could do. The alternative was disaster.

What had looked like a very straightforward project at the outset had come close to failure, not doable because little steps had gotten blocked, and people and priorities had turned out to be different than they'd seemed. Rocker had accepted too much at face value and hadn't examined the details. "Well," he thought, "I'll give it a hell of a try. If this fails, at least I'll know that I did my best."

PULLING IT TOGETHER

You started this chapter with the question, "What do they *really* want done?" Then you looked at what you have at your disposal to get the job done. Now you can define not only what has been asked of you but also what you think you can do. You know what you have enough of and what is short, where problems are likely to develop, and where opportunities lie. You have a more realistic grasp of the job.

Would you have accepted your job if you'd known then what you know now as a result of reviewing this chapter? If your answer is "no," or you are at all in doubt, think about what questions you should have asked then that you did not. What information were you missing? Would you ask similar questions if a different job were offered to you tomorrow? If your answer is "yes," it means you agree with the primary focus of this book, which is the exchange of more information and the establishment of greater candor in the employer/employee relationship.

People seldom ask enough questions about a new assignment or prospective job. They're excited about taking on bigger responsibilities and don't want to seem doubtful as they accept the challenge. But this enthusiasm undermines your ability to get a job done. You have too much dedication and not enough information.

Once you get all the facts and put them in perspective, you'll know, as far as it's possible to know, whether a job is doable or not. Succeeding at a very challenging job can add to your reputation, but failing in a difficult position, even through no fault of your own, can get you thrown right out of the saloon. You want to take on the "career-making" challenge and succeed, but you can't know everything in advance. Use the questions in this chapter to increase your chances of picking a winner.

A position isn't good or bad, but your perception of it changes when you ask enough questions. *Is your job doable for you?* You should feel by now that you know the answer to this, but a way of checking is to go back and review the main points in this chapter before you proceed to the next topic.

12

What Do You Get for What You Give?

Now it's time to examine what you gain for the effort you put into your job. Dollars immediately come to mind, of course, but there's much more than that. Some of the rewards you earn are provided directly by your company, but don't forget the other, less tangible benefits that make a difference to you. Sometimes listing just what you're getting can surprise you—hopefully favorably, but if not, at least you'll see where you're coming up short.

I've divided this chapter into "takehomeables" (such as cash and benefits), "enjoyables" (things that make most days a pleasure), and "business builders" (aspects of your job that make you stronger and deeper in your field). Any job provides something in each of these categories, most of which you take for granted. In this chapter, you'll look closely at each category, then at the balance between all three.

Compensation—dollars—is the scorecard, and you want to read behind the numbers. The heavy-hitters whose salaries are in the newspapers, and who don't need the big numbers they get, make this point over and over. Your compensation is management's appraisal of your performance, your cut of the pie that's divided each year between the stars management wants to make very happy, the above-average contributors who are important to the team, and the average contributors who aren't as noticed.

But there's a problem in considering compensation. Because it's very private, you think about it more than you talk about it. Discussions about who gets what in companies are discouraged. Still, you need to know where you stand and to confirm any gut feeling you have. Hopefully, you feel that your compensation is fair relative to your performance, what your colleagues are paid, and what your peers in other companies are receiving. Here you'll set your mind at ease about that fairness or determine what's less than fair in your situation.

Rather than just accepting management's offer with resignation, you owe it to yourself to evaluate the fairness of your compensation. Your boss may not tell you if you're being exploited, wanting you to think it's the normal pace of his department, or he may simply be trying to get the most he can from his budget. You should know which it is.

You're going to earn a million dollars, perhaps many millions, over the span of your career. Surprised? You shouldn't be, because a salary of $20,000 a year for 40 years brings you to $800,000, and surely you'll have some raises. It's the raises that make the difference, since each one establishes a new base for the next. A simple 5 percent raise each year increases that $800,000 to $2,415,995. If you factor in an additional 15 percent raise after 10 years, the total becomes $2,740,661. You see the cumulative impact.

That's the mathematical reality. I've also noticed lately that companies are deviating more frequently from rigid payroll charts. They seem more willing to grant big increases in bonus for big increases in performance, but this new pragmatism also leads them to release inefficient employees more readily.

The money is important, no doubt about it, but try not to get totally preoccupied with dollars. You get more than that for what you give—at least, you should. Furthermore, it never pays to evaluate a job solely on the basis of compensation. As we've already seen, you may be offered major money for a job that will do you in.

That said, I'm sure cash and benefits are still foremost in your mind, so let's look at them first. Don't be unsettled by the column for "outside offer" in the charts; this is only to make your comparisons easier if you're considering a job change.

TAKEHOMEABLES

In this section, we will consider the tangible rewards that come with your position: the dollars (both current and tax-deferred), the fringes and perks, the pension plan, insurance coverages, and assistance with relocation costs. In one way or another, these "takehomeables" all translate into money in your pocket.

What About Current Cash?

- ○ How many months has it been since your last raise?
- ○ What has the rate of inflation been since then?
- ○ Are you staying even with inflation?
- ○ Have you been paid with a title rather than with cash?
- ○ Have you been transferred laterally without an increase?

The easiest way to start your evaluation of your current cash is to note your figures for last year and this year on the accompanying chart.

	Last year	This year	Next year	Outside offer
Current cash				
Salary				
Commissions				
Bonus				
Profit sharing				
Cash spread forward				
Bonus				
Profit sharing				
TOTAL				

If your company has a profit-sharing plan, it's just as it says, a sharing of a percentage of profits, determined by management, either paid in cash or deferred. When the company flourishes, you essentially get a reward. *What profit-sharing arrangements do you have?*

Is your compensation up-to-date? Companies take care of good people, and if you're good, your boss won't let you go too long without a raise. A raise every 12 to 18 months is about average. More frequently is a plus for you; less frequently is obviously a minus. Good companies also want to make sure you aren't hurt if the rate of inflation is soaring.

If you're a star, your company will not try to hold you with a fancier title or lateral move and no increase. Highly driven, competent people won't take that, so if it's offered to you, read between the lines. You may have no alternative, and a lateral move can even be interesting, but know what the real message is.

Could you possibly be overpaid? Don't laugh! This happens by design in many fast-track companies and by accident in other companies, but it can hurt if you get accustomed to it. Sure, it's great for a while—say, four to six years—but if you don't make the cut into senior management and choose to stay anyway, you set yourself up for a jolt. At your exalted scale, there are few slots you can move into, and no one wants to offer you less than you're getting already and think you're worth. If your compensation is running high, keep the value of your performance in perspective and your relationships broad. You may need them.

Cash spread forward, also known as "golden handcuffs," means you get an award that is parceled out to you over a period of years—a third every year for three years or a quarter every year for four years. This is supposed to prevent you from jumping ship after a huge bonus.

Different companies have different personalities, as we've seen. Some have the attitude that you're lucky to get as much as you do and that you're privileged just to be on board. Some companies emphasize teamwork and are relatively democratic; others fight hard to keep their best performers, and the range in compensation is wider. *Given your company's attitude, what message is your compensation sending?*

There's pride that comes with a good salary and recognition for a job well done, and it's nice not to be in contention with your company over dollars. On the other hand, if you feel you're doing well but aren't being fairly compensated, then you have a problem that will distract you and divert your best energies away from your performance. Carefully analyze the factors that bring you to this conclusion and then see whether you can review the situation with your boss. You or he may have missed an important factor in the calculation. Clear this up if you can, before your resentment leads you to do something foolish.

Consider Your Tax-Deferred Compensation

- ○ Does your company have a plan by which you can defer earnings?
- ○ Is it worthwhile in your tax bracket?
- ○ Is the money invested well while it's deferred?
- ○ Are you up-to-date on the tax consequences?

Again, it may be simplest to start with the accompanying chart.

	Last year	This year	Next year	Out-side offer
Profit sharing				
Stock options				
Stock appreciation rights				
Other				
TOTAL				

Current cash is increasingly the dominant form of compensation, but tax sheltering—that constant wrestle between you and Uncle Sam—is still on the minds of many. Grants of stock options and stock appreciation rights and various arrangements to defer tax were the rage a few years ago, but changes in the tax laws have made deferring taxes less attractive. This is a complicated and often unpredictable area. For example, just when individual retirement accounts (IRAs) seemed to have become part of the fabric of our society, the 1986 Tax Reform Act made the money deposited into them taxable to the vast majority of taxpayers in 1987.

It's difficult for me to get too specific here, since so many variables exist in tax-deferred compensation. The important thing is to be aware of the tax-deferred benefits available to you, to reassure yourself that they are in fact beneficial for you, and to increase them if appropriate.

What Do You Receive in Benefits and Perks?

What benefits and perks does your company make available in the following or similar categories:

○ Savings plans?
○ Stock purchase plans?
○ Maternity leave?
○ Paid vacation?
○ Company automobile (or allowance)?
○ Club memberships?
○ Product samples?
○ Discounts on merchandise?
○ Tuition refund?

A caution before we get into benefits and perks. As a recruiter, I don't spend much time on them, and I get nervous if a job candidate emphasizes them too early. I know they're important once you're on board, but they should have a low priority if you're considering a big increase in job responsibility. Goodies tend to follow high performance, and the more of a hotshot you are, the more exotic your perks become.

So many benefits and perks are available now that some companies offer a "cafeteria" plan where you're given an allowance that you can spend on any combination of features you wish. This system is designed to make you happy but keep the company's costs down.

If you participate in a company-sponsored savings plan, what percentage of your salary may you contribute? What percentage of your contribution is matched by your company? How soon does the company contribution vest?

Stock purchase plans are popular in growing companies where employees want to own shares of rising stock. These plans often allow the employee to put away 10 percent of his salary and to buy a share as soon as his account has accumulated 85 percent of the market price. It effect, he receives a company-sponsored 15 percent discount. These plans can be attractive, but far more risky than a more conventional savings plan. *What percentage of your salary may you allocate toward stock purchases? Are shares available to you at a discount?*

How many weeks of maternity leave does your company allow? Paid or unpaid? Eight to twelve weeks is the accepted norm, although extensions are possible. Some companies grant longer leaves that are unpaid. Some respond to a doctor's recommendation that additional time is needed, and disability leave can be added to that if complications require it. These are generalizations; check your company's policy for specifics. Are you guaranteed your old position back when you return?

Vacation time is pretty straightforward. *How many weeks of paid vacation are you allowed? How many weeks are added for increasing years of service?*

Company automobiles are given to those who need them to fulfill their responsibilities. *Which costs are you responsible for? Are there limitations on your use of the company car?* If you don't get a company car, you may be given an allowance toward use of your own car instead.

Company-sponsored club memberships fall into the same category as company cars: Membership in a lunch, health, or country club is often considered appropriate if it will help you conduct your business. *What clubs do you have use of?*

These few entries alone make a fine wish list, but they're just a beginning as you look at all the things your company provides for you. Senior managers may get to pass along various personal expenses, from the cost of commuting to the cost of maintaining a separate residence. Small wonder that companies with good benefits and insurances often pay 30 percent of your salary to provide them.

Check Out the Pension Plan

○ Does your company have a pension plan?
○ Is it a defined-benefit or defined-contribution plan?
○ Is your fund portable in the event that you leave the company?
○ What is the basis on which benefits are awarded?
○ Are your vested benefits "frozen" if you leave the company before retirement?

You're naive if you don't look into the provisions of your company's pension plan. It's more important than you may now think, and plans vary greatly. I'm no expert on pensions, but I've seen enough things happen, both good and bad, to be able to alert you to some of the considerations.

What kind of plan do you have? The old standard pension plan said you would receive so much if you stayed with the company for so many years, and the maximum benefit generally worked out to about half your salary. This is a defined-benefit plan, and it's expensive for companies.

With a defined-contribution plan, the company invests a specific amount for you, but only rarely does it promise a specific benefit. This approach is cheaper for the company and also makes it easier for the company to give you your fund if you leave. One of your concerns with a defined-contribution plan, however, is how your funds are being invested—both the type of investment and the skill with which your funds are administered. Those who are young and early in their career are after growth, and some risk is appropriate; those near retirement who are about to draw their benefits prefer more stability and less risk. *How are your funds invested? Can you have your account segregated in an investment of your choice?*

Once your benefits are vested, they're yours. But if you leave a company prior to retirement, the company may want to keep your pension fund until you're entitled to it at retirement age. If you think you can invest it better than your company can, ask for it and see what happens.

In most instances, a company will freeze your vested benefits if you leave before retirement. The dollar amounts remain as they were the day you left. It's possible for you to have vested rights that you can't claim for 30 years. If they've been frozen, inflation could have eroded their original value by the time you get hold of them.

Because companies are taking more interest in pension plans, you should, as well. If your company is going to get creative with your retirement money, you certainly want to know what it's doing.

What Do You Receive in Insurance?

Which of the following types of insurance does your company provide for you:

- O Medical?
- O Hospitalization?
- O Major medical?
- O Dental?
- O Optical?
- O Life?
- O Disability?

As medical costs continue to escalate and more sophisticated treatments become available, protection from medical expenses has become imperative. The more protection your company offers you, the better. Insurance coverage is *not* all the same, and the time to understand the limits of your coverage is before you file a claim.

To put your health insurance in perspective, check the annual deductible for each type of coverage as well as the percentage you pay after the deductible has been satisfied. *Is there a maximum amount after which the company assumes all additional expenses?* Some companies will underwrite your membership in a health maintenance organization (HMO). Some policies cover psychiatric care; some specifically exclude it.

If you're considering having a baby, read the fine print. Find out what procedures and expenses aren't covered. Some plans offer reimbursement for midwife and alternative birth center care. Some even offer "rewards" for leaving the hospital early. You'll have to switch to a family plan, if you haven't already done so; bear in mind that if you try to switch after you're pregnant, or if you change employers while you're pregnant, the pregnancy may be regarded as a preexisting condition that's not covered.

Check how much life insurance your company carries for you. *What is the face amount? Does the policy provide for an increasing benefit? Can you buy more coverage at reduced rates?*

Disability insurance is designed to give you some financial support in the event that you cannot work, either short- or long-term, due to accident or illness. Are disability benefits based on a percentage of your annual salary or your total compensation (there can be a big difference!)? *For how many years are long-term disability benefits paid? Is there a maximum amount?*

Established and profitable companies generally give the most insurance benefits and struggling companies the least. Laws require that benefit plans be equal for all employees in a company, so there is no fear that you're getting less than someone else. Also, plans are often similar within an industry, unless there is a great disparity in the relative strength of the different companies in the industry.

What do you think of your insurance coverages? If you're not happy, what are your alternatives? Can you buy additional coverage at reduced rates?

What About Relocation Costs?

○ Are you aware of all the different kinds of assistance your company can provide with relocation costs?

○ How much assistance does your company offer?
○ Are relocation benefits less for new employees?
○ What level of benefits do you have?
○ Will you require spousal assistance when you move?

You probably know from experience that moving expenses can be staggering, from closing costs to the broker's fee to new appliances. If your company wants you badly enough, it will find a way to take the sting out of your relocation expenses. Senior managers can negotiate all kinds of favorable arrangements, even up to getting the corporation to absorb much of the cost of a new home.

See the following lists for a rundown of some of the ways in which your company can help you with relocation expenses. No company gives all these things, but you should be familiar with your options as you investigate what your company does provide.

Selling Your Old Home Your company may:

- Make arrangements with a relocation firm to ensure the sale of your home.
- Assist you financially if you're forced to carry two mortgages for a while.
- Pay the real estate broker's commission on the sale of your home.
- Contribute to closing costs (for example, pay legal fees).

Moving to Your New Home Your company may pay for:

- House-hunting trips.
- Temporary living arrangements.
- Inspection costs.
- Miscellaneous costs to make the new home livable (some companies will give you a month's salary).
- Shipment of household goods.

Loan Assistance Your company may:

- Provide you with an equity loan if the sale of your old home doesn't yield enough money to buy a new one.
- Provide payment assistance for a while because of the mortgage interest differential on your new home.
- Secure a preferential mortgage interest rate.
- Offer an interest-free loan.

If you're relocating to work for a new company, find out whether you're getting the benefits new hires receive (generally less favorable) or those existing employees receive. Management hires usually get the existing-employee plan.

Some of the items on the lists apply only during periods of high inflation. If you're having a tough time selling your old home because the market is poor, your company can bail you out in a number of ways. If relocating will cause your mortgage payments to leap because interest rates have zoomed, the company can offer payment assistance or perhaps get you a more favorable mortgage rate. If the company assists you in a manner that will cause you to pay additional income taxes, it may give you more money to compensate.

It pays to anticipate your costs as early as possible and to discuss the coverage your company will provide, since arrangements vary widely and can get complicated. When you do move, there are so many incidental expenses involved just in personalizing a new home that you want to make sure the administrative costs are covered. *How does your plan look?*

ENJOYABLES

This section will deal with your job's intangible rewards: the satisfaction you receive from doing your work, the desirability of your job's location within the country, job-related travel opportunities, and the pleasure you get from working with your colleagues. While these "enjoyables" cannot be deposited in your bank account, don't overlook their importance as you evaluate your current position or an outside offer.

Consider Your Job Satisfaction

○ Do you look forward to going to work every day?
○ Are you happy?
○ Are you distracted, envious, or unusually critical?

Job satisfaction is something you feel in yourself—something you don't want to lose once you have it. It doesn't come easily and doesn't relate to being with the biggest, fastest, or best, or even with being any of those things yourself. It's a feeling that is yours alone, and it's important.

If you're truly satisfied, you won't resent having to go to work, or get distracted easily, or feel envious of your colleagues, or criticize everybody. Happiness and personal satisfaction are powerful rewards and may lead to even greater achievements than dogged maneuvering for a competitive advantage.

Go back to Chapter 5 and see what your ideal job would be. *How close to it are you?*

What About Geographic Location?

○ Do you love where you are?
○ Are the sports you enjoy readily available?
○ Do the cultural aspects in your area coincide with your interests?
○ Do you like the climate?

Different areas of the country capture different people, and I mean capture. Once there, they find it impossible to leave. Once you get captured by a place, you'll be willing to give up many things to stay there. I've seen people pass up great opportunities in order to stay in a certain location—and for them, this was the correct decision.

If you are where you want to be, this will make your life more pleasant and full. You'll also be more inventive on your job to make sure you stay important where you are. Think carefully before leaving your ideal location.

Is Travel an Important Factor?

○ Does your job require you to travel?
○ How often?
○ How far afield?
○ Do you enjoy the places to which you're obliged to go?
○ Can you schedule private time there?
○ Could you afford to go to these places on your own?

This point is addressed to those who find company travel a pleasure. For you, it's an "enjoyable." If you're considering a job change, here's the place to compare the amount and type of travel required in your prospective job with what you have now.

Does your business travel enhance your expertise? Can you take your spouse along occasionally at not too much additional cost? If you enjoy the travel you do with your company, make an effort to keep the responsibilities that keep you traveling. In a strictly desk job, you might go nuts.

Are Your Associates a Plus?

○ Do your peers share your interests?
○ Do they inspire you?
○ Are you proud to work with them?

In Chapter 3, you took a close look at your relationship with your peers. This is the same point, but in the balance sheet. If you're with a group you enjoy, that's very important and hard to duplicate elsewhere.

Some people love to be in an environment that attracts a particular type. These people get an industry in their blood— whether it's academia or investing or theater or oil—and it's not something to take lightly.

If your peers turn you on, that's truly an "enjoyable" of your job. To put it in perspective, however, ask yourself whether it will last. *Is it the environment that makes the people special, or vice versa? Which could you find elsewhere?*

BUSINESS BUILDERS

Here you will examine those aspects of your job that promote your professional growth: the relevance of the challenges you face, the value of the experience you gain, the usefulness of the contacts you make, and the strength of the reputation you're building. Taken together, these "business builders" constitute a solid professional foundation that you should consider in evaluating any position.

Consider the Challenge and Experience Associated with Your Job

○ Are you being challenged almost to your limits?
○ Do you enjoy it?
○ Are the challenges in line with your career goals?
○ Is the experience you gain highly regarded in your industry?

Just enough challenge is tremendously stimulating, but too much is deadly. How much is too much is strictly a personal decision. As I describe the challenge of a job, some candidates will say "No, thanks," while others can't wait to start.

The outcome of a true challenge is not predictable. You want enough challenge in your job so that you have a chance to stretch, but not so much that you're out of your depth. The experience you gain from handling a challenge makes you more capable, and your pride upon mastering it is much like the exhilaration you feel after successfully running an obstacle course. *Are others impressed by your accomplishments? Do they think the experience you're gaining is important? Do you?*

Are Your Contacts Valuable?

○ Does your job allow you to meet people of importance?
○ Do they in turn introduce you to others?
○ Has this helped you professionally?

Contacts has become a tainted word, one implying something opportunistic. But contacts are a reality of business life, and they're no more opportunistic than any other aspect of business. The fact that I devoted all of Chapter 3 to your relationships illustrates the significance of networking as a "business builder."

You need a wide circle of people whom you can call on to help you solve your business problems. If your job puts you in an excellent position to make good contacts, that is a professional advantage worth noting. Consider why professionals and managers rotate from business to academia to government and back: They gain contacts, as well as reputation, which is the next point.

Don't Forget Your Reputation

○ Is your reputation growing?
○ Who knows what you're doing?
○ To whom is it important?
○ How can you leverage your present reputation?

You already considered the importance of visibility and recognition for your performance in Chapter 2. If your job provides you with the opportunity to build your professional reputation, that's a definite plus. You may even consider reputation a key element of your compensation, since the right reputation can be worth far more than the dollars you're paid.

You can build a good reputation by working with experts in your field and having your name associated with theirs, by working in a leading-edge company, by handling a special project or turnaround, by setting records, or by doing what you do best wherever you are. *Does your company afford you the opportunity to build your reputation?*

COULD THIS BE YOU?

Peter had just celebrated both his 10th anniversary with his company and his 35th birthday. He was beginning to think of himself as middle-aged, and he was a little glum. Things hadn't turned out as he'd expected. He hadn't made his million as so many hotshots his age already had, and in fact, he didn't see it happening at all.

The morning paper had carried an article about double-income couples with no children who had taken up polo because they found tennis and yachting too mundane. Peter shook his head. With two kids' college educations to worry about, he and his wife didn't qualify as "dincs," and they certainly weren't about to take up polo. They couldn't even afford to take up the old linoleum in the kitchen.

Peter thought it was time to look closely at his financial package, something he hadn't bothered to do when he'd come on board ten years ago. He'd come in on a fast track, and although he still had a good job, somehow his progress had slowed down.

Peter took out a pad and pencil and tried to pin down his compensation. He realized he didn't really know all the ins and outs of his insurance coverages, and he was a little vague about certain aspects of the company's pension plan, but all in all he knew enough to get started.

His starting place was his base salary—$50,000. He also had incentive compensation of $10,000 and an overall bonus of $6,000, for a total of $66,000 coming to him that year. Nothing spread forward. Peter had heard that middle-level executives on a fast track often received compensation equal to two times their age, but thinking about this just depressed him.

On the tax-deferred side, Peter had a small profit-sharing account to which the company contributed 3 percent of his salary each year. Nice, but insignificant. The stock purchase plan did nicely, though. He contributed 10 percent of his salary and bought company stock at a 15 percent discount. On a good stock like his company's, that made an impact.

The perks were pretty good. Peter never thought much about vacation. He just took what he wanted as he could fit it in and hadn't heard any grumbling about it from his boss. He had an automobile allowance, which not too many others had. He would have liked to have a club membership, but at least he could sign a vice-president's name at the club when he needed to entertain clients.

No doubt about it, Peter was getting older, and pensions were on his mind. He was vested now, but all that meant was that he would receive $8,400 a year starting at age 65 if he were to leave the company tomorrow. The benefit was defined, which he liked, and he knew it would increase the longer he stayed with the company. Still, he wished he could invest the money himself over the next 31 years. A college friend of Peter's had left a consulting firm a year ago and had been given a lump-sum distribution from the profit-sharing account. He'd increased it 27 percent last year. Peter didn't really know who took care of investing his company's pension funds, but since the benefits were defined and the company healthy, he wasn't concerned.

Insurance. His general feeling was that the coverages were good, but each one was different. He'd have to talk to someone in human resources and get the details straight for once. He knew there was a disability plan but had no idea what it would pay. Undoubtedly, it would be less than he was making. The thought made him nervous.

What else? All in all, Peter was satisfied with his job and liked his peers. What he really liked, though, was being able to live and work in an area that allowed him to participate in world-class sailing ten minutes from his house. He had to admit he'd maneuvered out of various business trips so he wouldn't miss races. The sailing was taking up a lot of his time. Maybe he'd been making a trade-off there. Maybe that was why he'd slid off the fast track.

Just how far off the fast track was he, anyway? Peter had come to the company for challenge, and for three or four years he'd had plenty. When had been his last real challenge, though? Too long ago. It didn't really show because the company was moving so fast, but he'd definitely gotten comfortable. If he got aggressive again, and took on something with a little more punch, maybe he could get his compensation up.

The situation wasn't dire. Peter was in pretty good shape, and he had a lot of good business contacts. He was constantly on the phone. Still, most of his calls seemed to be with the Steady Eddys who kept things moving rather than with the heavy-hitters. If he could get his hands on a project that would give him more visibility, maybe he could get through to some of the more important guys.

At this point, those guys wouldn't know who he was. That hurt. The truth was, although Peter had arrived ten years ago with a hot reputation, he'd let it slide. He winced. He'd become a Steady Eddy himself.

Peter had started this whole review by thinking about his financial package, and here he was taking a much broader look at himself and his job. He was happy, but now he didn't know if that was good or bad. He needed to figure out what he really wanted to be. He had some more thinking to do.

PULLING IT TOGETHER

Cash makes your life workable, but I hope you now see that there are a number of other things you get for all that you give. Even though some can't be measured in dollars, they have considerable value. Takehomeables, enjoyables, and business builders all have a role in making you stronger professionally and better for yourself and your family. An embittered or over-stressed achiever is no treat to anybody, including himself.

What trade-offs have you found? Like Peter, you may be enjoying yourself more than you should at the expense of your progress. Or maybe you're not enjoying your job enough. If you're lucky, the mix is right-on.

You may have turned up some things you hadn't fully appreciated before, which is nice. You may also have outlined some areas where your understanding isn't as complete as you thought it was. Maybe you've found that your compensation is generous by industry norms. If not, you may have joined the great majority who want more.

If you're trying to compare a prospective job with your existing position, you will know less about the new position and may be inclined to think of it in more glowing terms than is realistic. Ask for the data you need, and be sure to look beyond the obvious. For all that you are contemplating giving, take a careful look at the rewards that will be coming your way.

13

What Is Your Career Fitness Index?

That first time through should have been tough. Some of the questions made you face embarrassing answers, and others forced you to search for additional information. You probably looked at a number of things for the first time. This chapter will help you put them in perspective and make sense of your discoveries before you decide what you're going to do.

What follows is a list of all the points covered in *What Your Boss Can't Tell You.* Use it to summarize your career review, to evaluate the overall picture, and to make plans. Periodic use of the checklists in this chapter allows you to spot trends, compare the results of different reviews, and see if you are meeting your objectives. Use this chapter as a quick checkup in between thorough reviews and as a reference for finding your way around the book. You can also use it to compare a job you have against one you've been offered (more about this in Chapter 14). The checklists are a place to keep track; they are as important as you choose to make them.

Some encouragement: Performing a career checkup every year or so will alert you to how things are changing, and how fast, so you can take appropriate steps. A review when you're faced with a decision can help you make the right move for the right reasons. If you're alert, you'll be able to anticipate career crises, and whatever happens, you can be prepared with fallback plans.

Each time you review the checklists, you'll become more familiar with the range of variables that can affect you and your company. Each review will be easier and faster, since you'll have benchmarks from previous reviews in mind as a basis of comparison. If you want to go back and focus on a particular area, the following checklists will give the page number of the section you need.

Done annually, the career checkup can be a powerful tool. It can make you aware of whether you've been coasting. It may force you to admit that you didn't do much unusual last year. It will reveal whether your objectives are changing and can allow you to judge whether your value to your company is increasing or decreasing.

You probably have a gut feeling for how you're doing. This is your chance to quantify that feeling so you can do something constructive with your insights. You'll find that having one factor in great shape doesn't guarantee an overall clean bill of health, and you may find that a number of complaints you thought were unrelated are actually symptoms of a deeper illness. Isolated aspects of your situation may be irrelevant or overshadowed by other factors you've never before taken into account. You need to take a close look at the entire picture, but this is very difficult to do without help. Luckily for you, help has arrived.

If you want to score yourself on a chapter, rate yourself from one to ten on each section (one is terrible, ten is nirvana). Then add up the section points and divide this total by the number of sections in that chapter. Example: Chapter 1 has 12 sections, and your section point total is 60. Your Career Fitness Index (C.F.I.) for that chapter is 5 (60 divided by 12). To get an overall score, enter your Career Fitness Index for each chapter on the chart on pages 262 and 263, and generate your final Career Fitness Index in the same manner.

Working your career checkup down to a number is more of a fun thing to do than a truly helpful one, but at least a poor result will send you back to the text to see where the problems lie.

The checklists are designed to make sure you recognize all the variables affecting you and your company, keep them in perspective, and spot new trends early on. They are yours to tailor to your needs. You can add factors to the checklists or delete those that don't apply to you.

Review of Chapter 1

How Well Are You Managing Your Manager?

Instead of worrying about whether or not your boss likes you, focus on how to earn his respect. Your boss is busy with other concerns; it's up to you to create the best possible working relationship—and your boss isn't going to tell you how to do this. Try to recognize your boss's management style, his interests and priorities, and where he may be headed so you can plan accordingly. With a better understanding of how your boss operates, you'll be able to work with him more effectively—and to target strengths to acquire yourself.

Chapter Notes and Checkup Comments:

Checklist 1: Managing Your Manager

Page No.	Section	Date of review			
		Score			
5	Examine Your Relationship with Your Boss				
6	Consider Your Boss's Personal Interests				
7	Assess Your Boss's Management Style				
8	Study How Your Boss Handles Conflict				
10	Watch How Your Boss Develops Others				
11	Review Your Boss's Track Record				
13	Assess Your Boss's Corporate Goals				
14	Weigh Your Boss's Political Clout				
16	Represent Your Boss Effectively				
16	Acquire Your Boss's Strengths				
19	Does Your Boss Evaluate You Constructively?				
20	Do You Have the Potential to Succeed or Follow Your Boss?				
	TOTAL				
	Divide total by 12 to get your chapter C.F.I.				

Review of Chapter 2

Is Your Performance as Good as You Think It Is?

You need to determine whether or not you are making a significant contribution to your company's objectives, are doing all you can to optimize your performance, are a valuable member of your team, and understand exactly what your accomplishments have been. Your boss can give you some insights regarding the quality of your performance, but matters of great significance to you may interest him only minimally. An outstanding performance depends upon a wide range of factors; the variables are set forth here so you can gauge your achievements and strengths—or should you discover them, deficiencies. Be alert to the real reasons for your successes and try to analyze whether your performance would be as good—or better, or worse—in another setting.

Chapter Notes and Checkup Comments:

Checklist 2: The Quality of Your Performance

Page No.	Section	Date of review			
		Score			
25	Assess the Value of Your Performance				
27	How Close Are You to the Primary Business of Your Company?				
28	Determine Your Annual Plan				
30	Achieve Your Objectives				
31	Weigh Your Performance Relative to That of Your Peers				
33	Assess Your Performance as a Manager and Leader				
35	Consider Your Performance as a Developer of People				
36	What About Championing Something New?				
37	Assess Your Involvement in Outside Activities				
39	Examine Your Track Record				
41	Gain Recognition for Your Performance				
42	Consider the Transferability of Your Performance				
	TOTAL				
	Divide total by 12 to get your chapter C.F.I.				

Review of Chapter 3

Do Your Working Relationships Work?

It takes time and energy to cultivate an array of constructive working relationships, but they help you get the job done, they're essential for your progress, and they act as career insurance. They're also something no one else can maintain for you. Here's a checklist covering a whole range of relationships to nurture—including some you are probably neglecting.

Chapter Notes and Checkup Comments:

Checklist 3: Your Working Relationships

Page No.	Section	Date of review			
		Score			
49	Examine Your Relationship with Your Subordinates				
51	Consider Your Relationship with Political Factions				
53	Assess Your Relationship with Your Peers				
54	Think About Your Relationship with Your Boss's Peers				
55	Take Stock of Your Relationship with Senior Management				
57	Examine Your Relationship with a Mentor				
59	Consider Your Relationship with Your Company's Human Resources Department				
60	Assess Your Relationship with Your Customers or Clients				
62	Review Your Relationship with Experts in Your Field				
63	Study Your Relationship with Former Associates				
65	Think About Your Relationship with Your Family				
	TOTAL				
	Divide total by 11 to get your chapter C.F.I.				

Review of Chapter 4

How Do Others Perceive You?

I find that people are often oblivious to the impression they make. They never bother to find out how others perceive them. Since this is information that others seldom volunteer, particularly if the news is bad, you can't rely on your boss to tell you how you are perceived. To work effectively with others, you need to know what it's really like to work with you. Once you become aware of the many factors upon which you are being judged, you can correct any flaws in your presentation. The factors shown on the checklist are important to your long-term business relationships and career success.

Chapter Notes and Checkup Comments:

Checklist 4: Others' Perceptions

Page No.	Section	Date of review			
		Score			
71	Take Stock of Your First Impression				
72	Consider Your Body Language				
73	What About Your Eyes?				
75	Listen to Your Voice				
77	Assess Your Judgment				
78	Take Stock of Your Ability to Communicate				
79	Are You Persuasive?				
81	Consider Your Foresight				
82	Can You Handle Risk?				
83	What About Your Use of Humor?				
	TOTAL				
	Divide total by 10 to get your chapter C.F.I.				

Review of Chapter 5

How Well Do You Know Yourself?

Recognizing your own deepest desires isn't an indulgence, it's essential to your personal and professional well-being. If you are not suited to your job, you'll eventually lose out to someone who is. Take this opportunity to put your personality, abilities, values, and goals in perspective so you can identify a career path you'll pursue with enthusiasm; then monitor your career progress and changing goals over time. This is the most private chapter of all. No one, not even the most perceptive or sympathetic boss, can presume to know your personal goals and priorities.

Chapter Notes and Checkup Comments:

Checklist 5: Self-Knowledge

Page No.	Section	Date of review			
		Score			
89	What Are Your Natural Inclinations?				
91	Consider Your Private Goals				
92	Assess Your Personality				
94	What About Your Sense of Loyalty?				
95	What Is Your Area of Expertise?				
97	Determine Your Career Goals				
98	Take Steps to Achieve Your Career Goals				
100	So You Want to Be President				
101	So You Want to Be an Entrepreneur				
	TOTAL				
	Divide total by 9 to get your chapter C.F.I.				

Review of Chapter 6

What Makes the Company Tick?

Failing to examine the corporate environment in which you have chosen to work is a serious oversight, for you need to know if your company's operations are vigorous and if its personality and values are in tune with your own. Look at the checklist overview of how your company functions, its strengths and weaknesses, the source of its momentum, and where it may be headed. See if the company's organization and atmosphere are conducive to your best ideas and most productive work, and check for weak links and vulnerabilities.

Chapter Notes and Checkup Comments:

Checklist 6: The Company

Page No.	Section	Date of review			
		Score			
110	Take Stock of Your Company's Image and First Impression				
111	Consider Your Company's Personality				
112	Pinpoint Your Company's Driving Force				
113	How Well Is Information Distributed?				
115	How Much Cooperation Is Encouraged?				
116	Assess Your Company's Work Environment and People Programs				
117	How Is Your Company Structured?				
118	Look at Manufacturing and Production				
120	Consider Research and Development (R&D)				
121	What About Environmental Considerations?				
122	Examine International Operations				
	TOTAL				
	Divide total by 11 to get your chapter C.F.I.				

Review of Chapter 7

How Strong Are the Products and Markets?

You want to be in a dynamic company that has good products, strong markets, and the capacity to innovate and stay ahead. Try to identify the characteristics that make your company's products and services viable—or vulnerable. Your belief in your products may strengthen or weaken as a result of this chapter, but you will know where your company stands.

Chapter Notes and Checkup Comments:

Checklist 7: Products and Markets

Page No.	Section	Date of review			
		Score			
127	Take a Look at Your Company's Products				
128	Consider Product Quality				
130	What Are the Markets for Your Company's Products?				
131	What Is Your Company's Market Share?				
132	Assess Pricing Strategy				
133	Examine Profit Margins				
134	What About Advertising and Promotion?				
135	Consider Packaging				
136	How Are Sales and Distribution Handled?				
137	Take a Look at Your Company's Customers				
	TOTAL				
	Divide total by 10 to get your chapter C.F.I.				

Review of Chapter 8

How Good Are the People and How Well Does the Company Develop Them?

When it comes to people management, companies differ dramatically. One corporation chews up talent; another promotes it. One is quick to hire and fire; another makes an effort to develop its employees and build strength from within. You need to know whether or not your company can be depended upon to help your career progress. You can't predict the future, but you can tell a great deal about your chances of prospering with your company by examining the factors outlined in the accompanying checklist.

Chapter Notes and Checkup Comments:

Checklist 8: Hiring-Development-Separation Cycle of Employment

Page No.	Section	Date of review			
		Score			
143	Consider Your Company's Hiring Process				
144	Is College Recruiting Effective?				
145	What About Outside Hiring?				
147	How Effective Is In-House Training?				
148	Consider Your Company's Use of Outside Training				
150	Examine the Evaluation Procedures				
152	Take a Look at Succession Planning				
153	Is There a Good System for Posting Job Opportunities?				
154	How Are Firing and Separation Handled?				
	TOTAL				
	Divide total by 9 to get your chapter C.F.I.				

Review of Chapter 9

Who's in Charge Here?

This chapter helps you look carefully at your company's senior management and board of directors—those who set the tone of the company and determine its direction and policies. Look for patterns that will make you either more or less comfortable. There are things you should know about that your boss may not recognize or, if he does, may not wish to divulge.

Chapter Notes and Checkup Comments:

Checklist 9: Top Management

Page No.	Section	Date of review			
		Score			
161	Examine Your Company's Chief Executive Officer				
162	Consider Your Company's Owners/Controlling Interests				
163	What Is the Track Record of Top Executives?				
164	Check Out the Ethics of Senior Management				
165	What About Litigation?				
167	Assess the Goals of Senior Management				
168	Take a Look at the Age Spread in Senior Management				
169	Does Senior Management Share a Similar Background?				
170	Consider the Turnover in Senior Management				
171	Study Your Company's Board of Directors				
173	What Can You Learn from the Chairman's Toys?				
	TOTAL				
	Divide total by 11 to get your chapter C.F.I.				

Review of Chapter 10

How Good Is Your Company's Financial Health?

You need more than corporate reassurances about the financial well-being of your company. You need facts. Look carefully at your company's financial pressure points and try to identify trends, both favorable and disturbing. Look for financial inconsistencies that may hide dangers, and try to spot unusual assets or liabilities that don't show up on the balance sheet. Here you can compare your company's fiscal health to that of the competition and also consider whether your company can acquire—or may be acquired by—others.

Chapter Notes and Checkup Comments:

Checklist 10: The Financials

Page No.	Section	Date of review			
		Score			
181	What Are the Company's Revenues?				
183	What Are the Company's Earnings?				
184	What Is the Company's Cash Flow?				
186	What Is the Company's Debt Picture?				
187	What Unusual Financial Liabilities Exist?				
188	What Undervalued Assets Exist?				
189	What is the Company's Capital Structure?				
190	Who Owns the Company's Stock?				
192	What Is Wall Street Saying?				
	TOTAL				
	Divide total by 9 to get your chapter C.F.I.				

Review of Chapter 11

Is the Job Doable?

I find that people often assume in good faith that if they have been given a job to do, it must be doable. Not true! There may be certain factors built into your job that will prevent you from succeeding despite your best efforts. Your boss may or may not recognize these land mines, and may or may not tell you what you need to know. You must determine the availability of what you require in order to do the job and recognize situations that could sabotage you. Using this checklist, you'll be able to distinguish a job no one has done before but that is do-able from one that is impossible. If your job is difficult but practicable, you'll know what to ask for; if it's impossible, you'll know not to waste your time.

Chapter Notes and Checkup Comments:

Checklist 11: The Job's Doability

Page No.	Section	Date of review		
		Score		
200	What Are Your Specific Responsibilities?			
202	Have You Got Enough Authority to Do the Job?			
203	Must You Infringe on Anyone's Turf?			
204	How Broad Is the Commitment to Your Job?			
205	Are the Funds You Need Available?			
206	Do You Have Enough Time?			
207	Have You Got the Right People?			
208	Are There Attitude Problems in Your Group?			
209	Does Your Operation Have the Productive Capacity You Need?			
210	Is the Technology in Your Division Up-to-Date?			
211	Do You Have Assured Supplies of Raw Materials?			
212	What Has Been the Turnover in Your Position?			
	TOTAL			
	Divide total by 12 to get your chapter C.F.I.			

Review of Chapter 12

What Do You Get for What You Give?

Here is a concise compensation checklist that includes both the financial and psychological rewards of working. For your efforts you receive "take-homeables," "enjoyables," and "business builders." Any job provides something in each of these categories, most of which you take for granted. Look at each category and at the balance between all three. Recognize the trade-offs and consider what adjustments you'd like to make.

Chapter Notes and Checkup Comments:

Checklist 12: Your Compensation Picture

Page No.	Section	Date of review			
		Score			
	Takehomeables				
219	What About Current Cash?				
221	Consider Your Tax-Deferred Compensation				
222	What Do You Receive in Benefits and Perks?				
224	Check Out the Pension Plan				
225	What Do You Receive in Insurance?				
226	What About Relocation Costs?				
	Enjoyables				
229	Consider Your Job Satisfaction				
229	What About Geographic Location?				
230	Is Travel an Important Factor?				
230	Are Your Associates a Plus?				
	Business Builders				
231	Consider the Challenge and Experience Associated with Your Job				
231	Are Your Contacts Valuable?				
232	Don't Forget Your Reputation				
	TOTAL				
	Divide total by 13 to get your chapter C.F.I.				

Your Career Fitness Index

Enter in the chart below your career fitness index (C.F.I.) for each chapter. Then total your points and divide by 12 to arrive at your overall C.F.I.

		Date of review		
	Chapter	*Chapter C.F.I.*		
1	How Well Are You Managing Your Manager?			
2	Is Your Performance as Good as You Think It Is?			
3	Do Your Working Relationships Work?			
4	How Do Others Perceive You?			
5	How Well Do You Know Yourself?			
6	What Makes the Company Tick?			
7	How Strong Are the Products and Markets?			
8	How Good Are the People and How Well Does the Company Develop Them?			

9	Who's in Charge Here?				
10	How Good Is Your Company's Financial Health?				
11	Is the Job Doable?				
12	What Do You Get for What You Give?				
	TOTAL				
	Divide total by 12 to get your overall C.F.I.				

PULLING IT TOGETHER

Whether you used numbers and calculated your overall Career Fitness Index, or made notes to indicate strong and weak points, or merely let your eyes run over the checklists, you have just reviewed all the points covered in this book. Hopefully, you have found strengths to exploit. You may have spotted changing situations to watch more closely, weaknesses to correct, or even collisions about to occur.

On the big issues, it may be helpful to get together with a colleague from marketing and another from finance. If you all put your conclusions on the table, you'll have an even clearer idea of the strength of your company.

Without changing jobs, you are now in a position to contribute more constructively to your performance reviews and to the determination of your annual plans. You know how to align yourself with company goals and can now pursue your own peak professional performance by choosing where to expend your energy.

If you've found things are bad, at least you've gained lead time to explore alternatives before being forced to do so. See what you can do to improve the situation, and before you do anything drastic, read the next chapter.

14

How Do You Know If It's Time to Make a Move?

Congratulations. You've just finished an extremely thorough analysis of your job, your company, and your ambitions. You put familiar information in a new perspective, considered things you never thought of before, and have a clearer idea of what lies ahead. The beauty of your career checkup is that you've been honest with yourself, completely open, and have arrived at your own conclusions. No one has told you anything.

You've invested a lot of time in your checkup and have many new insights. You're burning to do something with them. What now?

Well, it depends. If you're happy in your job, turning in a strong performance, and handling enough challenges to keep upgrading your skills, then you're unusually fortunate. Say, "Hallelujah," but not too loud. Then ask yourself why you've been so successful and how you can continue to succeed. You need not make a move to another company, but isn't there a greater level of success to which you aspire? Are you using every tool at your disposal? Have you perhaps gotten a little bit complacent?

If you're feeling uneasy and want to do something bold, be careful! Don't move too fast with your new information. When your doctor puts away his stethoscope and gives you the results of your physical examination, you don't throw out your body because a few problems have turned up. Similarly, you shouldn't jump to another job just because your present one is less than perfect. Think of it this way: You've looked at all the factors in your situation, thought about the mix, and came up with an imbalance. What will it take to restore that balance? Take a moment to pinpoint which factors are out of whack. Are you at fault, or are you in the wrong spot? Can you correct the problems, or are they out of your hands? How much effort would it take to salvage your job? What would you like to gain by moving elsewhere?

A Good Match Is as Important to Keep as It Is to Find

Some advice: *Don't underestimate the value of your investment in your current position.* You've put a lot into your present company. You've nurtured relationships, you've learned the procedures, you understand the products and the company traditions, you know the company's strengths and weaknesses. This is all real and valuable information. And another thought. You had a lot to do with getting yourself where you are. The likelihood is that you won't move to a vastly different situation. I've seen too many people making wrong choices and moving when they shouldn't. Today there's too much talk about changing jobs and not enough about making the most of the job you have. Too many executives are actually standing on soggy milk cartons as they reach up to change a light bulb. They're so busy focusing on the benefits of more light that they're oblivious to the possible consequences of what they are doing.

If you're restless, what is really causing you to want to make a change? Every company has warts, and so does every boss, but you probably have your share, as well. Your career checkup may have turned up more flaws than you anticipated, but enough to change jobs? I don't think that's likely in most cases.

I've found that many executives get seduced by the idea of that one perfect job, as well as by one last challenge. They want to take all their years of experience and really wrap their arms around a job that will make them proud—maybe even run their own show. The problem is that many of them are naive. Often they've been in one company most of their working lives and are more dedicated than talented. While they have idealistic intentions and a glowing idea of their next move, they don't recognize all the risks involved.

Keeping Your Options Open

Now that I've given you my gospel on staying where you are, let me qualify my remarks. *Making the most of the job you have does not mean closing off your alternatives.* If you don't keep your visibility high and prepare backup plans, you're foolish.

Imagine how you might feel if you got tagged. A call from your boss leads to a pleasant chat, followed by a rational explanation of how bad things are. Your boss tells you how sorry he is to let you go and how eager he is to help . . . that is, until the next person walks into his office.

Sound too dramatic? Maybe. But it's close.

"Aha," you say. "I've read *What Color Is Your Parachute?*, I have a well-established network, and I also have a friend who will help me write a good résumé." Fine. You are entering the search phase, a period that can last from ten minutes to ten months or longer—a tedious time that is a drain on you, your family, and your friends. It's a wasteful exercise that can often be avoided.

Even if you think your job is the best in the world, that management loves you, and that your company is without equal, you still must be prepared to leave. Over the course of your career, you will probably change jobs four or five times, and at least one of these changes will not be at your instigation. Call it mutual agreement. Whatever you call it, you're still out.

It can happen for any number of reasons: business cycle turns, reorganization, management changes, bankruptcy, deregulation, worldwide competitive forces. All take their toll. The corporate environment is constantly changing, and your company is under no obligation to take care of you if you've outlived your usefulness.

Contingency planning is as close as you'll come to career insurance: It can head off the terrible waste that occurs if you are forced to change jobs and are not prepared. You don't question a fire drill, do you? The fact that an actual fire is unlikely is irrelevant. But be warned: Planning to change jobs is not simple.

I've heard many people say, "I've never looked for a job. I've always been sought." Well, they acted helpless. They didn't make the extra effort and take the extra time to plan for the unexpected and to keep their options open.

The best safety net is to be as valuable as you can where you are, to keep updating your skills, and to have a solid reputation that is recognized in your industry. Go back to Chapter 2 and reconsider what efforts you might make to increase your visibility, for this is the only way to make sure alternatives will be presented to you when you most need or want them. You want your name to come up in the event that you truly do wish to initiate a job change—or are forced to do so.

When Jumping the Track Is Not a Derailment

Another way to broaden your opportunities is to be receptive to alternative career paths. If your company is deteriorating, or your industry is contracting, or you just aren't happy with your present route, you may need to be particularly resourceful and open-minded as you investigate your options.

The fast track isn't the only track, and it isn't the right track for everyone. Since the ranks thin toward the top of any organization, the vertical ascent has always worked against the majority of people. These days management ranks are even thinner, since computers can do much of the synthesizing that managers used to do. You may stay on the upward path but end up doing the same thing longer with no assurance of getting to the next step. Or you can get off the fast track altogether. Today there are many career mobility options.

There's a difference between thinking in terms of a career and thinking in terms of a job. With a career, you're under the scrutiny of others; with a job, the decision is all yours. It's my observation that while career-minded executives are still the majority, more people are focusing on making a track record for their own satisfaction and not to the specifications of others. They become, to a greater or lesser extent, independent practitioners. If this appeals to you, there's no way to predict whether you will in the long run make more or less money than you would have following a more conventional route. What is certain is that both your performance and path are truly incumbent on you. Nobody else is doing quite what you're doing; nobody else knows where you're going.

Companies have become more receptive to hiring people for noncareer positions. The extreme is contracted work—for example, hiring a consultant for a short-term project— but it's also possible to do specialized work within a corporation, or to be essentially an in-house free-lancer. The independence of this approach gives you more flexibility about where, when, and on what you choose to work. It can be lonely, as well as risky, but it does provide many kinds of job alternatives.

Should You Accept the Offer?

Now, suppose you have a job offer in hand. Just the thought conjures up good feelings. You don't get a job offer very often, and when you do, it's a compliment. It makes you feel good, and you get a kick out of mentioning it to your family. It presents you with an alternative, and that can be tantalizing. But once you have a job offer, the decision process is at hand, and a lot rides on whether you make the right or wrong decision.

Evaluating a prospective job is a complex task, made all the more difficult by the warm feelings that come from being wanted. Suppose you've been approached by another company that wants you badly. This is a heady experience. Try being objective as limousines meet your plane and senior executives hold special meetings with you, followed by dinners at fine restaurants. It's difficult to think clearly when you're the focus of attention, and the whole ritual is designed to get you to accept the position. It reminds me of trying to make a decision when someone is making love to you. It's impossible! But you are going to do it.

When you're faced with an important career decision and emotions are running high, reviewing the checkup in this book will help you to separate fantasy from reality, to compare what is "out there" with what you now have. The special value of running a comparative checkup is that it will prevent you from being persuaded by the wrong factors. The questions in this book are a starting point from which you can attempt to gain an insider's view of the company. It's tough to see those things that will be so obvious six months after you change jobs—when it's too late.

I'm not trying to make you afraid of moving, since getting people to move is my livelihood. I'm talking about your taking an added step to make sure any new match has the highest chance of success, for everyone's benefit. You need to know what essential questions to ask a prospective employer. You need to think through the job more than the guy who has offered it to you.

In some cases, the more insistent your prospective company is that it *must* have you, the more wary you need to be. How long will this infatuation last? Does the company just have a critical short-term need, after which the party will be over? Are you really so unusual? Are you being offered a lot of money— or whatever—to distract you from asking the right questions? Upon reflection, you may find yourself refusing the offer you can't refuse.

To check out your job alternative, do the next four things— in an hour if you have to, but preferably over a period of days when you have enough time to probe for new information.

1. Walk your alternative through Part II of this book and see how your prospective company compares with your present one in work environment, products and markets, quality of people, quality of management, and financial health. If the other company isn't healthy, you have no reason to go further, but if it compares well with your present company, then . . .

2. Go to Part III and check the doability of the prospective job. How does it fit in with the company's priorities? Then review your compensation package, going beyond salary to the subtle elements you know are important once you're on board. If the comparison is still favorable, then . . .

3. Go back to Part I of the checkup and compare your ability to manage your prospective boss, your performance, the relationships you will need, how you think people will perceive you, and your personal priorities. How does the job mesh with the plan you set for yourself? Estimate how you will fit in, and if this, too, looks good, then . . .
4. Project how you'll feel three months from now when you've settled into your new office, the unusual attention from senior management has evaporated, and you're expected to perform. Then project out two years and estimate where you might be in either situation, and finally, step back a little further and do it for five years. How do things look?

Once you've gone through these four steps, you're no longer making a snap decision. That's a pretty careful analysis, and you've anticipated the advantages and disadvantages of each situation. If your job alternative passes these tests, grab that opportunity before it gets away! It must be good.

If You're Going to Quit, Quit While You're Ahead

One more cautionary note: *There is a best time to leave a job or company.* You leave when you're hot, when your company is hot. You leave when others aren't leaving. You leave on the upturn, near the peak, because you want to settle into your new position before any question arises about your previous company and what happened when you were there. Hiring bosses are just like anyone else: They want what they think they can't have, and what they can get easily they think is pedestrian.

Those who left General Electric in the seventies were thought to be management geniuses. But the vast numbers who were let go in the eighties were considered surplus, used up, accustomed to heavy staff assistance and not compatible with a lean and trim organization. But in truth, the executives weren't any different. What had changed was how they were perceived.

Where is the fast track for you in your industry? Do you want to be there? Are you going to stay where you are, give your best, and take your chances, or are you going to leave on an upturn and try to leverage your strength? Risks exist with either approach. There is no "right" answer.

Only You Can Decide

Managing your career is like cooking your favorite recipe: You're the cook, and the result has to please only you. I've given you my best thoughts and best questions, but now the ball is landing back in your court. The decision about whether or not to make a change, whether or not to accept the offer, is one you can't delegate. It's yours and yours alone.

Good luck.

I'd like to hear whether this book has been useful to you and how you think it could be improved. If you'd like to suggest additional topics that could be covered or have further insights about those that are already included, write to me, care of AMACOM Books (135 West 50th Street, New York, NY 10020).

Index

A

advertising, 134–135
American Express, 148
American Management
    Association, 150
American Society for
    Training and
    Development, 147, 150
annual plan, personal, 28–29
appearance, and first
    impressions, 71–72
assets, undervalued, 188–189
associates, former, 63–64
attitude problems, 208–209
authority, for job, 202
automobiles, company, 223
awards programs, 117

B

Beatrice Companies, 185
Bell Communications
    Research, 149
benefits, 222–224
board of directors, 171–173
body language, 72–73
Bolles, Richard, *What Color
    Is Your Parachute?*, 97
boss
    commitment by, 204

conflict handling by, 8–9
corporate goals of, 13–14
evaluation by, 19–20
management style of, 7–8
peers of, relationship with,
    54–55
personal interests of, 6, 7
power of, 14–15
relationship with, 4–6, 23
representing, 16
respect from, 5
role of, in career, 3
and staff development,
    10–11
strengths of, 16–18
track record of, 11–13

C

cafeteria plan, 223
capital structure, 189–190
career
    evaluation of, xii
    goals for, 97–100
    vs. job, 268
career fitness index, 236–264
cash compensation, 219–221
cash flow, 184–185
challenge from job, 231
chief executive officer, 159,
    161–162
    toys of, 173–174

clients, *see* customers
clothes, and first impressions, 71–72
club memberships, 223
college recruitment, 144–145
commitment, 204–205
communications, 50
    abilities of, 78–79
    within company, 113–115
    technology in, 211
company
    advertising by, 134–135
    board of directors of, 171–173
    capital structure of, 189–190
    cash flow of, 184–185
    communication within, 113–115
    controlling interests of, 162–163
    cooperation within, 115–116
    customers of, *see* customers
    debt of, 186–187
    driving force of, 112–113
    earnings of, 183–184
    environmental concerns in, 121–122
    environment within, xiv
    finances of, 178–195
    goals of, boss and, 13–14
    image and first impression of, 110–111
    international operations of, 122–123
    manufacturing division of, 118–119
    market share of, 131–132
    operations and priorities of, 109–125
    owners of, 162–163
    packaging by, 135–136
    personality of, 111–112
    pricing strategy of, 132–133
    products and markets of, 126–140
    profit margins of, 133–134
    research and development in, 120
    revenues of, 181–183
    sales and distribution of, 136–137
    structure of, 117–118
    undervalued assets of, 188–189
    work environment of, 116–117
company automobiles, 223
compensation, 217–218
    benefits as, 222–224
    cash, 219–221
    overpayment of, 220
    tax-deferred, 211–222
conflicts, handling of, by boss, 8–9
constructive criticism, 19–20
contacts, from job, 231–232
Continental Can Company, 153
contingency planning, 267–268
contracted work, 269
controlling interests, 162–163
cooperation, 203–204
    within company, 115–116
corporate environment, xiv

corporate goals, of boss, 13–14
corporate politics, 51–53
customers, 137–138
  relationship with, 60–61
  service for, 129

D

deadlines, 206
debt, of company, 186–188
debt-to-equity ratio, 186
decision making, 77
defined-contribution pension
  plan, 224
dilution, 183
directors, 171–173
disability insurance, 226
distribution, 136–137
dress, and first impressions,
  71–72

E

earnings, 183–184
Eastman Kodak, 167
education, *see* training
Emerson Electric Company,
  131
employment at will, xiv
entrepreneur, as goal, 101–102
environmental concerns,
  121–122

equipment, technology and,
  211
ethics, of senior management,
  164–165
evaluations, 142
  by boss, 19–20
  procedures for, 150–152
Executive Qualities (Fox), 77
exit interview, 155
expertise, 95–96
experts, relationship with,
  52–53
eye contact, 73–75

F

family, relationship with,
  65–66
Feinberg, Mortimer, on
  management, 164
financial information sources,
  179
firing, 154–155
first impressions, 71–72
  of company, 110–111
Ford Motor Company, 115
foresight, 81–82
former associates, 63–64
Forum Corporation, 150
Fox, Joseph M., *Executive
  Qualities*, 77
free-lancer, 277
full-employment policy, 155

G

Geneen, Harold
   Managing, 173
   on planning, 31
General Electric, 151
geographic location, 229
goals, 90
   career, 97–100
   corporate, boss and, 13–14
   entrepreneur as, 101–102
   president as, 100–101
   private, 91–92
   of senior management,
      167–168
GTE, 148

H

health insurance, 225–226
hiring
   outside, 145–146
   process for, 143–144
house buying and selling,
      assistance with, 227–228
human resources department,
      59–60
humor, 83–85

I

individual retirement
      accounts, 222

Industrial Investor, 181
information
   access to, 113–115, *see also*
      communication
   financial, sources of, 179
in-house training, 147–148
institutional reports, 192
insurance, 225–226
international conditions, and
      raw materials, 212
international operations,
      122–123
interview, exit, 155
inventories, 119
investment banking firms,
      192–193

J

job
   authority for, 202
   vs. career, 276
   challenge of, 231
   commitment to, 204–205
   contacts from, 231–232
   cooperation in, 203–204
   current, investment in, 274
   experience from, 231
   funding for, 206
   possibility of completing,
      199–216
   responsibilities of, 200–201
   staffing for, 207–208
   time requirements for,
      206–207

job offer, xii
  accepting, 269–270
job openings, posting of,
    153–154
job satisfaction, 229
job security, xii
Johns Manville, 188
judgment, 77–78

K

Kepner-Trego, Inc., 149–150
Kets de Vries, Manfred F. R.,
    Unstable at the Top, 176

L

labels, 96
Lazarus, Harold, on training
    facilities, 148
leader, assessing performance
    as, 33–35
Levi Strauss, 117
liabilities, 187–188
liability suits, product,
    129–130
life insurance, 226
listening, 79
litigation, 165–167
loyalty, 94–95

M

management
  boss's style of, 7–8
  see also senior management
manager, assessing
    performance as, 33–35
Managing (Geneen), 173
manufacturing, 118–119
markets, of company, 130–131
market share, 131–132
maternity leave, 223
MBWA (management by
    walking around), 53
Mellon Bank, 172
mentor, relationship with,
    57–58
Miller, Danny, *Unstable at
    the Top,* 176
Mostek, 120
moving expenses, 227
Myers-Briggs Type Indicator,
    93

N

natural inclinations, 89–90
networking, 35, 63–64
new concepts, 37
niche products, 128
nonoperating and
    nonrecurring revenues,
    182

O

objectives, achievement of,
30–31
Ogilvy & Mather, 117
outside activities, 37–38
overtime, 206
owners, of company, 162–163

P

packaging, 135–136
peers, 204, 230
of boss, relationship with,
54–55
relationship with, 53–54
Pennzoil, 188
pension plan, 224–225
perceptions, 69–87
performance
comparison of, 31–33
evaluation of, 24–46
as manager and leader,
33–35
value of, 25–27
perks, 222–224
personal chemistry, 47, 48
personality, 92–94
of entrepreneurs, 102
personnel management, 59–60
persuasiveness, 79–81
PERT (Performance
Evaluation and Review
Technique) chart, 207

planning, contingency,
267–268
Polaroid, 167
political factions, 51–53
posted job openings, 153–154
power, of boss, 14–15
power stare, 75
president, as goal, 100–101
pricing strategy, 132–133
private companies, financial
information from,
179–180
private goals, 91–92
productive capacity, 209–210
products, 126–140
liability suits from, 129–130
life cycles of, 127
quality of, 128–130
technology and, 210–211
profit margins, 133–134
profit-sharing plan, 220
Prokesch, Steven, on
management style, 160
promotion, 11, 54–55
psychological tests, 144
public speaking, 78–79

Q

Quality College, 149
quitting, 271–272

R

raw materials, 211–212
recognition, 41–42

relationships, working, 47–68
relocation costs, 226–228
reputation, job and, 232
research and development, 120
  technology in, 211
respect
  from boss, 5
  from subordinates, 50–51
responsibilities, job, 200–201
résumé, vs. track record, 39
revenues, 181–183
  nonoperating and nonrecurring, 182
rewards, 217–235
risk, 82–83
Robinson-Patman Act, 132

S

salary, *see* compensation
sales, 136–137
Securities and Exchange Commission, 179
self-awareness, lack of, xii
self-knowledge, 88–105
senior management, 159–177
  age spread of, 168–169
  background of, 169–170
  ethics of, 164–165
  goals of, 167–168
  relationship with, 55–57
  stock ownership by, 191
  track record of, 163–164
  turnover in, 170–171
separation, 154–155

service for products, 129
The Soul of a New Machine, 92
speeches, 78–79
staff development, 35–36
  boss and, 10–11
staffing, for job, 207–208
staff positions, 203
stock ownership, 190–191
stock purchase plans, 223
subordinates, relationships with, 49–51
succession planning, 21, 142, 152–153

T

takeovers, 191
Tandem Computers, 114, 153
tax-deferred compensation, 221–222
team spirit, 50
technology, 210–211
telephone manner, 75–76
testing, psychological, 144
Texaco, 187–188
time requirements, for job, 206–207
Toastmasters Club, 80
track record, 39–40
  of boss, 11–13
  of senior management, 163–164
training, 10, 148–150
  in-house, 147–148
transferability, 43

travel, 230
Treybig, Jim, 114
tuition refund plans, 150
turnover, 212–213
  in senior management,
    170–171
typecasting, 96

U

Unstable at the Top (Kets de
  Vries and Miller), 176

V

vacation, 223
vested pension plans, 225
voice, 75–76

W

Wall Street, 192–193
Watson, Thomas, Jr., on risk-
  takers, 83
*What Color Is Your
  Parachute?* (Bolles), 97
white collar crime, 165
Wilson Learning, 150
women, xvii
work environment, 116–117
working relationships, 47–68
W.T. Grant Company, 185

X

Xerox Corporation, 133, 166